Complete Korean

Complete Korean

Mark Vincent and
Jaehoon Yeon

For UK order enquiries: please contact
Bookpoint Ltd, 130 Milton Park, Abingdon, Oxon OX14 4SB.
Telephone: +44 (0) 1235 827720. *Fax:* +44 (0) 1235 400454.
Lines are open 09.00–18.00, Monday to Saturday, with a 24-hour message answering
service. Details about our titles and how to order are available at www.teachyourself.
co.uk

For USA order enquiries: please contact
McGraw-Hill Customer Services,
PO Box 545, Blacklick, OH 43004-0545, USA.
Telephone: 1-800-722-4726. *Fax:* 1-614-755-5645.

For Canada order enquiries: please contact
McGraw-Hill Ryerson Ltd, 300 Water St, Whitby,
Ontario L1N 9B6, Canada.
Telephone: 905 430 5000. *Fax:* 905 430 5020.

Long renowned as the authoritative source for self-guided learning – with more than 50
million copies sold worldwide – the **teach yourself** series includes over 500 titles in the
fields of languages, crafts, hobbies, business, computing and education.

British Library Cataloguing in Publication Data: a catalogue record for this title is available from the British Library.

Library of Congress Catalog Card Number: on file.

First published in UK 1997 as *Teach Yourself Korean* by Hodder Education,
part of Hachette UK, 338 Euston Road, London NW1 3BH

First published in US 1997 by The McGraw-Hill Companies, Inc.

This edition published 2010.

The **teach yourself** name is a registered trade mark of Hodder Headline.

Typeset by MPS Limited, A Macmillan Company.

Printed in Great Britain for Hodder Education, an Hachette UK Company, 338 Euston
Road, London NW1 3BH, by CPI Cox & Wyman.

The publisher has used its best endeavours to ensure that the URLs for external websites
referred to in this book are correct and active at the time of going to press. However,
the publisher and the author have no responsibility for the websites and can make no
guarantee that a site will remain live or that the content will remain relevant, decent or
appropriate.

Hachette UK's policy is to use papers that are natural, renewable and recyclable products
and made from wood grown in sustainable forests. The logging and manufacturing proc-
esses are expected to conform to the environmental regulations of the country of origin.

Impression number 10 9 8 7 6 5 4 3 2 1

Year 2014 2013 2012 2011 2010

Contents

Credits

Front cover: © IMAGEMORE Co. Ltd/Getty Images

Back cover and pack: © Jakub Semeniuk/iStockphoto.com, © Royalty-Free/Corbis, © agencyby/iStockphoto.com, © Andy Cook/iStockphoto.com, © Christopher Ewing/iStockphoto.com, © zebicho - Fotolia.com, © Geoffrey Holman/iStockphoto.com, © Photodisc/Getty Images, © James C. Pruitt/iStockphoto.com, © Mohamed Saber - Fotolia.com

Pack: © Stockbyte/Getty Images

Meet the authors

I began studying Korean in the early 1990s at the University of London, and I have to admit that at first it was something of a shock! I'd always loved foreign languages at school, and had studied quite a few of them, including Russian, Spanish, and Greek. But that didn't prepare me for how different – and also how exciting – Korean would be! Korean works very differently from the European languages and it comes with a completely unique script to boot. And while that certainly makes things challenging, it also makes them fascinating and wonderfully enriching. The real secret is to refuse to be bewildered and put off by all the new things you will learn at the outset (even though it is indeed confusing at first!), and to stick at it, a little a day. I remember after my first week of classes I thought I would never make it but in the end I did, becoming at the time only the second British citizen to major in Korean. It was definitely worth all the effort, and in this book we do our best to give you as many tips as we can, and to provide down-to-earth explanations of the way the language works (as well as colloquial expressions that you will use all the time if you go to Korea). Koreans are an enthusiastic and friendly people who will warmly welcome and encourage your attempts to speak their language. Learning Korean is certainly difficult; we wouldn't pretend otherwise. But it is also lots of fun, and will give you a real sense of achievement as well as many new friendships and an infinitely richer experience if you travel to Korea, not to mention a wider view of language and the wonder of human communication.

Mark Vincent

I have been teaching Korean since 1989 at the School of Oriental and African Studies (SOAS), University of London, and have taught many European students. They find Korean very difficult, but interesting and rewarding when they make it to the end. I met

Mark Vincent as a SOAS student in the early 1990s, and he is one of the best students I have met so far. We came up with an idea of writing up an interesting Korean language textbook for beginners, and Hodder and Stoughton accepted our manuscript. This is how this book came into being. I love learning foreign languages, and have studied quite a number of them, including German, French, Russian, and Japanese. I am also currently learning Chinese for fun. The regrettable thing is, however, that I cannot fluently speak these languages except for a little bit of Japanese – I can read them much better though! The aim of the book, when we were writing it, was to make readers talk actual Korean! We tried to provide readers with up-to-date colloquial competence as well as structural reading knowledge. Mark, as a former learner himself, added many useful insights on the way you understand and learn an exotic language like Korean. We have provided you with easy-to-understand explanations of grammar and as many tips as possible. Do not give up and try a little a day, then you will find it fun and rewarding.

Jaehoon Yeon

Only got a minute?

Korean is a fascinating language to study. For a start, it has a completely different alphabet from ours, a writing system which is unique among the languages of the world. Its grammar is entirely different from English – everything seems to be expressed backwards in Korean! It also has sounds which are alien to any that we have in European languages. Then there are the different cultural assumptions which underlie the different languages ...

There are now several introductory Korean courses on the market, and our aim has been to make this one stand out in the following ways. First, it focuses on real-life situations, with dialogues which feature authentic Korean as it is spoken on the street. We have tried to make the book be led by the dialogues while maintaining a logical progression through the basics of the grammar. Apart from the first few units, in which we have deliberately simplified things, the dialogues contain real Korean with colloquial phrases and idiomatic expressions left in and explained.

Our second aim has been to make the lesson notes as clear as possible, drawing comparisons with English to illustrate how Korean is both similar and different rather than introducing a lot of grammatical terminology. We have tried to explain in detail the crucial grammar points and also provide a taster for a few more advanced matters without letting these intrude. Much non-essential grammar has been omitted. The exercises have been designed to test the essential grammar thoroughly, and to give lots of practice with practical language use.

Korean is not an easy language to learn but the challenges that it presents are what make communicating in it so rewarding. When you begin to communicate in Korean, we are sure you will find it both entertaining and fulfilling.

5 Only got five minutes?

Who speaks Korean, and why should you?

If you learn Korean, you will be speaking the language of 80 or 90 million other people, the language of the only nation on earth which remains divided, the language spoken by a country with one of the world's strongest economies, the language of a people of rich and diverse culture still largely unknown in the West. Koreans will appreciate it when you try to speak with them using their language, and they will be delighted to communicate with you. Korean is the eleventh largest language in the world in terms of the number of native speakers.

Being in Korea and speaking in Korean is both exciting and challenging. Although many Koreans are learning English, most do not speak it, and of those who do, many are not able to speak coherently, even though they know lots of English words. If you want to have a truly rewarding time when you visit Korea (whether for business or pleasure), learning Korean is the way forward.

And even in the West you can practise, too. There are now many Korean companies in Europe and the States, and there are growing communities of Koreans in Britain, on the West Coast of America and elsewhere.

A potted history of Korean

Grammatically, Korean is related to Japanese and Mongolian (the structure of the three languages is quite similar). Korean is thought to belong to the Altaic family of languages, meaning that it is also related to Tungusic and Turkish. This may all come as a surprise, since many people assume that Korean will be like Chinese. Grammatically, Korean is totally different from Chinese. There is no connection between them.

However, many Korean words (as opposed to grammar) come from Chinese, since China has been the major influence in Korea's literature and culture. Probably 50 per cent of Korean words are originally of Chinese origin. This is a bit similar to the way in which English has many words which are borrowed from Latin.

Some tips for learning Korean

The first thing to remember is this: don't be put off by how different and difficult it all seems at first. It is different, and it is difficult. But, as long as you keep going, you will quickly begin to spot the patterns and come to understand the way that Korean sentences work. It is quite possible for a westerner to learn to speak Korean fluently – even a westerner with little previous experience of language learning. With a course like this one, you will find that although there are always new challenges along the way, you will progress rapidly and logically through the basics of the Korean language.

One of the exciting things about learning Korean is that there are so few westerners who can speak it. Despite Korea's rapid economic growth, and despite the constant American military presence in Seoul, there are still few westerners to be seen on the streets of even the largest cities. Very few of those can speak any Korean at all.

Koreans are absolutely delighted when you try to speak their language and they will bend over backwards to try to help and encourage you. They won't make you feel silly, and they won't take your efforts to speak Korean for granted, no matter how good you are.

Contrariwise, many Koreans are eager for opportunities to practise their English. If you go to Korea and are keen to improve your command of the language, it is best to be clear in your mind that you will try to speak Korean, no matter how hard someone might try to persuade you to speak English! It is the best way to learn quickly.

10 Only got ten minutes?

The Korean alphabet

The Korean alphabet is unique among the writing systems of the world. This is because it is the only known alphabet which was specifically invented or made to order. From ancient times literacy in Korea had existed only among the ruling classes, and consisted of classical Chinese, or sometimes of using Chinese characters and adapting some of them for use in a Korean context. Among the majority of the people, there was no literacy at all – not even Chinese.

However, in 1443 King Sejong, the most famous of all the Korean kings and queens, invented 28 letters especially designed for writing Korean, called 'Hunmin Chong'um'. After the invention, King Sejong commanded extensive research to be conducted in order to explain the philosophical background of the invention and how to utilize the alphabets for writing Korean. This was carried out by a team of scholars, and the accuracy and sophistication of their research and phonological analysis is still a source of amazement to scholars today. The Korean alphabet, *han'gul*, is perhaps the most outstanding scientific and cultural achievement of the Korean nation.

If you are to take seriously the task of learning Korean, there is no substitute for learning to read the Korean script. It is not especially difficult (certainly not as difficult as it looks), and you will soon come to appreciate both its uniqueness and its elegance.

The Korean script (*han'gul*) is indeed an alphabet, but it has one special feature which sets it apart from most others. In English we start writing at the beginning of a word and write a sequence of letters, each one following the next, until we reach the end. Usually (apart from the case of silent letters and other peculiarities) we pronounce each letter in turn in the sequence running from left to right.

Korean, however, instead of writing a string of letters in sequence, writes its letters in syllable blocks. Thus, take the Korean word which is pronounced as **komapsumnida**. It means *thank you*. In English we write the letters left to right, k-o-m-a-p-s-u-m-n-i-d-a, but Korean breaks the word into syllables: **ko-map-sum-ni-da**. Don't worry about the form of the letters, but simply have a look at the way this works below.

고맙습니다

Fig. 1

Most Korean syllables begin with a consonant letter (if the syllable begins with a vowel then a special 'null' or silent consonant symbol is inserted instead). This consonant letter has a vowel letter, usually either to the right or underneath. Every syllable must have the consonant letter plus a vowel letter. Some syllables have another consonant letter written underneath the first consonant and the vowel, and occasionally you will meet syllables that have two consonants next to each other in this final, underneath position.

All the dialogues in this book appear first in Korean script, followed by a romanized version. For the first few lessons you may well want to rely on the romanized version so that you can quickly begin to speak Korean words and sentences without being troubled by the initial difficulty of being slowed down by the writing system. But you must constantly practise reading the dialogues in the Korean script as well without relying on the romanization. You should see romanization as a crutch to help you on your way as you learn Korean writing. By the time you have passed the first few lessons, you should be going first to the Korean texts, and looking at the romanization to test your pronunciation.

Some key phrases

For now, though, here are a few key phrases and expressions to tuck under your belt: greetings, *please* and *thank you*, and other essential expressions. Since we won't be studying the alphabet properly until the next section ('Foundations'), let's dive right in with some Korean phrases written in romanization (English script):

Annyong haseyo!	*Hello!*
Mannaso pangapsumnida!	*Pleased to meet you!*
Oraeganman-ieyo	*Long time, no see!*
Komapsumnida	*Thank you*
Kamsa hamnida	*Thank you (alternative)*
Shille hamnida	*I'm sorry/excuse me*
Annyong-hi gaseyo	*Goodbye (to someone who is leaving)*
Annyong-hi gyeseyo	*Goodbye (to someone who is staying)*

How to use the course

Most of the 14 units of this course follow the same pattern.

Introduction An introduction in English that explains what you will learn in the unit.

Dialogue In each unit there are two dialogues, followed by a list of new vocabulary and some simple comprehension questions in English or Korean. Each dialogue is followed by grammar notes which explain how to use the language patterns that have come up.

Phrases and expressions This section gives you expressions that are commonly used as set phrases, and also gives you translations of snippets of dialogue which contain difficult grammar patterns which you are not yet ready to analyse and which you must learn simply as set expressions for the time being.

Vocabulary New words from the dialogues will go into the vocabulary section. The list of words in the vocabulary follows the order in which they appear in the dialogue. Sometimes we also give you additional words which are closely related to the ones that occur in the dialogues.

The units are meant to teach you how to use Korean practically in everyday situations – how to order in a restaurant, how to complain when your hotel room isn't quite what it should be, how to express opinions and disagreements, and so on.

Grammar To be able to do these things, however, you need to have a good understanding of grammar. This is the purpose of the commentary sections. Do not be put off by the quantity of grammar explanations, therefore. You do need these in order to speak Korean properly. We have done our best to keep unnecessary details and minor exceptions to rules out of the text. Do not worry if you don't understand every single bit of grammatical structure in the Korean dialogues. The important thing is that you learn the dialogues thoroughly, and that you understand the main grammar points of each unit.

Practice Please do the exercises! Don't be tempted to skip to the next unit until you've done them, checked them in the key at the back of the book, understood your mistakes and learned the correct answers.

Take time to learn the Korean alphabet properly, and make sure you write the exercises out in Korean script, even if you also do them in romanization. In the second half of the book you will find that the romanization has been largely dropped.

Listening exercises If you want to have a good command of spoken Korean, you will find the recording essential. Listen to it as often as you can. Listen back over units that you studied previously; listen to future units – to make yourself familiar with the sounds and intonations – picking out what you can, even though you won't understand everything.

Although the going will seem tough at times, Korean is a fun language, and studying it can be very rewarding. Remember to enjoy yourself – the best way to do so is to follow the maxim 'a little and often'!

Insight boxes Throughout the main text of the units you will find these boxes which give learning tips and advice – both linguistic and cultural – that our students have found useful.

Ten things to remember At the end of each unit there is a summary of the most important things to remember.

Foundations: alphabet and pronunciation

The Korean alphabet

We're going to divide looking at the alphabet and pronunciation into three sections: first, to introduce you to the letters of the alphabet, then to look at the way that we have romanized those letters in this book, and finally to look at important rules of sound changes in pronunciation. First, then, the letters of the alphabet and principles of Korean writing.

The Korean alphabet writes its letters in syllable blocks, as explained above, in 'Only got ten minutes?' What we will be learning about first, then, is how to write Korean syllables. These syllables are then placed next to each other to make up words and sentences.

Writing Korean

Every Korean syllable begins with a consonant letter (if the syllable begins with a vowel then a special null consonant symbol is inserted in place of the consonant letter; this looks like a zero, and is the last consonant letter in Fig. 2). This consonant letter has a vowel letter either on its right or underneath it (some vowels go both to the right and underneath; we will deal with those later). Every syllable must have the consonant letter plus a vowel letter. Some syllables have another consonant letter written underneath the first consonant and the vowel, and occasionally you will meet syllables that have two consonants next to each other in this final, underneath position.

For now we will just concentrate on syllables that have one consonant letter and one vowel letter. Here are some consonant letters:

ㄱ ㄷ ㅂ ㅈ ㅁ ㄴ ㅇ

Fig. 2

These are pronounced as follows: **k** as in *kitchen*; **t** as in *toad*; **p** as in *potty*; **ch** as in *chamber*; **m** as in *miser*; **n** as in *nanny*; the last letter is the zero or null consonant, which means the syllable begins with a vowel sound – you must always write this null consonant whenever the syllable begins with a vowel sound.

Remember that we can add a vowel letter either to the right or underneath these. First, the vowels that go to the right-hand side. In Fig. 3 you will see the vowels **a** as in *bat*, **ŏ** as in *hot*, **ya** as in *yap*, **yŏ** as in *yonder*, **i** as in *hit* or *ea in heat* (this is why you need the recording to tell which one is to be used where!). On the next line we have made up syllables with the consonants you have learned. These are, respectively: **ka, kŏ, kya, kyŏ, ki, tya, ti, pa, pŏ, chi, chŏ, ma, mŏ, nyŏ, nŏ, i, ya.**

ㅏ ㅓ ㅑ ㅕ ㅣ
가 거 갸 겨 기 댜 디
바 버 지 저 마 머 녀
너 이 야

Fig. 3

There are also other vowels which have to be written under the consonant letter. Some of these are in Fig. 4, and underneath are some syllables for you to practise. The vowels are pronounced **o** as in *boat* (note that this is different from the vowel **ŏ** which you have learned above); **u** as *oo* in *pool*; **yo** as in *yokel*; **yu** as in *yuletide*; **ŭ** as *u* in *curd* or *e* in *berk*. The syllables we have given you are: **to, tu, tyo, tyu, tŭ, ko, kŭ, pu, pyo, cho, chŭ, mu, myu, nyu, no, o, yo.**

ㅗ　ㅜ　ㅛ　ㅠ　ㅡ

도　두　됴　듀　드　고　그

부　뵤　조　즈　무　뮤　뉴

노　오　요

Fig. 4

You are now in a position to do Exercises 1 and 2 and you should do these at this point.

Exercise 1

◀) **CD 1, TR 1, 01:10**

Read the following Korean words written in Korean script and listen to the recording.

1 바보　　　　　2 바나나

3 마마　　　　　4 가도

5 자주　　　　　6 아이

7 고교　　　　　8 묘기

9 드무오　　　10 머기

Exercise 2

◀) **CD 1, TR 1, 01:50**

Read the following Korean words written in Korean script and listen to the recording.

1 아버지　　　　2 어머니

3 너야　　　　　4 가구

5 두부   **6** 모유

7 거기   **8** 모기

9 모자   **10** 나가자

Now, as we remarked earlier, you can add another consonant underneath the first consonant and the vowel letter, to give three-lettered syllables. We need at this point to tell you that the null consonant symbol (the little circle) has two functions. At the beginning of the syllable it tells you that the syllable begins with a vowel sound. However, in last place in a syllable it represents the sound **ng** as in *bring*. Some combinations are illustrated in Fig. 5. The syllables we have given are: **kim, pak, min, chŏm, kŏn, pyŏng, kom, chun, yop, tŭm, pang** and **ûng**.

김   박   민   점   건   병

곰   준   욥   듬   방   응

Fig. 5

It is now time to learn some more consonants. These are given in Fig. 6, and they are, respectively: **l** as in *ladle*, **h** as in *hope*, **s** as in *sat*.

ㄹ   ㅎ   ㅅ   ㅋ   ㅌ   ㅍ   ㅊ

Fig. 6

The final four consonants on the list are aspirated versions (made with a puff of air) of the four consonants you have met already: **k, t, p** and **ch**. We romanize the aspirated versions as **k', t', p'** and **ch'**. To make these aspirated sounds, shape your mouth as you would to make the normal **k, t, p** or **ch** sound, and then make the sound by forcing air out of your mouth in a rush. If you put your hand to your lips as you make them (or hold up a sheet of paper) you should feel the puff of air as you make the sound (or should see the paper move). Imagine the difference between saying the **c** in *of course* if you were saying it calmly and naturally, and saying it again when you were irritated with someone: 'don't be ridiculous, *of course* it's not, stupid!'. The first would be the Korean letter **k**, and the second would be **k'**. The difference can be important; as an example, the word **pi** means *rain*, but the word **p'i** means *blood*!

In addition, the four consonants **k**, **t**, **p** and **ch**, along with **s** can also be doubled (that is, one written immediately after the other). This is a bit more difficult to explain than aspiration. Here you make your mouth (lips and tongue) very tense and make the sound lightly, without a puff of air. Once again the difference is important, and the best way to pick it up is to listen to the recording or a Korean speaker, and try to imitate the sounds. We romanize these by **kk**, **tt**, **pp**, **cch**. The consonant **s** can also be doubled to give **ss**. Fig. 7 has examples of syllables containing the double and aspirated consonants.

김 킴 낌 돈 톤 똔 분 푼 뿐
잔 찬 짠 산 싼

Fig. 7

There are also a few more vowels to learn. Fig. 8 contains the vowels **ae** as *a* in *care*; **e** as in *hen*; **yae** as in *yesterday*; **ye** also as in *yesterday* (there is no significant difference in sound between **yae** and **ye**). These sounds are illustrated in the syllables **maen**, **p'en**, **yae**, **kye**.

ㅐ ㅔ ㅒ ㅖ
맨 펜 얘 계

Fig. 8

Finally, certain vowels are made up of combinations of others (you read the one underneath first, then the one on the right-hand side). You can probably work out the pronunciations of these for yourself, but we give you them in any case. They are as in Fig. 9: **wa** (o + a) as in *wag*; **wo** (u + ŏ) as *wa* in *wanted*; **wae** (o + ae) as the word *where*; **we** (wu + e) as *we* in *wet*; **oe** (o + i) as in German *Goethe*; **wi** (u + i) as in French *oui*; **ŭy** (ŭ + i, say them together, fast), sometimes pronounced as **e**.

와 궈 왜 궤 뇌 귀 긔

Fig. 9

Occasionally you will meet syllables that have two consonants in the final place. Unless we tell you otherwise (by missing one of them out in the romanization), both of these should be pronounced. You will find a couple of examples, along with some examples of the vowels in the last paragraph, in Fig. 10. The syllables we have given you are: **ilk, wae, kwon, hwan, palk, kwi, mwo, oen** and **ŏps**.

읽 왜 권 환 밝 귀 뭐 왼 없

Fig. 10

You have now learned the entire Korean alphabet, and are ready to tackle all the exercises.

You can also now look up in a dictionary any word you find written in the Korean script. The order of the Korean alphabet is given in Fig. 11. Notice that all the words beginning with vowels are grouped together under the null consonant symbol. This means that all the vowels (the last 21 symbols on the list), occur in the dictionary at the place marked by the asterisk.

ㄱ ㄲ ㄴ ㄷ ㄸ ㄹ ㅁ ㅂ ㅃ ㅅ
ㅆ ㅇ* ㅈ ㅉ ㅊ ㅋ ㅌ ㅍ ㅎ
ㅏ ㅐ ㅑ ㅒ ㅓ ㅔ ㅕ ㅖ ㅗ ㅘ
ㅙ ㅚ ㅛ ㅜ ㅝ ㅞ ㅟ ㅠ ㅡ ㅢ ㅣ

Fig. 11

Exercise 3

The following Korean words written in Korean script are the names of countries which you should be able to recognize. Read the names and write down what the English equivalent is.

1 파키스탄   **2** 멕시코

3 뉴질랜드   **4** 네덜란드

5 스웨덴   **6** 덴마크

7 인도네시아   **8** 폴란드

9 캐나다   **10** 아메리카

Exercise 4

The following Korean words written in Korean script are loan words from English which you should be able to recognize. Read the names and write down what the English equivalent is.

1 호텔   **2** 피아노

3 컴퓨터   **4** 텔레비전

5 라디오   **6** 택시

7 레몬   8 아이스크림

9 햄버거   10 샌드위치

11 오렌지 주스   12 테니스

13 카메라   14 토마토

Exercise 5

◆) **CD 1, TR 1, 02:30**

Read the following Korean words and listen to the recording.

1 빵   2 시내

3 오징어   4 과일

5 안녕하세요   6 선생님

7 사업   8 말씀

9 일본   10 영국

Romanization of Korean

This book gives you a romanized version of all the Korean
dialogues and the lesson notes it contains (that is, written in
English letters). In addition, Korean scripts are given for all the
dialogues and the new vocabularies.

This is not because we believe the Korean alphabet to be
unimportant. On the contrary, as we have already stressed, it is
very important that you learn it. However, there are two reasons
why we have consistently used romanization, in addition to

printing the dialogues and the vocabularies in the Korean script. The first is that we want you to move quickly through the course and become competent at handling Korean as a spoken language as soon as possible.

The second reason is that often Korean letters are not pronounced exactly as they are written, or rather, certain letters are pronounced in a different way under certain circumstances. We could explain all the rules for this and let you work out the pronunciation for yourself. However, by using the romanization guidelines, most of this is done for you.

There are several different methods of romanizing Korean, and the one we have used is a modified version of what is known as the McCune-Reischauer system.

You have already seen the way we romanize most of the letters from the previous explanation of the Korean alphabet, but there are a number of points to notice:

1 **k, t, p** and **ch** are all written as such at the beginning of a word; however, in actual pronunciation, they can be pronounced **g, d, b** and **j** if they are preceded and followed by vowel sounds. We do not indicate this in the romanization so that you can be sure where you should be looking up words in dictionaries or glossaries. If you listen to the recording (as you should), you will be reminded when these letters should be pronounced in the different way.
    However, in the middle of a word, these letters **k, t, p, ch** are written as **g, d, b** and **j** when they occur between vowels. Therefore, the word which is written in Korean letters as **ha-ko** (the dash marking the syllable break) will be romanized here as **hago**.

2 The consonants **m** and **n** are romanized as such; double consonants are written as **kk, tt, pp, cch**; aspirated consonants are written as **k', t', p', ch'**; the zero or null consonant is not romanized since it has no sound – remember to write it in the

Korean script when a syllable begins with a vowel, however. As the last consonant in a syllable, we romanize it as **ng**, which is the way it is pronounced (as in *bring*).

3 The letter **h** is sometimes not pronounced; in those cases we do not romanize it, although we indicate its presence in the vocabularies by writing it in brackets as in the word **man(h)i**, pronounced **mani**. When the letter **h** occurs as the last consonant in a syllable and the following syllable begins with **k, t, p or ch**, then those sounds become aspirated. Instead of writing **hk** in romanization, therefore, we write **k'**, which is the way in which the Korean is actually pronounced.

4 The consonant **s** is pronounced **sh** (as in *shall*) when it is followed by the vowel **i**, and we romanize it as **sh** in such instances. Note that **ss** + **i** is pronounced **sshi**, but we romanize it as **ssi**.

5 Finally, the consonant **l** is a little tricky. Sometimes it is pronounced **l** (when one of the letters to the side of it is a consonant), but between vowels it is pronounced **r**. We romanize it as **l** or **r** according to the pronunciation. Take the word **il** for example, which means *day*. When the word is followed by the subject particle -**i**, the **l** is pronounced as an **r**, so we romanize it as **ir-i**. What you have to remember is that in the vocabulary this will be listed under **il**, and not **ir**. It sounds a bit puzzling at first, but you will soon get used to it, and there is no real difficulty.

The vowels are straightforward, and are romanized in the way we described when going through the letters of the Korean alphabet. Be careful to watch the two os, **o** and **ŏ** (as in over and other); also remember that **ŭ** is pronounced as the **u** in *burn*; **u** is pronounced as the **u** in *lute*. You should look over the description of the vowels again at this point to ensure that you are happy with them.

In conclusion, a word about double consonants. By this we mean two syllables in which the first ends with the same consonant as the initial consonant of the second (**om-ma; man-na; hal-la**). In these cases, hold on to the consonant sound a little longer than you would if there was just one, for example, with **omma**, say 'om', then, keeping your mouth closed and still making the humming sound of the **m**, make a little pause before you say 'ma'. Listen to this on the recording; don't get anxious about it, just remember to try to make the consonant sound a little longer than you would if there were only one of them.

You are now in a position to do the exercises on romanization.

Exercise 1

Write the following in Korean script.

1	Jaemin	**2**	kayo
3	chigŭm	**4**	yangju
5	marŭn anju	**6**	chungguk
7	mashida	**8**	pap
9	chinccha	**10**	uri

Exercise 2

Put the following Korean words in romanization form.

1	어때요	**2**	사람
3	선생님	**4**	아니요
5	사무실	**6**	만나다
7	미국	**8**	학교
9	대사관	**10**	점심

Pronunciation

Although Korean writing is consistent (that is, a word is always spelt in the same way), some syllables are pronounced in different ways in certain contexts (if surrounded by certain other syllables or sounds). For example, an **n** can, given certain conditions, be pronounced like an **l**. In Korean script the letter would still be written as an **n**, but Korean speakers would know to pronounce it as an **l**. You will know, not only because we are now going to tell you the most important of the pronunciation rules, but also because our romanization will tell you.

Rule 1

When the letters **k**, **t** and **p** precede **m** or **n** or **l**, they are pronounced (and romanized) as **ng**, **n** and **m** respectively. If the letter they precede is an **l**, then the **l** also changes to an **n** sound. The following examples show in the left column how they would be spelt in *han'gul*, and in the right-hand column, the way they are pronounced and romanized. We have put dashes in to indicate the syllable breaks.

hak-nyŏn (학년)	**hang-nyŏn**
tat-nŭn-da (닫는다)	**tan-nŭn-da**
hap-ni-da (합니다)	**ham-ni-da**
tok-lip (독립)	**tong-nip**

Rule 2

l is pronounced as an **n** when immediately preceded by any consonant except **l** or **n**. Thus we have **tong-nip** as above (from **tok-lip**), shimni (from **shim-li**).

Whenever an **l** appears next to an **n**, either as **nl** or **ln**, the resulting pronunciation is **ll**: **chilli** from **chin-li** (진리), **illyŏn** from **il-nyŏn** (일년).

Rule 3

If a word ends in a consonant and it is not followed by a particle (a little word that attaches to nouns), or the verb -**ieyo** (to be learned in Unit 1), then the last consonant is pronounced in a special way. The last consonant is not released. That means that you say the word as you would in English, moving your mouth into position to make a final consonant sound (see below) and beginning to say it, but stopping short of releasing any air. It would sound to an English speaker almost as if the consonant had been swallowed.

If the last consonant is a **ch**, **ch'**, **s**, **ss** or **h**, then the sound that you begin to make at the end of the word is the sound **t** (again, you don't release it).

We felt it was important to include these rules, because they make the book accurate and enable you to understand what is going on when it seems that the Korean text does not match up to the romanization or to what Korean speakers actually say. But we don't want you to become overly worried about it. If you listen to the recording regularly, and look carefully at the Korean script and the romanization, then you will soon pick up the rules, and the explanations we have given in this section will help you as you go.

There is a practice exercise, however, to enable you to practise the rules of this section. If you prefer, you can skip it and get straight on with the lessons themselves.

Exercise 1

◀) CD 1, TR 1, 03:20

The following examples show in the left column how they would be spelt in *han'gul*, and in the right-hand column, the way they are pronounced and romanized. Listen to the recording and practise them.

1 먹는다	mŏng-nŭn-da	6 작문	chang-mun
2 한국말	hang-gung-mal	7 국민	kung-min
3 숙녀	sung-nyŏ	8 심리	sim-ni
4 갑니다	kam-ni-ta	9 앞문	am-mun
5 닫는다	tan-nŭn-da	10 십만	sim-man

Exercise 2

◀) CD 1, TR 1, 04:00

A Korean never releases a consonant at the end of a syllable except when the word is followed by a particle or ending that begins with a vowel. The following examples show in the left column when the last consonant is not released, and in the right column when the last consonant is released before vowels. Listen to the recording and practise them.

1 집	chip	집에	chib-e
2 앞	ap	앞에	ap'-e
3 옷	ot	옷이에요	osh-ieyo
4 낮	nat	낮은	nach-ŭn
5 낮	nat	낮이	nach'-i
6 낫	nat	낫이	nash'-i
7 국	kuk	국이에요	kug-ieyo
8 밖	pak	밖에	pakk-e
9 밭	pat	밭에	pat'-e
10 꽃	kkot	꽃이에요	kkoch'-ieyo

1

Where are you off to?/Cheers!

In this unit you will learn
- *how to talk about where you are going and why*
- *how to ask questions*
- *how to order drinks and snacks*
- *basic structure of Korean sentences*
- *how to make polite requests*
- *how to form what is known as the polite style of speech*

Where are you off to?

◀) **CD 1, TR 2**

Sangmin meets his friend Jaemin in the street and asks him where he is off to.

상민	재민씨! 안녕하세요!
재민	네. 안녕하세요! 잘 지냈어요?
상민	네, 네. 어디가요?
재민	지금 시내에 가요.
상민	뭐 하러 시내에 가요?
재민	빵 사러 가요.
상민	나도 빵 사러 시내에 가요.
재민	그럼 같이 가요.
상민	네. 같이 가요.

Sangmin	Jaemin-ssi! Annyŏng haseyo?
Jaemin	Ne. Annyŏng haseyo! Chal chinaessŏyo?
Sangmin	Ne, ne. Ŏdi kayo?
Jaemin	Chigŭm shinae-e kayo.
Sangmin	Mwo ha-rŏ shinae-e kayo?
Jaemin	Ppang sa-rŏ kayo.
Sangmin	Na-do ppang sa-rŏ shinae-e kayo.
Jaemin	Kŭrŏm kach'i kayo.
Sangmin	Ne. Kach'i kayo.

1 How is Sangmin getting on?
2 Where is Jaemin going?
3 Why?
4 Who else is going there?
5 What does Jaemin suggest?

Phrases and expressions

annyŏng haseyo?	*hello!/how are you?*
annyŏng haseyo!	*hello!/fine* (note: this phrase is both a question and a reply)
chal chinaessŏyo?	*how have you been doing (getting on)?*
chal chinaessŏyo.	*fine, thanks (I've been getting on well).* (question and reply)
ŏdi kayo?	*where are you going?*
mwo ha-rŏ . . . kayo?	*what are you going to . . . to do?*

(name) -ssi	씨	*(title used with people's names; see note 2)*
ne	네	*yes*
chal	잘	*good, well* (adverb)
ŏdi	어디	*where?*
ka-	가-	*go* (verb stem)
kayo	가요	*go* (stem plus polite ending **-yo**)
chigŭm	지금	*now*

QUICK VOCAB

2

QUICK VOCAB (cont.)

shinae	시내	*town centre*
-e	–에	*to (particle, attaches to nouns)*
mwo	뭐	*what?*
ha-	하–	*do (verb stem)*
haeyo	해요	*do (stem plus polite ending **-yo**, irregular form)*
(verb stem)-**rǒ**	–러	*in order to (verb)*
ha-rǒ	하러	*in order to do*
ppang	빵	*bread*
sa-	사–	*buy (verb stem)*
sayo	사요	*buy (stem plus polite ending **-yo**)*
na	나	*I/me*
-do	–도	*too, also (particle, attaches to nouns)*
kǔrǒm	그럼	*then, in that case*
kach'i	같이	*together*

Grammar 1

1 *Korean names*

Korean names usually consist of three syllables. The first syllable is the surname (the most common Korean surnames being Kim, Lee and Pak), and this is usually followed by a two-syllable first name. There are odd exceptions: sometimes the first name will only contain one syllable. The two names in this dialogue, Jaemin and Sangmin, are both first names.

In Korean, the surname (when it is used) always comes first, the opposite of the English order. Therefore, Mr Pak Jaemin's surname is Pak, and his first name Jaemin. In this book we shall always use the Korean order (Pak Jaemin) rather than the English (Jaemin Pak). When you are writing Korean names in the Korean script, remember also that Koreans put no space between the surname and the first name – they are treated almost like one word.

Insight

Korean names usually have three syllables: a one-syllable surname which comes *first*, and a two-syllable first name which *follows* the surname.

2 *Talking to friends and talking about them*

When referring to someone you know well in a friendly situation, either to address them directly or to talk about them, it is quite acceptable to use their first name, just like we do in English. Following the name you should use the polite title -씨 (-ssi). You can refer to friends you know quite well and with whom you are on a similar social level as John-ssi, Deborah-ssi, Jaemin-ssi, Kyuthae-ssi, and so forth.

It is only when you are speaking to a very close friend that this -씨 (-ssi) can be dropped and you can just use their name (though if other people are present it is best to carry on using it). If you use -씨 (-ssi) you won't make any mistakes or offend anyone, whereas if you try dropping it, you could make a social mistake.

3 *Korean verbs*

All the sentences (except the first) in the dialogue end with a verb (a 'doing-word' like *walk, go, kick, steal*). Korean sentences always end with verbs in this way. In English, the position of the verb is quite different: we would say, for example, *I go to the shops*, whereas a Korean will say *I shops-to go*. Main verbs always come at the end of the sentence, and getting used to this major difference in sentence structure takes a little while, since it can seem as though you are having to say everything backwards!

The dialogue also contains other verbs which occur in the middle of a sentence. Even these are at the end in a sense, however, because they are used to end a clause. A clause is a part of a sentence which has its own verb and which could stand on its own as a sentence if it were changed a little bit. For example, the sentence *If you come then I'll go* is made up of two clauses, both of which could stand on their own as sentences (*you come* and *I'll go*). To summarize, Korean clauses and Korean sentences must always have a verb at the end. More about clauses and clause endings later.

Insight

Remember, in a Korean sentence the verb *always* comes at the end. Confusing at first, but you'll soon get used to waiting until the end of a sentence to find out what it's all about!

You will notice that all the verbs have endings to them. The verbs at the end of the sentences all end in -요 (**-yo**). This is a polite way of ending a sentence. The mid-sentence verbs in this lesson all end with -러 (**-rŏ**). This is explained in note 7.

Korean verbs are made up of stems onto which endings can be added. Every verb has a stem; it is the most basic part of a Korean verb. Sometimes you might want to add as many as seven different endings at once onto a verb stem! In the vocabulary sections of this book we shall usually list verbs by their stem forms, and this is the form in which you should learn them. By the rules we teach you, you will learn how to make the other forms of the verb from these stems. In the first few lessons we shall remind you when we are teaching you the stem form. If we don't tell you a stem, it is because there is something odd (irregular) about it, or because we only want you to learn one particular form of the verb in question for the time being.

> ## Insight
> Every Korean sentence has a verb at its end, and every verb
> has an ending on it! Sometimes other particles are inserted
> between a verb and its ending, but you should always think
> of a verb as consisting of these basic parts:
>
> Verb stem / (one or more optional particles)/Verb ending

Verbs are listed in a dictionary in what is known as the 'dictionary
form'. This is simply the stem with the syllable ㅡ다 (-ta) after it.
You can use verbs that you learn from the dictionary simply by
taking off this -ta and using the stem as normal with the endings
described in this book. There are some verbs which behave a bit
oddly, however, and we will not go systematically through all the
different kinds of verb stems until Unit 7, so you should hold fire a
bit with the dictionary until that point. Otherwise you could make
some bad mistakes!

The verbs in this lesson, 가ㅡ (ka- [go]), 하ㅡ (ha- [do]), 사ㅡ
(sa- [buy]), all occur with quite simple endings, and we will look at
these now.

4 Polite sentences with ㅡ요 (-yo)

The verb stems of this dialogue all end in vowels (ka-, ha- and
sa-), and to these you can add what is called the polite sentence
ending, -yo, to form a sentence. This polite sentence ending in -yo
is also known as a particle, and it is sometimes called the 'polite
particle'. Note that the verb 하ㅡ (ha-) is irregular, and the polite
sentence form is 해요 (haeyo), not 하요 (hayo) as you would have
expected.

가요 (kayo) is in itself a complete sentence (or clause) which means
I go, he goes, she goes, we go, etc, depending on the context. There
is no need to specify precisely who does the going in order to
make a good Korean sentence. Thus, if you are talking about your

mother, for example, and want to say that she goes somewhere, Korean only requires that you say 가요 (**kayo**) – you don't need to use a word for *she*.

We ought to explain the term 'polite sentence ending' (or 'polite particle'). Korean has various styles or levels of speech which are used according to the social situation in which you are speaking. For example, when you are having a drink with close friends, you will use a very different speech style from that which you would use if you were addressing a meeting, or talking to somebody for the first time. The speech style is shown in Korean principally by the verb endings. Although we have formal and informal language in English, we do not have anything as systematic and widespread as the Korean system of verb endings. These verb endings are crucial to every Korean sentence, since you cannot say a Korean sentence without selecting a speech style in which to say it. You have now begun to learn the most common, **-yo**, which marks the polite style of speech. This can be used in most social situations, particularly if it is neither especially formal nor intimate. It is, if you like, a middle-of-the-road style!

Verbs in the polite style may be statements, questions, suggestions or commands – this is expressed in the tone of voice that you use to say the sentence rather than being shown explicitly in the form of the verb. You have seen this several times already in the dialogue. The phrase 같이 가요 (**kach'i kayo**) is first a suggestion, then when it is used a second time it is a statement. 잘 지냈어요 (**chal chinaessŏyo**) can be both a question, asking how someone is, or a statement, saying that you are fine. 안녕하세요 (**annyŏng haseyo**) can also be both a question and a statement, depending on the way in which you say it.

Insight

The most important verb ending you will ever come across is the polite style ending −요 (**yo**). It's the most common way of ending sentences in everyday conversation. Sometimes it is even added to nouns also, to ask or confirm something (빵요 [**ppang-yo**]? *Bread?*). It's just a great way to end a sentence!

5 Who are you talking about?

As we've already mentioned, Korean does not need you to specify
the subject of the sentence, i.e. precisely who is doing the action
the sentence describes. You can specify it if you want to for special
emphasis, but as long as it is clear from the context, Korean does
not require it. 어디 가요? (ŏdi kayo?) therefore, means *where are
you going* – but it is not necessary to say 'you', because the context
makes it clear that the speaker is asking the hearer. If you look at the
last seven sentences in the dialogue (from line 3), you'll see that only
one uses a subject 나도 빵 사러 가요 (na-do ppang sa-rŏ kayo). The
subject of that sentence 나도 (na-do) is stated for emphasis.

6 Word order

We have seen that the word order of Korean sentences is very
different from English. 잘 지냈어요? (chal chinaessŏyo?) is a nice
example, as it literally means 'well have you been getting on?',
which is the opposite of what we would say in English. Usually the
order is *subject – object – verb* (*SOV* for short). This gives, *Peter
the ball kicked, Mary the shops-to went.*

7 To go to do

The other verb ending introduced in this dialogue is -러 (-rŏ)
which means *in order to*. You add this onto a verb stem at the
end of a clause, just as you added -요 (-yo) to verb stems at
the end of sentences. Note that, with verb stems which end in
consonants (you haven't learned any yet, but will soon), you add
the form -으러 (-ŭrŏ) (rather than just -러 (-rŏ)) to the verb
stem.

The most complicated part here is sorting out the word order.
Let's look at the English sentence 'I'm going to the shops in order
to buy bread'. Korean says this by putting the two clauses the
other way round: *in order to buy bread I'm going to the shops.*

However, that's not all! Remember that in addition, Korean puts its verbs at the end of clauses and sentences, and puts verb and clause endings after that. This gives us *I [bread buy-in order to] to the shops go*. Notice the way one clause is embedded inside the other. Usually the subject of the sentence comes first (in this case, *I*), then the in-order-to clause, then the place where you're going, then the main verb:

I (subject)	*go to the shops*	*in-order-to buy bread*	*(English)*
I (optional)	*bread buy – in-order-to*	*shops-to go*	*(Korean)*

Therefore, the Korean sentence order is 나도 빵 사러 가요 (**na-do ppang sa-rŏ kayo** [*I-too bread buy-in-order-to go*]). In other words, the main verb of the sentence is the *going*, for example, **kayo** or **shinae-e kayo**. The other part of the sentence, the *in order to . . .* bit comes first, as in 빵 사러 가요 (**ppang sa-rŏ kayo**), or 빵 사러 시내에 가요 (**ppang sa-rŏ shinae-e kayo**). This is the correct order. Don't be tempted to try other orders – they will probably be wrong!

Note: This construction is only used with verbs of 'going' and 'coming'. It cannot be used with other verbs at the end of the sentence.

Cheers!

◄） CD 1, TR 2, 01:02

Sangmin goes to a bar with his friends and orders from the waiter.

상민	아저씨, 소주 있어요?
아저씨	네, 네. 있어요. 소주, 맥주, 양주 다 있어요.

상민	그럼, 맥주 하나하고 소주 하나 주세요.
아저씨	네. 알겠어요.
상민	그리고 안주도 주세요. 뭐 있어요?
아저씨	과일하고 오징어하고 마른안주하고 파전하고 . . . 다 있어요.
상민	그럼 과일하고 오징어 주세요.

A little while later, the waiter brings the order . . .

아저씨	여기 있어요. 맛있게 드세요.
상민	감사합니다.
상민	*(to friends)* 건배!

Sangmin	Ajŏssi, soju issŏyo?
Ajŏssi	Ne, ne. Issŏyo. Soju, maekchu, yangju – ta issŏyo.
Sangmin	Kŭrŏm, maekchu hana-hago soju hana chuseyo.
Ajŏssi	Ne. Algessŏyo.
Sangmin	Kŭrigo anju-do chuseyo. Mwo issŏyo?
Ajŏssi	Kwail-hago ojingŏ-hago marŭn anju-hago p'ajŏn-hago . . . ta issŏyo.
Sangmin	Kŭrŏm, kwail-hago ojingŏ chuseyo.

A little while later, the waiter brings the order . . .

Ajŏssi	Yŏgi issŏyo. Mashikke tŭseyo.
Sangmin	Kamsa hamnida.
Sangmin	*(to friends)* Kŏnbae!

1 What drinks does the waiter have?
2 How many drinks does Sangmin order?
3 What else does he ask about?
4 What side dishes does he order?
5 What does the waiter wish his guests?

있어요 (issŏyo). This is one of the most useful words you will ever learn, as it can be used to ask that most important of questions: *Do you have any . . .? Have you got . . .? Is there any . . .?* 빵 있어요 (**ppang issŏyo**)? 있어요 (**issŏyo**). *Do you have any bread? (Yes,) we do (have it).*

Phrases and expressions

. . . issŏyo?	*do you have . . .?*
. . . chuseyo	*please give me . . .*
algessŏyo	*fine/understood/right away*
kamsa hamnida	*thank you*
yŏgi issŏyo	*here you are/here it is*
mashikke tŭseyo	*have a good meal/enjoy your food*
kŏnbae	*cheers!*

ajŏssi	아저씨	*waiter!*
soju	소주	*soju, Korean wine/vodka*
iss-	있-	(1) *exist, there is/are* (stem) (2) *have* (stem)
issŏyo	있어요	(as above, polite style)
maekchu	맥주	*beer*
yangju	양주	*spirits, western liquor*
ta	다	*all, everything*
hana	하나	*one*
-hago	-하고	*and*
chu-	주-	*give* (stem)
chuseyo	주세요	*please give* (polite request form)
kŭrigo	그리고	*and* (also) (used to begin a sentence)
anju	안주	*snacks or side dishes for drinks*
-do	-도	*also*

QUICK VOCAB

kwail	과일	*fruit*
ojingǒ	오징어	*squid*
marǔn anju	마른 안주	*dried snacks*
p'ajǒn	파전	*Korean-style pancake*
yǒgi	여기	*here*

Grammar 2

1 *There is/there are*

The verb 있어요 (**issǒyo**) means *there is* or *there are*, depending on what you are talking about (*there is a book, there are some sheep*). The stem of this verb is 있- (**iss-**), and before the polite particle 요- (**-yo**) can be added, the vowel 어- (**-ǒ**) has to be inserted. This is because 있- (**iss-**) ends with a consonant, whereas the verbs from the first dialogue all ended with vowels. To repeat, stems ending in vowels usually make the polite form by adding -요 (**-yo**). An exception is the verb 하- (**ha-** [*do*]), which, as you will remember, becomes 해요 (**haeyo**) not 하요 (**hayo**). Stems ending in consonants add the ending -어요 (**-ǒyo**) to form the polite style, unless the last vowel in the stem is an -아 (**-a**) or -오 (**-o**), in which case -아요 (**-ayo**) is added to make the polite style.

> *Polite style*
> vowel-stem   **+ yo**
> consonant-stem   **+ ayo**   *if last vowel is -a or -o*
> consonant-stem   **+ ǒyo**   *otherwise*

The opposite of the verb 있- (**iss-**) is 없- (**ǒps-**) (*there isn't or there aren't*). From the rules given earlier, you can work out that its polite style form is 없어요 (**ǒpsǒyo**).

This pair of verbs, as well as expressing existence and location (as in 저기 있어요 [**chǒgi issǒyo**], (*it's over there, it exists over there*), have another meaning of have. 있어요 (**issǒyo**) can mean *I have/he* *has (one/some)*, and 없어요 (ŏpsŏyo) can mean *I don't have*. You can tell by the context which is the relevant meaning.

You will notice again that you can make a complete sentence just with a verb (like 있어요 [issŏyo]). You don't need to specify the subject (who has), and you don't even need to specify what it is that you are talking about, provided that the context makes it clear. In English we usually do need to specify this sort of thing, but Korean likes to be economical and to cut out any unnecessary information.

2 Waiters and shopkeepers

The word 아저씨 (ajŏssi) literally means *uncle*, but it is used as a general term to refer to a shopkeeper, waiter, or even a man in the street on occasions when formality is not called for. It can only be used for males. For females the term is 아줌마 (ajumma) which literally means *aunt*, but is used for any woman who is, say, over 35. The term 아가씨 (agassi) should be used to refer to and attract the attention of young women.

3 Korean particles

In the introduction we talked about the way Korean adds little words called particles to the ends of words. You can see this clearly in the dialogues. We have shown the particles by inserting a dash between the word and the particle, as in 나-도 (na-do [*me-too*]), 시내-에 (shinae-e [*town centre-to = to town*]). Notice that the particle always comes after the noun that it relates to. English often does the opposite of this. We would say 'with me' or 'to school', but Korean says *me-with* and *school-to*.

4 Giving lists, and saying 'and'

The Korean word for *and* is the particle -하고 (-hago). Imagine that you want to say one thing *and* another: *cigarettes and matches*. In Korean, the particle −하고 (**-hago**) attaches to the first noun of the pair, so that you would say: *cigarettes*-**hago** *matches*. The 하고 (**hago**) becomes a part of the word *cigarettes*, since as a particle it has to be attached to a noun. If you want to pause between the two words, you must pause after saying 하고 (**hago**), not before, e.g. *cigarettes*-**hago** (pause) *matches*. You must not say *cigarettes* (pause) **hago** *matches*. Once again, this is because −하고 (**-hago**) belongs to the noun it is with; it is not a free word like the English 'and'.

If there are more than two items in a list, each word is followed by 하고 (**hago**), with the exception of the last, e.g.:

cigarettes-**hago** *matches*-**hago** *ashtray*-**hago** *lighter*

However, you can also add −하고 (**-hago**) onto the last noun of the group if you want to. This gives the sequence a vaguer ring – as though there might be even more items in the list, but you are deciding to stop there (or can't think of any more for the time being).

The particle −하고 (**-hago**) can also mean 'with'. Thus you can say 재민하고 시내에 가요 (**Jaemin-hago shinae-e kayo** [*I'm going to town with Jaemin*]). Once again, you can add more names to the list, e.g. 재민하고 상민하고 시내에 가요 (**Jaemin-hago Sangmin-hago shinae-e kayo**). When you are using −하고 (**-hago**) to mean *with*, you can also use a slightly extended form of the particle, −하고 같이 (**-hago kach'i**), e.g.:

재민하고 같이 시내에 가요 (**Jaemin-hago kach'i shinae-e kayo**).

5 Asking for things

You have learned about Korean verb stems and the polite ending −요 (**-yo**). You will see that this dialogue contains the verb 주세요 (**chuseyo**). The stem here is 주− (**chu-**), and the usual polite style ending is −요 (**-yo**). The bit in the middle, however, you will learn about later. It is a form used to make polite requests, but for now simply memorize the form 주세요 (**chuseyo**) as a word meaning *please give me*. You have also seen the same ending in the phrase 맛있게 드세요 (**mashikke tŭseyo**). 맛있게 (**mashikke**) means *tastily*, and 드세요 (**tŭseyo**) comes from a verb stem which means *imbibe* or *take in*. Therefore, the literal meaning is 'please eat tastily'.

6 Asking for 'one'

In the dialogue, an order is made for a beer and a **soju**. Notice how the number 하나 (**hana** [*one*]) comes after what is being ordered. To ask for one beer you say 맥주 하나 주세요 (**maekchu hana chuseyo**). To ask for one tea you can say 차 하나 주세요 (**ch'a hana chuseyo**).

Korean drinking habits

Koreans love to get together and drink and the most popular drink particularly among men is **soju**, Korean wine/vodka, which has about a 20% alcohol content. The normal form of **soju** does not have an especially strong taste, though recently it is being drunk more and more in fruit flavours like cherry (*ch'eri soju*) and lemon (*lemon soju*), and there is even cucumber flavour (*oi soju*). Beer is becoming increasingly popular, with Korean beers being typically sweeter and lighter than their Western counterparts. Another favourite is **makkŏlli**, which is also made from rice, and has a thick, milky consistency. It is the kind of drink that you will probably either love or hate.

Soju is usually drunk in shots like vodka, and the phrase *one shot!*, spoken in a quasi-American accent, is very popular in Korean bars (the word for bar is **sulchip**, literally *booze house!*). If you go out to drink with Korean friends there will be toasts before each shot, and you will be expected to give one (English will be quite acceptable, at first!). Another popular habit is for each person to sing a song, so be ready with a few Elvis or Beatles numbers, no matter how bad your singing voice might be! Another alternative is the national anthem!

Practice

You will need the following words for the exercises.

chungguk	중국	*China*
ilbon	일본	*Japan*
sulchip	술집	*pub*
hakkyo	학교	*school*
pap	밥	*rice* (cooked rice)
kŭ-daŭm-e	그 다음에	*after that . . .*
kage	가게	*shop*
mashi-	마시–	*drink* (verb stem)
anj-	앉–	*sit* (verb stem)
mŏk-	먹–	*eat* (verb stem)

As you are doing these exercises, don't be tempted to try to use any words we haven't given you. You shouldn't need any!

1 Unjumble the following sentences: write them in the correct order first in romanization, then in Korean script for practice. Don't forget to work out the meaning!

a 가요 (kayo) 일본에 (ilbon-e) 지금 (chigŭm)

b 있어요 (issŏyo) 맥주 (maekchu) 아저씨 (ajŏssi)

c 사러 (sa-rŏ) 가게에 (kage-e) 뭐 (mwo) 가요 (kayo)

d 주세요 (chuseyo) 오징어 (ojingŏ) 양주하고 (yangju-hago)

e 그리고 (kŭrigo) 주세요 (chuseyo) 안주도 (anju-do)

f 나도 (na-do) 가요 (kayo) 가게에 (kage-e)

g 마른 (marŭn) 다 (ta) 밥 (pap) 안주하고 (anju-hago) 있어요 (issŏyo) 맥주하고 (maekchu-hago)

2 Make up Korean sentences to say that there is or there are the following things.

What other meaning could these sentences have?

3 Imagine that the following Korean sentences were spoken to you. Make up an appropriate response in each case.

1 어디 가요?

2 여기 있어요.

3 안녕하세요!

4 잘 지냈어요?

5 뭐 마시러 술집에 가요?

6 소주, 맥주, 양주 다 있어요.

4 Give the polite style form of the following verbs. Try making a short sentence out of each one.

- **a** ka-
- **b** iss-
- **c** sa-
- **d** mŏk- *(eat)*
- **e** ŏps-
- **f** ha-
- **g** anj- *(sit)*

5 Translate the following sentences into Korean.

- **a** *What are you going to buy at the shop?*
- **b** *Hello Mr Kim! How are you?*
- **c** *What are you doing after that?*
- **d** *Are you going to the town centre now?*
- **e** *Where are you going?*
- **f** *We have beer, fruit and bread – all of them!*
- **g** *Please also give me some rice.*
- **h** *Here is your squid. Enjoy your meal!*
- **i** *We don't have Western spirits. Then give me a beer, please.*
- **j** *Some Korean pancake and a soju, please.*

6 Get the attention of the following people and ask them to give you the following things.

7 Read the following notes made by a waiter for two orders. What is required at each table?

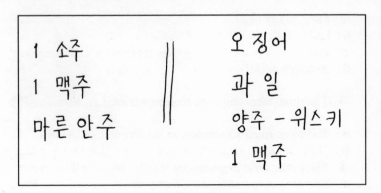

1 소주
1 맥주
마른 안주

오징어
과일
양주 - 위스키
1 맥주

8 Make up two dialogues, based on the following scenarios.

a *You meet a friend who is going to the shop. Greet him and ask where he is going. Suggest that you go together. He agrees and suggests that after that you go to the pub for a beer.*

b *You are in a pub where you meet a friend. Ask how he's been and order a beer and a soju for the two of you. Ask the waiter what snacks he has, make up an appropriate response and order some fruit.*

TEN THINGS TO REMEMBER

1 How to say *hello*.

2 How to ask someone how they are (hint: it's the same as the previous point!).

3 The three most common Korean names: Lee, Kim and Pak.

4 The basic rule of Korean word order: verb at the end.

5 The polite style of sentences, which always ends in **-yo**.

6 How to say *there is/there are* (and *there isn't / there aren't*).

7 Every verb is made up of a stem, to which endings (like **-yo**) are added.

8 How to order drinks and snacks with **chuseyo**.

9 The difference between the ways of calling for a waiter or waitress (**ajŏssi, ajumma, agassi**).

10 How to say *and*.

2

Long time, no see!/It's not me!

In this unit you will learn
* *how to meet, greet and introduce people*
* *how to find where you want to be*
* *how to say that something is or isn't something else*
* *how to give your sentences subjects and topics*

_____

Long time, no see!

◆) CD 1, TR 3

Mr Kim meets an old friend Mr Pak and is introduced to Mr Pak's wife.

박선생	김 선생님, 안녕하세요?
김선생	아! 박 선생님! 안녕하세요!
박선생	오래간만이에요!
김선생	네. 그래요. 진짜 오래간만이에요.
박선생	잘 지냈어요?
김선생	네. 잘 지냈어요. 요즘 사업은 어때요?
박선생	그저 그래요.

(*pointing to his wife*) 우리 집사람이에요.

김선생	아! 그래요? 반갑습니다. 말씀 많이 들었어요.
박선생 부인	반갑습니다. 저는 장윤희에요.
김선생	저는 김진양이에요. 만나서 반갑습니다.

Mr Pak	Kim sŏnsaengnim, annyŏng haseyo?
Mr Kim	A! Pak sŏnsaengnim! Annyŏng haseyo!
Mr Pak	Oraeganman-ieyo!
Mr Kim	Ne. Kŭraeyo. Chinccha oraeganman-ieyo.
Mr Pak	Chal chinaessŏyo?
Mr Kim	Ne. Chal chinaessŏyo. Yojŭm saŏb-un ŏttaeyo?
Mr Pak	Kŭjŏ kŭraeyo.

(*pointing to his wife*) **Uri chipsaram-ieyo.**

Mr Kim	A! Kŭraeyo? Pangapsumnida. Malssŭm mani turŏssŏyo.
Mr Pak's wife	Pangapsumnida. Chŏ-nŭn Chang Yunhŭy-eyo.
Mr Kim	Chŏ-nŭn Kim Jinyang-ieyo. Mannasŏ pangapsŭmnida.

1 How long is it since they met?
2 How is Mr Pak's business doing?
3 What does Mr Kim say about Mr Pak's wife?
4 What is Mr Pak's wife's name?

Phrases and expressions

oraeganman-ieyo	*long time, no see!*
yojŭm saŏb-ŭn ŏttaeyo?	*how's business these days?*
kŭjŏ kŭraeyo	*so-so*

22

malssŭm mani tŭrŏssŏyo (mannasŏ)pangapsŭmnida		*I've heard a lot about you pleased to meet you!*

Kim sŏnsaengnim	김 선생님	*Mr Kim* (**sonsaengnim** 진생님 *also means teacher)*
a!	아!	*ah!*
Pak	박	*Pak (Korean surname)*
kŭraeyo (?)	그래요?	*really (?), is it/it is so (?) (question and reply)*
chinccha	진짜	*really*
yojŭm	요즘	*nowadays*
saŏp	사업	*business*
-ŭn	-은	*(topic particle: see note 4)*
ŏttaeyo?	어때요?	*how is it?*
uri	우리	*we/our*
chip	집	*house*
saram	사람	*person*
chipsaram	집사람	*wife*
(noun)-ieyo	-이에요	*it is (equivalent to) (noun)*
malssŭm	말씀	*words, speech*
man(h)i	많이	*much, many, a lot*
chŏ	저	*me*
-nŭn	-는	*(topic particle)*
Jang Yunhŭy	장윤희	*woman's name (surname first)*
Kim Jinyang	김진양	*man's name (surname first)*

Grammar 3

1 Korean surnames and titles

When you want to address Korean men politely, you can use the title
선생님 (**sŏnsaengnim**), which literally means *teacher*, but in practice

means Mr, Sir. The title can be used on its own to speak to someone you don't know, with the surname (김 선생님 [Kim sŏnsaengnim], 박 선생님 [Pak sŏnsaengnim]), or with the full name (박 재민 선생님 [Pak Jaemin sŏnsaengnim]). It is never used just with someone's first name, so you cannot say 진양 선생님 (Jinyang sŏnsaengnim) (nor, for that matter, can you say 김씨 [Kim-ssi] or 김진양씨 [Kim Jinyang-ssi], both of which would be considered to be quite rude). Notice that, like the polite title —씨 (-ssi) used with first names, the title comes after the person's name, not before as in English.

The title 선생님 (sŏnsaengnim) originally meant the one who was born first, and it therefore shows respect in addressing the person being spoken about as an elder. It is also the normal word for a teacher, and the context is the only way of telling whether it means that someone is a teacher, or whether they are simply being addressed as Mr.

Addressing women is a little more complex. Often women are addressed as being their husbands' wives. This means that Mrs Cho who is married to Mr Kim (Korean women keep their own surnames rather than taking their husbands) may be addressed as 김 선생님 부인 (Kim sŏnsaengnim-puin) (*Kim-Mr-wife*). You could even say the English Mrs Cho (Misesŭ Cho), and sometimes Miss is also used (Misŭ Pak).

Insight

Surnames. Korean women keep their maiden name as their surname, even after marriage.

2 The copula

When you want to say that something *is* something else (e.g. *Mr Kim is a Japanese teacher, this (thing) is a table, this office is the Korean department office*), you use a special verb form called the copula. Like other Korean verbs, it comes at the end of the sentence. However, it behaves a little differently from ordinary verbs. To say 'A is B' (as in, *this is a Chinese book*), you would say:

A   B-ieyo (or B-eyo)
this Chinese book-ieyo

The form −이에요 (**-ieyo**) is used when 'B' ends in a consonant, and −에요 (**-eyo**) is used when 'B' ends in a vowel:

선생님이에요 **sŏnsaengnim-ieyo**   *is a teacher*
맥주에요 **maekchu-eyo**   *is beer*

Please note that 'is' in this sense means 'is equivalent to, is identical with'; it does not mean 'is located in' or 'is a certain way' (e.g. *is green, is angry*). English does not make this distinction. Look at the following sentences:

this is a book
the book is on the table
the book is green

All these use the English 'is', and yet only the first 'is' means 'is identical to'. The second 'is' expresses location, the third describes the book. It is only for the first, when you are saying that 'one thing is equivalent to' or 'the same as' something else that the copula (이에요 [**ieyo**]) is used in Korean. You must be very careful with this, as when you start to learn Korean it can be tempting to use the copula where you should not.

We have described the form *A-B*-**ieyo**, but the simple form *B*-**ieyo** is just as common. This occurs several times in this lesson, and in all cases there is an implied *A* which is unspoken. Look at the following examples (we have put the implied *A* in brackets):

오래간만이에요 (**oraeganman-ieyo**)   *(a matter of) long time no see – it is*
우리 집사람이에요 (**uri chipsaram-ieyo**)   *(this person) my wife – is*

This is the same thing which we saw in unit 1: the context tells you what the subject of the sentence is, therefore you don't have to say it explicitly as you do in English.

Insight

The term *copula* is just a fancy word for the verb *to be*, when you want to say that something *is* something else. In Korean, this takes the form:

<something> <something else> (이)에요 ([i]eyo)

---

3 어때요 (Ŏttaeyo) and 그래요 (Kŭraeyo)

Korean has a group of words which mean 'is (a certain way)'.
어때요 (Ŏttaeyo) means *is how?*, as in:

선생님 어때요? **sŏnsaengnim ŏttaeyo?**	*what is the teacher like?, how is the teacher?*
사업은 어때요? **saŏb-ŭn ŏttaeyo?**	*what's business like, how's business?*

그래요 (kŭraeyo) means *is like that*. It can be used as a statement, e.g. 그래요 (kŭraeyo) (*it is like that, that's right, it is [so]*). As a question, 그래요? (kŭraeyo?) means *is it like that? is that so? really?*

4 Topics

Korean has a particle which can be attached to a noun or a phrase to emphasize that it is the topic of the sentence, that is to say, the thing which is being talked about. Sometimes we do this in English with an expression like *as for . . .*, for emphasis. We might say, for example, *As for my business, it's going pretty well at the moment, or As for me, I don't like cake*. Korean does this kind of thing very frequently with the topic particle −은/−는 (**-ŭn/-nŭn**). In the two sentences above, the nouns *my business* and *me* would both be followed by the topic particle in Korean to show that they are the topics of their sentences.

The particle has two forms, −는 (**-nŭn**) when the noun you are making a topic ends in a vowel, and −은 (**-ŭn**) when it ends in a consonant. Examples are 소주는 (**soju-nŭn**) (*as for soju*), 재민씨는 (**Jaemin ssi-nŭn**) (*as for Jaemin*), 선생님은 (**sŏnsaengnim-ŭn**) (*as for teacher*), 사업은 (**saŏb-ŭn**) (*as for business*).

Insight

Particles are little word-fragments which carry important meaning and are always added to the *end* of words in Korean. To say *books* (i.e. book + plural) we would use the Korean word for *book* and then add the plural particle at the end. To say *for Mr Kim* we would say *Mr Kim* and then add the particle *for* at the end.

To say *to the store* we use the word for *store* and add to it the particle −에 (**e**) which means *to*. Notice that in English the preposition comes first, but in Korean it comes *after* the noun (literally 'store-to').

5 Wives and family

There are at least three words for wife, and they can be divided into two categories, honorific words and non-honorific words. Koreans are very concerned about politeness, and therefore when they are referring to someone else's wife they use an honorific term 부인 (**puin**). This term is never used to refer to your own wife, however. In Korean culture you are meant to downplay yourself, your family and your possessions, therefore to speak about your own wife as 부인 (**puin**) would be inappropriate and possibly even arrogant. Instead, you use either the word 집사람 (**chipsaram**) (literally *house person*), or 아내 (**anae**). It would be very rude to speak about someone else's wife with these non-honorific words.

Furthermore, when referring to your relatives, and even your house, you are expected to say 우리 (**uri**) (*our*) rather than 내 (**nae**) or 제 (**che**), both of which mean *my*. Thus, you would say 우리 집사람 (**uri chipsaram**) (*our wife*) when you want to talk about your wife, even though she is no one else's. Everybody is expected to do this when they talk about their family members.

It's not me!

◀) CD 1, TR 3, 01:02

Mr O is looking for the Korean teacher, Mr Kim. However, first he meets Mr Lee.

오선생	실례합니다
이선생	네?
오선생	한국말 선생님이에요?
이선생	아니요. 저는 한국말 선생님이 아니에요. 저는 일본말 선생님이에요.
오선생	아, 죄송 합니다. 여기가 한국학과 사무실이 아니에요?
이선생	네. 한국학과가 아니에요. 여기는 일본학과에요.
오선생	그럼 한국학과 사무실이 어디에요?
이선생	저기 있어요.

Mr O goes over to the Korean department.

오선생	실례지만, 여기가 한국학과 사무실이에요?
김선생	네. 무슨 일이세요?
오선생	한국말 선생님 만나러 왔어요.

Mr O	Shillye hamnida.
Mr Lee	Ne?
Mr O	Hangungmal sŏnsaengnim-iseyo?
Mr Lee	Aniyo. Chŏ-nŭn hangungmal sŏnsaengnim-i anieyo.
	Chŏ-nŭn ilbonmal sŏnsaengnim-ieyo.
Mr O	A, choesong hamnida. Yŏgi-ga hanguk hakkwa samushir-i anieyo?
Mr Lee	Ne. Hanguk hakkwa-ga anieyo. Yŏgi-nŭn ilbon hakkwa-eyo.
Mr O	Kŭrŏm, hanguk hakkwa samushir-i ŏdi-eyo?
Mr Lee	Chŏgi issŏyo.

Mr O goes over to the Korean department.

Mr O	Shillye-jiman, yŏgi-ga hanguk hakkwa samushir-ieyo?
Mr Kim	Ne. Musŭn ir-iseyo?
Mr O	Hangungmal sŏnsaengnim manna-rŏ wassŏyo.

1 What does Mr O ask Mr Lee?
2 Who is Mr Lee?
3 Where are Mr O and Mr Lee having their conversation?
4 Where does Mr O go next?
5 Why has he come?

Phrases and expressions

shillye hamnida	*excuse me, please*
. . . iseyo?	*are you . . . , please?* (i.e. the person I'm looking for)
choesong hamnida	*I'm sorry*
. . . ŏdi-eyo?	*where is . . . ?*
shillye-jiman . . .	*excuse me, but . . .*
musŭn ir-iseyo?	*what is it? how can I help you? what's the problem?*
. . . manna-rŏ wassŏyo	*I came to see . . .*

hanguk	한국	Korea(n) (pronounced **han-guk** 항국)
mal	말	language
hangungmal	한국말	Korean language
aniyo	아니요	no
-i	-이	(subject particle: see notes)
anieyo	아니에요	is not (opposite of **-(i)eyo**, negative copula)
ilbon	일본	Japan
ilbonmal	일본말	Japanese language
-ga	-가	(subject particle)
hakkwa	학과	department (of college/university)
samushil	사무실	office
ŏdi	어디	where?
chŏgi	저기	(over) there
musŭn	무슨	what, which
il	일	matter, business, work
manna-	만나-	meet (stem)
wassŏyo	왔어요	came (past tense form)

Grammar 4

1 More on verb endings

We have seen that Korean verbs take many different endings. This lesson contains the phrase 실례합니다 (**shillye hamnida**) (*excuse me*), which is made from the verb stem 실례하- (**shillye ha-**). The polite style form of this, as you would expect from the last lesson, is 실례해요 (**shillye haeyo**), since 하-(**ha-**) is irregular. The 합니다 (**hamnida**) form is what is known as the formal style, and usually when you are asking someone to excuse you, this is the form you will want to use. The formal and polite styles can be interchanged in many cases; but the formal is generally more suitable when speaking to someone older or higher in status than you. You will learn about how to make the formal style later.

This lesson also contains the form 실례지만 (**shillye-jiman**). This is an abbreviation of 실례하지만 (**shillye ha-jiman**), the -지만 (-**jiman**) ending meaning *but*. The complete expression means *I'm sorry, but . . .* Don't worry about the -jiman ending for now; you will learn it thoroughly later. Simply remember 실례지만 (**shillye-jiman**) as a set expression.

2 Joining nouns together

As you know, Korean attaches all kinds of particles on the end of nouns to give particular meanings. We have indicated particles by putting a dash between the noun and its particle. However, Korean also allows many nouns to be strung together in a sequence. Examples are 한국 (**hanguk**) + 말 (**mal**), which gives 한국말 (**hangungmal**) (*Korean language*) and 한 국 학 과 (**hanguk hakkwa**) which means *Korean department*. We write some of these as one word (like 한국말 [**hangungmal**]), and flag the individual words and the compound form in the vocabulary.

Insight

Combining nouns and particles. Notice that many Korean words are made by combining smaller words, and sometimes particles too. The term 선생님 (**sǒnsaengnim**) is made of up 선생 (**sǒnsaeng**) and –님 (**-nim**) (an honorific particle). But we can add 일본 (**ilbon**) to the front (일본 선생님 [**ilbon sǒnsaengnim**]). 일본 (**ilbon**) means *Japan*, so the full expression means *(esteemed) Japanese teacher!*

3 Finding the person you want

The copula is Korean's special verb form which allows you to ask if something is something else. You could use it, therefore, to ask a person if they are Mr Kim, say, or Mr Pak. However, when you do this, it is normal to use a special form of the copula –이세요? (**-iseyo?**) This form is an honorific form – it shows politeness to the other person. For the moment simply learn it as a phrase: … **iseyo?** For example:

박 선생님이세요? (**Pak sǒnsaengnim-iseyo?**)
Are you Mr Pak?

한국말 선생님이세요? (**Hangungmal sǒnsaengnim-iseyo?**)
Are you the Korean teacher?

4 Sentence subjects

In the previous dialogue you met the topic particle, and this dialogue introduces you to the subject particle, which is similar. The subject particle –이 (**-i**) attaches to the end of nouns which end in a consonant, and the subject particle –가 (**-ga**) attaches to nouns which end in a vowel. This gives: 맥주가 (**maekchu-ga**) (*beer*), 학교가 (**hakkyo-ga**) (*school*); 선생님이 (**sǒnsaengnim-i**) (*teacher*), 과일이 (**kwair-i**) (from **kwail**, *fruit*).

Naturally enough, the particle marks out the subject of the sentence. For example, in the sentence *The man kicked the dog*, 'the man' is the subject. In the sentence *The man is fat*, 'the man' is again the subject.

However, unfortunately, things are not quite so simple! In both of these sentences, the man could also be the topic, if the topic particle 는 (-nŭn) were used instead of the subject particle. What is the difference between the subject and topic particles?

When something is mentioned for the first time, usually the subject particle is used. Later on, when the subject is repeated in the conversation, you can switch to use the topic particle instead.

The topic particle, you will recall, is particularly for emphasis like the English 'as for'. It is particularly common when comparing two things, e.g. *as for me* (me-**nŭn**), *I hate shopping. As for Mum* (Mum-**nŭn**), *she just loves it.*

Do not worry too much about whether, in a given sentence, it is more correct to use the subject or the topic particle. Most sentences will be correct with either, although some will sound more natural to a Korean (and eventually to you) with one rather than the other. Gradually you will get the feel of which particle to use as your sense of the language develops. It is important that you do use one or the other in your sentences whenever you can, however. Do not just leave off particles, as it can tend to confuse Koreans when foreigners do so, even though they often leave them out themselves in casual speech.

Insight

Articles. Remember, Korean has no word for *a* or *the*, that is, no definite or indefinite article. It's one respect in which Korean is easier than English, so make the most of it!

5 Negative copula

You have learned how to say 'A is B' (this thing-A is a book-B).
Now you must learn the negative copula, 'A is not B', as in 'this
thing is not a book', 'Mr Kim is not my teacher', 'this book is not a
Chinese book'. The form is:

(A-subj/top)	아니에요 (anieyo)	(subj = *subject particle*; (B-subj) top = *topic particle; you can use either*)
저는 선생님이 아니에요	chǒ-nǔn sǒnsaengnim-i anieyo	*I am not a teacher*

(B-subj) **anieyo**

한국학과가 아니에요	**hanguk hakkwa-ga anieyo**	*(this) is not the Korean department*

Look at the examples in the dialogue very carefully to be sure that
you have understood this pattern.

6 When 'yes' means 'no'

Answering questions that require 'yes' and 'no' answers can be a
bit tricky in Korean.

If the question is positive (*Do you like mushrooms?*) then you
answer as you would in English (*Yes, I like them/No, I don't*).

However, if the question is negative (*Don't you like mushrooms?*),
then the answer you give will be the opposite to what you would
say in English, e.g.:

Don't you like mushrooms?

English	*Yes, I do like them*	*No, I don't*
Korean	*No, I do like them*	*Yes, I don't*

Aren't you going out tonight?

| English | *Yes, I am going out* | *No, I'm not* |
| Korean | *No, I am going out* | *Yes, I'm not* |

It goes without saying that you need to think very carefully when answering negative questions in Korean!

7 Where is it?

To ask where something is in Korean, you say: (*B-subj*)
어디에요? (ŏdi eyo?)

However, confusingly, you can also say (*B-subj*) 어디 있어요?
(ŏdi issŏyo?)

When you answer a *where is … ?* question, you must always use the verb 있어요 (issŏyo) e.g.:

| 학교가 거기 | hakkyo-ga kŏgi | *the school over there is / exists,* |
| 있어요 | issŏyo | *the school is over there* |

Being introduced

Koreans are very concerned about politeness, and this characteristic is especially noticeable when you meet people for the first time. It is wise to bow slightly when you shake hands with people, and be sure not to shake hands too hard. The Korean style is for the more senior person to do the shaking, while the other person allows their hand to be shaken. Phrases such as 만나서 반갑습니다 (mannasŏ pangapsŭmnida), which literally means *I've met you, so I'm pleased*, are very common. The form 처음 뵙겠습니다 (ch'ŏŭm poepkessumnida) is even more polite, and literally means *I am seeing you for the first time*.

Practice

For the exercises you will need the following additional vocabulary:

kŏngang	건강	health
hoesa	회사	company (i.e., the company, business)
kajok	가족	family
miguk	미국	America(n)
adŭl	아들	son
hakkyo	학교	school
taehakkyo	대학교	university
shinmun	신문	newspaper
chapchi	잡지	magazine
chigŭm	지금	now

1 The following Korean sentences have gaps where particles and word endings should be. Insert the appropriate word endings into the gaps from the selection given. If there is a choice A/B, make sure you use the correct form. Then work out the meanings of the sentences.

   a 상민(Sangmin)____! 나(Na)___ 시내(shinae)___ 가요 (kayo). (e, do, ssi)

   b 뭐 하(Mwo ha)____ 학교(hakkyo)___ 가(ka)___? (yo, e, -rŏ)

c 김 선생님(Kim sŏnsaengnim)_____ 어때요(ŏttaeyo)?
(ŭn/nŭn)

d 여기(Yŏgi)_____ 사무실이에요(samushir-ieyo)?   (i/ga)

e 아니에요(Anieyo). 여기(Yŏgi)_____ 사무실(samushir)_____
아니에요(anieyo). (i/ga, ŭn/nŭn)

2 Say hello to the following people, and ask about how things are
with them. For example, for the first one you would write the
Korean equivalent of *Hello Mr O, how's the company?* (As for
the company, how is it?).

a *Mr O*	*the company*
b *Mrs Cho*	*business*
c *Mr Pak*	*the family*
d *Taegyu*	*school*
e *Miss Pak*	*her health*

3 Fill in the missing bits of the following dialogue with appropriate
Korean sentences. Remember to check what comes after as well as
what comes before, so that the whole conversation makes sense.

a 백 선생님, 오래간만이에요 (Paek sŏnsaengnim,
oraeganman-ieyo)!

b _____

a 네, 네(Ne, ne). 요즘 사업은 어때요(Yojŭm saŏb-ŭn
ŏttaeyo)?

b _____

a 지금 어디 가요(Chigŭm ŏdi gayo)?

b _____

a 사무실이 어디에요(Samushir-i ŏdi eyo)?

b _____ (*over there*)

a 무슨 일이 있어요(Musŭn ir-i issŏyo)?

b _____

4 Look at the following drawings. Imagine that you are teaching a child the names of the objects and, pointing at each one in turn, you say *this thing* (이것이 [i-gŏsh-i]) *is* ....

Now make up five more sentences, saying that this thing is *not* what you see in the picture.

5 Translate the following dialogue into English.

a 실례합니다. 박 선생님이세요?

b 아니에요. 저는 박 선생님이 아니에요. 박 선생님은 중국 선생님이세요. 여기는 중국학과 사무실이에요.

a 아! 죄송합니다. 실례지만 한국학과는 어디에요?

b 저기 있어요. 나도 지금 선생님 만나러 한국학과에 가요.

a 그럼, 같이 가요.

6 Make up five questions for the following five people. For the first two, ask if they are so-and-so. For the last three, ask negative questions (*you aren't so-and-so are you?*). For all five of your questions make up positive and negative answers. Make sure that you get the words for 'yes' and 'no' the right way round with the last three!

a *an American person*
  b *Mr Lee*
  c *a Chinese teacher*
  d *Mr Paek's son*
  e *a school teacher*

7 Translate the following sentences into Korean. Remember that you should not be translating literally, but getting across the meaning with the words, phrases and constructions you have been learning.

◀) **CD 1, TR 3, 02:10**

  a I'm Pak Sangmin. *Oh, really? Pleased to meet you.*
  b How is school nowadays?
  c Excuse me, are you the Japanese teacher?
  d Waiter! Do you have any squid? *How is the squid?* It's not bad.
  e Isn't this the Korean department office? No, it isn't.
  f I'm not Mrs Woo. *Oh, really? I'm sorry.*
  g This is our Chinese teacher? *Really? I've heard a lot about you.*
  h Is this the Japanese shop?
  i I'm going to see the Korean teacher too.
  j I came to meet Mr Pak's wife.
  k Where is the Korean department?
  l Where is the school office?

8 Make up a short dialogue in which two old friends meet and ask each other how they are getting on. One of them has his son with him and introduces the son to the other person.

9 Kim Dukhoon is looking for the Chinese teacher in the Chinese department, but finds himself talking to the wrong person in the wrong place.

Dukhoon approaches the teacher and says:

실례지만 여기가 중국학과 사무실이에요 (shillye jiman yŏgi-ga
chungguk hakkwa samushir-ieyo)? 중국말 선생님 만나러 왔어요
(chunggung mal sŏnsaengnim manna-rŏ wassŏyo).

How might the teacher respond?

TEN THINGS TO REMEMBER

1 The word for *Mr*.

2 How to ask someone how they've been or how things are.

3 How to say *Pleased to meet you!*

4 How to introduce someone.

5 How to address someone with surnames and titles.

6 The copula – the verb *to be*, and how it is used; how to say something is or isn't something.

7 What the topic particle looks like (**-ŭn/-nŭn**), and how/why it is used.

8 How to apologize and say *excuse me*.

9 How to ask where something is.

10 Subjects of sentences, and how they are marked with the particles **-i/-ga**.

3

....

Sorry, wrong number!/Are you ready to order yet?

In this unit you will learn
- *how to make phone calls*
- *how to make arrangements to meet people*
- *about dining out in Korea*
- *how to ask for what you want*
- *how to discuss what you like and dislike*
- *numbers and counting*
- *how to say 'but'*
- *honorifics*
- *how to make suggestions and say that you can't do something*

_____

Sorry, wrong number!

◆) CD 1, TR 4

Tony is trying to contact his old Korean friend, Mr Kim, but at first he dials the wrong number.

토니	여보세요? 죄송하지만 김선생님 좀 바꿔주세요.
박	여기 그런 사람 없어요.
토니	거기 삼팔구의(에) 이오공육 아니에요?

| 박 | 아니에요. 전화 잘못 거셨어요. |
| 토니 | 죄송합니다. |

At last Tony gets through, has a brief chat to Mr Kim, and arranges to meet him for lunch.

토니	여보세요? 죄송하지만, 김선생님 좀 바꿔주세요.
김선생 부인	잠깐 기다리세요.
김선생	네. 말씀하세요.
토니	아, 안녕하세요? 저는 영국대사관의 토니에요.
김선생	아, 안녕하세요. 오래간만이에요.
토니	오늘 점심에 시간 있어요?
김선생	네, 있어요.
토니	그럼, 제가 점심을 사고 싶어요.
김선생	네, 좋아요. 열두시에 롯데 호텔 앞에서 만납시다.
토니	좋아요. 그럼, 이따가 봅시다.

Tony	Yŏboseyo? Choesong ha-jiman, Kim sŏnsaengnim chom pakkwo-juseyo.
Mr Pak	Yŏgi kŭrŏn saram ŏpsŏyo.
Tony	Kŏgi sam-p'al-ku ŭy(e) i-o-kong-nyuk anieyo?
Mr Pak	Anieyo. Chŏnhwa chalmot kŏshyŏssŏyo.
Tony	Choesong hamnida.

At last Tony gets through, has a brief chat to Mr Kim, and arranges to meet him for lunch.

| Tony | Yŏboseyo? Choesong ha-jiman, Kim sŏnsaengnim chom pakkwo-juseyo. |

Mr Kim's wife	Chamkkan kidariseyo.
Mr Kim	Ne. Malssŭm haseyo.
Tony	A, annyŏng haseyo? Chŏ-nŭn yŏngguk taesagwan-ŭy Tony-eyo.
Mr Kim	A, annyŏng haseyo. Oraeganman-ieyo.
Tony	Onŭl chŏmshim-e shigan issŏyo?
Mr Kim	Ne, issŏyo.
Tony	Kŭrŏm, che-ga chŏmshim-ŭl sa-go ship'ŏyo.
Mr Kim	Ne, choayo. Yŏldu shi-e Lotte Hot'el ap'-esŏ mannapshida.
Tony	Choayo. Kŭrŏm, ittaga popshida.

1 Who does Tony ask for?
2 What number did he mean to dial?
3 Who does Tony identify himself as?
4 What does Tony ask Mr Kim?
5 Why does he want to know this?
6 Where do they decide to meet?

Phrases and expressions

choesong ha-jiman	I'm sorry, but; excuse me, but ...
choesong hamnida	I'm sorry; I apologize; excuse me
... chom pakkwo-juseyo	can I have/speak to ..., please?
(chŏnhwa) chalmot kŏshyŏssŏyo	you've got the wrong number (you've misdialled)
(chŏnhwa) chalmot kŏrŏssŏyo	I've got the wrong number
chamkkan kidariseyo	please wait a moment
malssŭm haseyo	please speak (I'm listening!)
shigan-i issŏyo?	do you have (free) time?
(issŭseyo?)	(polite form)
... -ŭl sago ship'ŏyo	I want to buy ...
... ap'esŏ mannapshida	let's meet in front of ...
ittaga popshida	we'll see each other later/ see you later/let's meet later

yŏboseyo	여보세요	*hello* (on the telephone)
chom	좀	*a little; please* (see note 2)
kŭrŏn	그런	*such a, that* (particular)
sam	삼	*three*
p'al	팔	*eight*
ku	구	*nine*
i	이	*two*
o	오	*five*
kong/yŏng	공/영	*zero*
yuk	육	*six*
chŏnhwa	전화	*telephone*
chalmot	잘못	*wrongly, mis-*
chal	잘	*well* (adverb)
chamkkan	잠깐	*a little* (while)
kidari-	기다리-	*wait*
yŏngguk	영국	*England, British*
taesagwan	대사관	*embassy*
-ŭy	-의	*belonging to*
chŏmshim	점심	*lunch*
-e	-에	*at* (a certain time)
shigan	시간	*time, hour*
che-ga	제가	*I* (humble form) (subject)
choh-	좋-	*good* (stem)
choayo	좋아요	*good, fine, OK* (polite style, notice the **h** is not pronounced)
yŏl	열	*ten* (pure Korean number)
tu	두	*two* (pure Korean number)
yŏldu	열두	*twelve* (pure Korean number)
shi	-시	*o'clock*
hot'el	호텔	*hotel*

ap'esŏ	앞에서	*in front of*
manna-	만나-	*meet* (stem)
ittaga	이따가	*in a little while*
po-	보-	*see, look* (sometimes: *meet*)
pwayo	봐요	*see, look* (polite style, irregular)

Grammar 5

1 *Sentences with 'but'*

In Unit 2 you learned 실례합니다(shillye hamnida), and a similar form 실례지만(shillye-jiman), which meant *I'm sorry, but …* or *Excuse me, but …* This unit takes another verb, 죄송합니다 (choesong hamnida), and puts it in the −지만(-jiman) form: 죄송하지만(choesong ha-jiman), to mean *I'm sorry, but …* As you will have guessed, -jiman is a verb ending which means *but*, and it can be attached to any verb base.

Here are a few other verb stems you have learned, each put into the -jiman form:

가−(ka-)	*go*	가지만(ka-jiman)	*goes, but …*
하−(ha-)	*do*	하지만(ha-jiman)	*does, but …*
사−(sa-)	*buy*	사지만(sa-jiman)	*buys, but …*
있−(iss-)	*is/are, have*	있지만(it-jiman)	*has, but …*
마시−(mashi-)	*drink*	마시지만 (mashi-jiman)	*drinks, but …*
먹−(mŏk-)	*eat*	먹지만 (mŏk-jiman)	*eats, but …*
앉−(anj-)	*sit*	앉지만(anj-jiman)	*sits, but …*

Notice the form with 있−(iss-), where the double ss becomes pronounced as a t when −지만(-jiman) is added. In Korean *han'gul* you still write the double ss, but the word is pronounced **itjiman**.

Can you work out the meanings of the following sentence?

김 선생님 맥주 잘 마시지만, 저는 양주 잘 마셔요
(Kim sŏnsaengnim maekchu chal mashi-jiman, chŏ-nŭn yangju chal mashyŏyo).

2 Making requests more polite

The word 좀 (chom) is flagged in the vocabulary as meaning *please*. It is not, however, of itself the direct equivalent of our English word 'please', because some of its uses are quite different. However, if you insert the word **chom** in a request immediately before the verb at the end of the sentence, it does have a similar effect to 'please'. It is most frequently used when asking to be given something, that is, before the verb 주- (chu-) (*give*). In this unit you meet it in the sentence: 김 선생님 좀 바꿔 주세요 (**Kim sŏnsaengnim chom pakkwo-juseyo**) (*Can I speak to Mr Kim, please*). You might use it in a sentence such as 맥주 좀 주세요 (**maekchu chom chuseyo**) (*Please give me some beer*). It softens the request, and consequently makes it more polite.

3 Numbers and counting

◄》 **CD 1, TR 4, 02:10**

Korean has two completely different sets of numbers which makes things very awkward for the language learner. There is a Korean set, often called pure Korean numerals, and another set which are of Chinese origin, usually called Sino-Korean numerals. Numbers are used for counting things, and which set you use in any situation depends on what it is that you want to count! To count hours, for example, you use the pure Korean numbers, but to count minutes, the Sino-Korean numbers must be used. You just have to learn which set of numbers are used with which objects. Taking an example from the next dialogue, someone orders two portions of something and two dishes of something else. You simply have to know that the word *portion* takes the Sino-Korean numbers (so the word for *two* is 이(i)), and that *dishes* takes the pure Korean numbers (so the word for *two* is 둘(**dwul**))! There is no shortcut, and we will tell you more about this as the course progresses. In this unit you will meet the Sino-Korean numbers only. They are as follows:

공/영(kong/yŏng)	0				
일(il)	1	십일(shibil)	11	이십일(ishibil)	21
이(i)	2	십이(shibi)	12	이십이(ishibi)	22
삼(sam)	3	십삼(shipsam)	13	이십삼(ishipsam)	23
사(sa)	4	십사(shipsa)	14	(*etc.*)	
오(o)	5	십오(shibo)	15		
육(yuk)	6	십육(shimnyuk)	16		
칠(ch'il)	7	십칠(shipch'il)	17		
팔(p'al)	8	십팔(shipp'al)	18		
구(ku)	9	십구(shipku)	19	이십구(ishipku)	29
십(ship)	10	이십(iship)	20	삼십(samship)	30

Once you have learned 1 to 10, everything is straightforward. Twenty is just 'two-ten', 30 'three-ten', etc.:

이십(i-ship)	20
삼십(sam-ship)	30
사십(sa-ship)	40 (*etc.*)
구십(ku-ship)	90
백(paek)	100
천(ch'ŏn)	1000
만(man)	10000

Here are a few more complicated examples for you to pick up the pattern:

구십팔(ku-ship-p'al)	98
오십육(o-shim-nyuk)	56
백십일(paek-shib-il)	111
삼백팔십사(sam-paek-p'al-ship-sa)	384
이천구백칠십(i-ch'ŏn-ku-baek-chi'l-ship)	2,970
삼만오천육백이십오(sam-man-o-ch'ŏn-nyuk-baek- i-shib-o)	35,625

As you will have observed, there are a number of oddities in the pronunciation of numbers when they are put together, especially concerning the number 6. However, we will always indicate these in the romanization. Just remember that the number 6 can be pronounced in any of the following ways, depending on the surrounding syllables: **yuk, yung, nyuk, nyung, ryuk, ryung, lyuk, lyung!**

Phone numbers are given in Korean by listing the digits in their Sino-Korean form. Seoul numbers have seven or eight digits, and speakers usually give the first three or four, then the sound ―에(-e), then the second four. In English, one might quote the area code, then say ―에(-e), then the telephone number:

352–0873   삼오이―에 공팔칠삼(**sam-o-i-e kong-p'al -ch'il-sam**)

966–3491   구륙륙―에 삼사구일(**ku-ryung-nyug-e sam-sa-ku-il**)

01535 568326   공일오삼오―에 오륙팔삼이륙(**kong-il-o-sam-o-e o-ryuk-p'al-sam-i-ryuk**)

Insight

Korean has two different sets of numbers – one which is Korean in origin, and the other which is Chinese. For everything that you want to count you just have to learn which set of numbers it goes with – the Korean or the Sino-Korean (Chinese).

4 Introducing honorifics

In this unit you meet several verbs that end with −세요(-seyo).
The ones you have seen are: 하세요(haseyo) (from 하−(ha-)),
기다리세요(kidariseyo) (from 기다리−(kidari-)), and 있으세요
(issuseyo) (from 있−(iss-)). These verbs are in what we call the
polite honorific form which is shown by the ending −세요(-seyo).
All you have to do is add −세요(-seyo) to a verb stem which ends
in a vowel, and −으세요(-ŭseyo) to a verb stem which ends in a
consonant, like this:

마시−(mashi-)   마시세요(mashiseyo)   있−(iss-)   있으세요
(issŭseyo)

하−(ha-)   하세요(haseyo)   앉−(anj-) 앉으세요
(anjŭseyo)

기다리−(kidari-) 기다리세요(kidariseyo)

The most common use for this ending is as a polite request asking
someone to do something, e.g. *please (do it)*, so that 기다리세요
(kidariseyo) means *please wait*. Notice that we've called the ending
the polite honorific. You've met the polite ending −요(-yo) before,
and this ending also has it, hence the name **polite** honorific. But
it also has an -s- in it, which is the **honorific** bit. This serves to
honour the person you are talking to, that is, the person you are
requesting to do whatever it is. It is a form of respect, and it is this
honorific part that makes the ending −(으)세요(-[ŭ]seyo) into a
polite request.

Although for the next few units this is the most common use you
will meet for the polite honorific, there is another way in which it
can be used, either to ask a question of somebody you particularly
esteem, respect or wish to honour, or simply to make a statement
about them. Thus the sentence 김 선생님이 학교에 가세요(**Kim
sŏnsaengnim-i hakkyo-e kaseyo**) means *Mr Kim is going to school*,
and shows special respect or honour to Mr Kim. You will meet this
usage in the next dialogue.

For now you should make sure that you are completely happy with
the polite request meaning, but also be aware of the other use in
the back of your mind, since these honorifics are something that we
shall return to later on.

5 Saying what you want to do

The form -고 싶어요(-ko ship'ŏyo) (the form 싶어요[ship'ŏyo]
coming from the stem 싶-[ship'-]) can be added onto any verb
stem which describes an action, to produce the meaning *want
to* (verb). Thus 나는 먹고 싶어요(na-nŭn mŏk-ko ship'ŏyo)
means *I want to eat*. The -고(-ko) attaches straight to the verb
stem, whether it ends in a consonant or a vowel, and there are
no irregularities other than that the **k** of the -고(-ko) becomes
pronounced as a **g** after vowels, as you would expect. Note that
you can't put any other words between the -고(-ko) and the
싶어요(ship'ŏyo) parts. Treat them as if they are inseparable,
even though there is a space between them. Here are a couple
of examples:

먹-(mŏk-)   *eat*   저는 점심 먹고 싶어요(chŏ-nŭn
                             chŏmshim mŏk-ko ship'ŏyo)
                             I want to eat lunch
만나-(manna-)   *meet*   진양 만나고 싶어요(Jinyang
                             manna-go ship'ŏyo)
                             I want to meet Jinyang

Insight

Many Korean verbs consist of two words, the second of
which is 하- (ha-) which literally means *to do*. You've met
this verb in expressions like 좋아해요 (choa haeyo) where
the underlying verb is 좋아하- (choa ha-); and 안녕하세요
(annyŏng haseyo) where the underlying verb is 하- (ha-),
and the expression means *to do well* or *peaceably*; and
미안하지만 (mian hajiman …). Note the 하- (ha-) stem in
that expression too, *I'm sorry, but*….

6 *Making suggestions*

A final verb-ending pattern to learn from this dialogue is ㅡ(으)
ㅂ시다(-[ŭ]pshida). ㅡㅂ시다(-pshida) is added onto a verb stem
ending in a vowel, and ㅡ읍시다(-ŭpshida) is added if the verb stem
ends in a consonant. This pattern of using the vowel 으(ŭ) to add
to nouns or verb stems that end in consonants is one that you are
becoming familiar with. The example you have seen is the ending
(으)세요([ŭ]seyo), but the topic particle 는/은([n]ŭn) is similar.
You will meet many, many examples as you work through this
book.

The meaning of 읍시다([ŭ]pshida) is *let's do (such-and-such)*, and
it is a relatively polite or formal form, as opposed to something you
would say in a very informal or colloquial conversation. Note once
again that you can only add this form onto a verb which describes an
action, just as you saw with ㅡ고 싶어요(-ko ship'ŏyo). Thus you can
say 'let's go for a walk', since that describes an action, but you can't
say 'let's be pretty' using ㅡ(으)ㅂ시다(-[ŭ]pshida), since being pretty
is a state and not an action. Here are a couple of examples of the
form:

열두시에 같이 시내에 갑시다
(yŏldu shi-e kach'i shinae-e kapshida)
Let's go to town together at 12

음료수 마십시다
(ŭmryosu mashipshida)
Let's have a drink

Eating out

The first dialogue was all about arranging to meet up for lunch, and
this is a common enough Korean habit, just as it is in the West. You
will actually find that Koreans tend to eat out a little more often than
Westerners, and also that eating out can be done more cheaply in Korea.

In the West we tend to eat out for special occasions or for a treat and, of course, Koreans do this too and are prepared to spend quite a bit of money. But they will also often take an ordinary meal out and this can be done quite cheaply.

When eating out with Koreans, it is very rare to 'go dutch' and split the bill as we might among friends in our culture. In Korea it is normally one person who pays the bill, either the person who has done the inviting, or the most senior figure (in age or status). It is generally regarded as the senior person's job to pay for everyone else, and you must not offend Koreans by insisting on breaking their cultural tradition. After all, everyone ends up being the senior party at some time or other, so everything works out fairly in the end!

Are you ready to order yet?

◀ CD 1, TR 4, 06:27

Tony and Mr Kim meet up and go to a restaurant for lunch. They order drinks, and then have a discussion about their culinary likes and dislikes.

종업원	어서 오세요. 이쪽으로 앉으세요.
김선생	고맙습니다.
종업원	음료수 하시겠어요?
김선생	우선 맥주 좀 주세요.
김선생	한국 음식 좋아하세요?
토니	네, 아주 좋아하지만, 매운 거 잘 못 먹어요.
김선생	그럼 불고기나 갈비를 먹읍시다.
토니	네, 좋아요. 그리고 저는 냉면도 먹고 싶어요.

The waiter arrives to take their food order.

종업원	주문하시겠어요?
토니	불고기 이인분하고 냉면 두 그릇 주세요.
종업원	물냉면 드릴까요? 비빔냉면 드릴까요?
토니	물냉면 주세요.

A little while later the waiter arrives with the food.

종업원	맛있게 드세요!

During the meal, to the waitress:

토니	아가씨, 물하고 김치 좀 더 주세요.

Chongŏpwon	Ŏsŏ oseyo. I cchog-ŭro anjŭseyo.
Mr Kim	Komapsŭmnida.
Chongŏpwon	Ŭmryosu hashigessŏyo?
Mr Kim	Usŏn maekchu chom chuseyo.
Mr Kim	Hanguk ŭmshik choa haseyo?
Tony	Ne, aju choa ha-jiman, maeun kŏ chal mon mŏgŏyo.
Mr Kim	Kŭrŏm pulgogi-na kalbi-rŭl mŏgŭpshida.
Tony	Ne, choayo. Kŭrigo chŏ-nun naengmyŏn-do mŏk-ko ship'ŏyo.

The waiter arrives to take their food order.

Chongŏpwon	Chumun hashigessŏyo?
Tony	Pulgogi i-inbun-hago naengmyŏn tu kŭrŭt chuseyo.
Chongŏpwon	Mul naengmyŏn tŭrilkkayo? Pibim naengmyŏn tŭrilkkayo?
Tony	Mul naengmyŏn chuseyo.

A little while later the waiter arrives with the food.

Chongŏpwon	Mashikke tŭseyo!

During the meal, to the waiter:

Tony	Agassi, mul-hago kimch'i chom tŏ chuseyo.

1 Do they order wine?
2 What does Tony think about Korean food?
3 Tony is content with Kim's suggestion. True or false?
4 What does Tony ask the waiter for?

Phrases and expressions

ŏsŏ oseyo	*welcome!*
i cchog-ŭro anjŭseyo	*please sit over here (over this side)*
komapsŭmnida	*thank you*
ŭmryosu hashigessŏyo?	*would you like something to drink?*
chumun hashigessŏyo?	*would you like to order?*
... tŭrilkkayo?	*would you like ...? (lit: shall I give you ...?)*

chongŏpwon	종업원	*waiter, assistant (remember **ajossi** is the term to call him over)*
cchok	쪽	*side ('k' is pronounced 'g' when followed by a vowel)*
-(ŭ)ro	-(으)로	*towards, in the direction of*
anj-	앉-	*sit (stem)*
ŭmryosu	음료수	*drink*
usŏn	우선	*first*
ŭmshik	음식	*food*
choa ha-	좋아하-	*like (stem)*
aju	아주	*very*
maeun	매운	*spicy (adj)*

QUICK VOCAB

kŏ	거	*thing, object, fact* (abbreviation of **kŏt**, spelt **kŏs**)
mot	못	*cannot* (nb **mot** + **m-** = **mon m-**)
pulgogi	불고기	*pulgogi, Korean spiced marinated beef*
-na	-나	*or* (particle)
kalbi	갈비	*marinated and fried spare ribs* (usually pork, cheaper than *pulgogi*)
naengmyŏn	냉면	*thin noodles with vegetables*
chumun ha-	주문하-	*order* (stem)
i	이	*two*
-inbun	-인분	*portion*
tu	두	*two (pure Korean number)*
kŭrŭt	그릇	*dish/bowl*
mul-	물-	*water*
mul naengmyŏn	물 냉면	*thin noodles in cold soup* (spicy and refreshing!)
pibim	비빔	*mixed*
tŭrilkkayo	드릴까요	*would you like?* (lit: shall I give you?)
agassi	아가씨	*waitress!* (lit: girl, unmarried woman)
kimch'i	김치	*classic Korean side dish, marinated cabbage, spiced strongly with chillies*
tŏ	더	*more*

Grammar 6

1 좋아요 Choayo *and* 좋아해요 choa haeyo

There is an important difference between these two verbs. 좋아요 (**choayo**) is a kind of verbal adjective which means 'is good'. It may by implication mean that you like it, but the root meaning is that something is good. It is important to see the distinction, and here is an example to illustrate the difference. 김치 좋아요(**Kimch'i choayo**) means that the kimch'i is good. You might conceivably recognize it as being good kimch'i (as far as kimch'i goes …) without actually wanting to say that you like it. Even if you hate kimch'i, you might still be able to discern between good and bad examples.

Contrariwise, 좋아해요(choa haeyo) means 'like'. 김치 좋아해요 (Kimch'i choa haeyo) means that you, or whoever else is being spoken about, actually likes the stuff. It might be the case that you like kimch'i, even if it's not quite at its best. You can say you like something without commenting on its relative quality.

Can you explain the difference, therefore, between 김 선생님 좋아요(Kim sŏnsaengnim choayo) and 김 선생님 좋아해요(Kim sŏnsaengnim choa haeyo)?

The first means that Mr Kim is a good man, a good guy. The second means that you (or whoever) actually likes him.

Insight

Liking. To say something is good you use 좋아요 (choayo). To say you like something you use 좋아해요 (choa haeyo). For instance: 맥주 좋아요 (maekchu choayo) *the beer is good*. 맥주 좋아해요 (maekchu choa haeyo) *I like beer*. Both of these expressions come from the verb 좋- (choh-). Notice that it has a silent 'h' at the end – important for writing, but not for speaking.

2 Or

-(이)나(-[i]na) can be added after a noun to mean 'or', just like -하고(-hago) can be added after nouns to mean 'and'. (noun) -(이)나(-[i]na) (noun), therefore, means (noun) or (noun). 갈비나 불고기 먹읍시다(kalbi-na pulgogi mŏgŭpshida) means 'let's eat kalbi or pulgogi'.

You can make this *either … or* idea sound even more vague by adding -(이)나(-[i]na) to both nouns. Then the translation would be something like 'let's eat kalbi or pulgogi or something'. In a similar way you can have just one noun plus -(이)나(-[i]na)to make the

sentence more vague so that it means '(noun) or something'. Take the
sentence 갈비나 먹읍시다(**kalbi-na mŏgŭpshida**). This would mean
that you are not all that bothered about what exactly you eat, you are
just suggesting kalbi. Something else might be just as acceptable.

3 When you can't do it

The little word 못(**mot**) can be added to a sentence to give the
meaning that something cannot be done: 시내에 못 가요(**shinae-e
mot kayo**) (*I can't go to the city centre*). Note that your inability to
do something is being described – you can't do it, rather than that
you aren't able to or you won't. If you simply choose not to go to
the city, or if you aren't going, don't want to go or refuse to go,
you can't use this construction. It expresses impossibility. Whether
you want to go or not, you can't.

The word 못(**mot**) goes as close to the verb as possible, right near
the end of the clause immediately before the verb.

Watch out for the sound change that occurs at the end of 못(**mot**)
when the verb following begins with an **m**. 못(**mot**) plus 만나-
(**manna-**) gives [몬만나요]**mon mannayo** (*I can't meet*).

4 Measuring and counting

We will have a detailed section on measuring and counting later
on, but for now, notice the two patterns in this lesson which will
give you the key:

불고기(**pulgogi**)	이(**i**)	인분(**inbun**)
냉면(**naengmyŏn**)	두(**tu**)	그릇(**kŭrŭt**)
(*noun*)	(*number*)	(*measure*)

This is important. First you state the substance you are measuring,
then the number you want, then the unit that you are measuring it
by (here portions and dishes).

About Lotte, department stores and food

Lotte Hotel is one of the famous buildings in Seoul, and is situated right next to the Lotte Department Store (Korea's biggest) between Myŏngdong and Shich'ŏng (City Hall). Lotte is one of Korea's **chaebŏl** or large conglomerates.

A Korean department store is a little different from its Western equivalent. It contains literally hundreds of sales assistants (mainly female), with at least one on every single counter throughout the store. At first it can seem as though you're under pressure to buy, but this isn't really the case any more than in the West, and you soon get used to it!

This lesson also introduced two famous Korean foods. 김치 (**kimch'i**) is the marinated pickled cabbage – very spicy with lots of chilli powder – eaten as a side dish with virtually every Korean meal. There are certain other varieties, like 물김치 (**mul kimch'i**) or water kimch'i which is less spicy and consists of kimch'i in liquid, and 무김치 (**mu kimch'i**) which is made of white radish (**mu**) instead of cabbage. You also met 냉면 (**naengmyŏn**) which is a kind of clear, thin noodle, rather like vermicelli, usually eaten in a cold soup as 물냉면 (**mul naengmyŏn**). It is spicy (and is one of the few Korean dishes to contain mustard or something similar), but is extremely refreshing in the hot summer as it is served with lots of ice. 비빔냉면 (**pibim naengmyŏn**) is another form, without water this time, and mixed with other vegetables.

Practice

Additional vocabulary for these exercises is as follows.

shiktang	식당	*restaurant*
paekhwajŏm	백화점	*department store*
wain	와인	*wine*
mal ha-	말하-	*speak, say*

1 Make up a sentence for each of the following sets of information, saying that you want to do A and B. For example, for the first, your Korean sentence will say 'I want to meet Mr Pak and Mrs Kim'.

a	*Mr Pak*	*Mrs Kim*	*meet*
b	*bread*	*fruit*	*buy*
c	*pulgogi*	*kalbi*	*eat*
d	*English teacher*	*Japanese teacher*	*wait for*
e	*beer*	*whisky*	*drink*
f	*octopus*	*naengmyŏn*	*order*

Now repeat the exercise, saying that you want to do either A or B.

2 The following is an excerpt from a page in someone's telephone book. Write out the names of each person and their number, in Korean script and in romanization (*doctor:* 의사[*ŭysa*]).

3 The following sentences are jumbled up. Can you unscramble them?

a 하세요(haseyo)? 음식(ŭmshik) 좋아(choa) 한국(hanguk)

b 힐튼(Hilton) 이에요(ieyo) 저는(chŏ-nŭn) −의(-ŭy) 상민(Sangmin) 호텔(Hot'el)

c 앞에서(ap'esŏ) 학교(hakkyo) 만납시다(mannapshida) 열두시에(yŏldushi-e)

d 오늘(onŭl) 시간이(shigan-i) 점심(chŏmshim) 있으세요(issŭseyo)? −에(-e)

e 물(mul) 주세요(chuseyo) 우선(usŏn) 좀(chom)

f 먹어요(mŏgŏyo) 매운(maeun) 잘(chal) 거(kŏ) 못(mot)

g 냉면(naengmyŏn) 갈비(kalbi) 두 그릇(tu-kŭrŭt) 삼인분(saminbun) 주세요(chuseyo) −하고(-hago)

4 Change the following sentences to say that they can't be done. For example, for the first you will write a Korean sentence saying that you can't go to the Japanese embassy.

a *I'm going to the Japanese embassy.*

b 지금 점심 먹으러 식당에 가요(Chigŭm chŏmshim mŏg-ŭrŏ shiktang-e kayo).

c 재민씨, 상민씨 기다리세요(Jaemin-ssi, Sangmin-ssi kidariseyo)?

d *Sangmin eats spicy food.*

e *I am meeting Mrs Jang in front of the Chinese embassy.*

f 백화점에 가요(Paekhwajŏm-e kayo).

5 Put the following verbs into the polite honorific form (ending in −세요[-seyo]), and also into the 'let's do' form. Then make up four sentences, two with each of the two verb forms (you can use any verbs you want to make the sentences).

a 가-   **c** 보-   **e** 기다리-   **g** 만나-
b 주문하-   **d** 앉-   **f** 사-

6 What is the difference between the following two pairs of sentences?

    a 이 갈비가 아주 좋아요(I-kalbi-ga aju choayo).
       이 갈비를 아주 좋아해요(I-kalbi-rŭl aju choa haeyo).
    b 박 선생님의 아들 좋아요(Pak sŏnsaengnim-ŭy adŭl choayo).
       박 선생님의 아들 좋아해요 (Pak sŏnsaengnim-ŭy adŭl choa haeyo).

7 The following sentences should be translated into Korean. They are intended to practise suggestions and also how to say 'but'.

    a *Let's speak in Chinese.*
    b *Let's go to the department store.*
    c *Let's drink some beer or wine.*
    d *I want to go to America, but I can't.*
    e *I like whisky but I can't drink it. (implication: it isn't good for me or it makes me too drunk!)*
    f *I want to telephone Mr Kim, but I misdialled.*

8 What are the following numbers in English?

    a 구십칠(kuship-ch'il).
    b 오십삼(oship-sam).
    c 이백칠(ibaek-ch'il).
    d 팔백육십일(p'albaeng-nyukship-il).
    e 삼만사천 사백구십오 (samman-sach'ŏn-sabaek-kushib-o).

9 Translate the following sentences into English.

    a 매운 거 좋아하지만 한국음식 잘 못 먹어요.
    b 실례지만 영국 대사관이 어디 있어요?

c 이쪽으로 앉으세요. 음료수 하시겠어요?
d 시간이 있으세요? 그럼 이따가 만납시다.
e 김선생님? 잠깐 기다리세요.
  죄송하지만 여기 그런 사람 없어요. 잘못
   거셨어요.
f 거기 팔육삼의 공오사이에요?

10 You are arranging to meet your friend. She asks you
where you should meet. Answer her, suggesting a place
and a time.

TEN THINGS TO REMEMBER

1 How to ask to speak to someone on the telephone

2 What to do if someone has got the wrong number

3 How to say *Please wait a moment!*

4 How to say you want to do something

5 The way to make arrangements to meet someone

6 How to say *See you later!*

7 Forming *but ...* sentences

8 The verb ending which is used to make suggestions

9 How to say *thank you*

10 What to say before tucking into a meal

4

**How much is it altogether?/
Finding the way**

In this unit you will learn
- *simple shopping*
- *finding your way around*
- *more about negation*
- *how to say 'if'*
- *use of the direct object particle*
- *how to say where something is and where some activity
  takes place*
- *more numbers and money in Korean*
- *basic use of classifiers when counting things*

How much is it altogether?

◀) **CD 1, TR 5**

Chris goes to a Korean bookstore to buy some dictionaries and
unfortunately has a little trouble over the price.

점원	뭘 찾으세요?
크리스	사전 있어요?
점원	네. 한영사전 드릴까요?
크리스	네, 한영사전하고 영한사전 둘 다
주세요.

점원	여기 있어요.
크리스	얼마에요?
점원	한 권에 만원씩, 모두 이만원이에요.
크리스	한자 사전도 있어요?
점원	한자 사전은 세 가지 종류가 있어요.
크리스	제일 싼 거 주세요.
점원	잠깐 기다리세요 . . . 여기 있어요.
크리스	고맙습니다. 모두 얼마에요?
점원	한자 사전 삼만원 . . . 그러니까 모두 오만원이에요.
크리스	제일 싼 게 삼만원이에요? 그럼, 제일 비싼 건 얼마에요? 십만 원이에요?
점원	아! 죄송합니다. 착각했어요. 모두 삼만원이에요. 영수증도 드릴까요?
크리스	네, 주세요.
점원	알겠습니다. 여기 있어요. 안녕히 가세요!
크리스	안녕히 계세요.

Chŏmwon	Mwol ch'ajŭseyo?
Chris	Sajŏn issŏyo?
Chŏmwon	Ne. Han-yŏng sajŏn tŭrilkkayo?
Chris	Ne han-yŏng sajŏn-hago yŏng-han sajŏn tul ta chuseyo.
Chŏmwon	Yŏgi issŏyo.
Chris	Ŏlma-eyo?
Chŏmwon	Han kwon-e man won-ssik, modu i-man won-ieyo.
Chris	Hanja sajŏn-do issŏyo?
Chŏmwon	Hanja sajŏn-ŭn se kaji chongnyu-ga issŏyo.
Chris	Cheil ssan kŏ chuseyo.
Chŏmwon	Chamkkan kidariseyo … yŏgi issŏyo.
Chris	Komapsumnida. Modu ŏlmaeyo?

Chŏmwon	Hanja sajŏn sam-man won … kŭrŏnikka modu o-man won-ieyo.
Chris	Cheil ssan ke sam-man won-ieyo? Kŭrŏm, cheil pissan kŏn ŏlma-eyo? Shim-man won-ieyo?!
Chŏmwon	A! Choesong hamnida. Ch'akkak haessŏyo. Modu sam-man won-ieyo. Yŏngsujŭng-do tŭrilkkayo?
Chris	Ne, chuseyo.
Chŏmwon	Algesssŭmnida. Yŏgi issŏyo. Annyŏnghi kaseyo!
Chris	Annyŏnghi kyeseyo.

1 How many dictionaries does Chris want to buy?
2 How much are the first two volumes?
3 What choice is he later offered?
4 What kind of Chinese character dictionary does he require?
5 Whose fault is the confusion over cost?
6 What sarcastic remark does Chris make?

Phrases and expressions

mwol ch'ajŭseyo?	*what are you looking for? can I help you?*
(modu) ŏlmaeyo?	*how much is it (altogether)?*
algesssŭmnida	*I understand; okay, right, fine (formally)*
ch'akkak haessŏyo	*I have made a mistake*
annyŏnghi kaseyo	*goodbye (to someone who is leaving)*
annyŏnghi kyeseyo	*goodbye (to someone who is staying)*

mwol	뭘	*what* (object form)
ch'aj-	찾–	*look for*
sajŏn	사전	*dictionary*
han-yŏng	한–영	*Korean–English*
yŏng-han	영–한	*English–Korean*
tul	둘	*two* (when you mean 'the two of them', 'both')
ŏlma	얼마	*how much*

han	한	*one* (pure Korean, when used with a counter or measure word)
kwon	권	*volume* (measure word)
man	만	*10,000*
won	원	*won* (unit of Korean currency)
-ssik	–씩	*each, per* (see note 3)
modu	모두	*altogether, everything, everyone*
hanja	한자	*Chinese characters*
se	세	*three* (pure Korean)
kaji	가지	*kind, example* (counter for the noun **chongnyu**)
chongnyu	종류	*type, sort, kind*
cheil	제일	*the most*
ssan	싼	*cheap* (adjective)
ssa-	싸–	*is cheap*
kŭrŏnikka	그러니까	*therefore, because of that*
pissan	비싼	*expensive* (adjective)
pissa-	비싸–	*is expensive*
kŏn	건	*thing, object* (abbrev of **kŏt** 것 + topic particle)
ch'akkak ha-	착각하–	*make a mistake*
yŏngsujŭng	영수증	*receipt*

Grammar 7

1 *Counters*

In English, we sometimes use counters (counting words) to count objects. We might say, for example, two *cups* of coffee, or three *packets* of soup. Cups and packets are counters or measures by which we count and measure things like coffee and soup. On other occasions we do not use counters, for example, we say two books, three houses. However, in Korean, counters are frequently used when English does not use them. To say the two previous sentences, for example, a Korean might say:

책 두 권 (**ch'aek tu kwon**) *book two volumes* *two books*
집 세 채 (**chip se ch'ae**) *house three buildings* *three houses*

This is the usual pattern in Korean for counting things, or for talking about a certain number of something. Here are some common Korean counters which take the Sino-Korean numbers you have already learned:

분(**pun**) *minute* 삼분(**sam pun**) *three minutes*
초(**ch'o**) *second* 이십초(**iship ch'o**) *twenty seconds*
일(**il**) *day* 삼십일(**samshib il**) *thirty days*
년(**nyŏn**) *year* 사년(**sa nyŏn**) *four years*
층(**ch'ŭng**) *floors* 삼층(**sam ch'ŭng**) *three floors,*
     (in building)   *third floor*
원(**won**) *won (Korean* (*etc.*)
     money)
명(**myŏng**) *person*

Note that the word 명(**myŏng**) can also be used with pure Korean numbers.

You can ask how many of something there are with the word 몇(**myŏt**), for example: 몇 명(**myŏn-myŏng**)? 몇 년(**myŏn-nyŏn**)? 몇 분(**myŏt-pun**)?

This is not to say that Korean always uses counters. There are some words which do not take a special counter, that is to say, the word itself is the counter, as it is in English with books and houses. Thus, for counting days with 일(**il**) (*day*) you don't need to say 일삼일(**il sam il**). In fact, that would be wrong. You simply say

삼일(**sam il**). If a counter is not used, therefore, the number comes before what you are counting, instead of after it.

Insight

Korean has a set of particles known as *counters*. For example, if you want to count books, the counter is –권 (**-kwon**), which means something like 'volume'. If you wanted to say 'three books' you would say:

Item	Number	Counter
Book	three	volumes (**kwon**)

2 Pure Korean numbers

◄» CD 1, TR 5, 02:08

You now need to know the pure Korean numbers. We teach you up to 49. If you need more than that, you can simply use the Sino-Korean numbers instead. In fact, there are no pure Korean numbers above 99, so Sino-Korean numbers have to be used for 100 and over. For smaller numbers, however (say, below 50), it is important to know the pure Korean numbers and to use them when they are required, since otherwise you will be easily misunderstood (or not understood at all!) by Koreans.

하나(**han[a]**)	1	열하나(**yŏlhan[a]**)	11
둘(**tu[l]**)	2	열둘(**yŏldu[l]**)	12
셋(**se[t]**)	3	열셋(**yŏlse[t]**)	13
넷(**ne[t]**)	4		
다섯(**tasŏt**)	5		
여섯(**yŏsŏt**)	6		
일곱(**ilgop**)	7		
여덟(**yŏdŏl**)	8	스물(**sŭmu[l]**)	20
아(**ahop**)	9	서른(**sŏrŭn**)	30
열(**yŏl**)	10	마흔(**mahŭn**)	40

The letters in brackets are only used when the number is not followed by a noun or a counter to which it refers.

Most counters are used with pure Korean numbers, so with the exception of those you have already learned which take Sino-Korean numbers, you are safe to use pure Korean numbers. Here are some examples of common counters which are used with pure Korean numbers:

시 (shi)	*o'clock*
시간 (shigan)	*hours* (duration)
살 (sal)	*years of age*
사람 (saram)	*person*
분 (pun)	*person* (honorific)
마리 (mari)	*animal*
권 (kwon)	*volume* (for books)
잔 (chan)	*cup (ful)*
상자 (sangja)	*box*
병 (pyŏng)	*bottle*

3 Prices

This lesson introduces you to a construction for saying how much things cost, using the word 씩(ssik), which is difficult to translate, but gives the sentence the flavour of so much each, so much apiece, or so much *per* such and such a quantity. Study the following sentences to see how it is used:

한 권에 만원씩	(han kwon-e man won-ssik)	*10,000 won per book* (volume)
사과 오백원씩	(sagwa o-baek won-ssik)	*apples 500 won each*
사과 한 상자에 천원씩	(sagwa han sangja-e ch'ŏn won-ssik)	*apples 1,000 won a box*

To make sentences out of these, all you have to do is add the copula:

사과가 오백원씩이에요   **(Sagwa-ga o-baek**   *Apples are 500*
                         won-ssig-ieyo)   *won each*

4 Introducing adjectives

You have now met several Korean words that function in the way that adjectives do in English. In Korean they are usually called modifiers, but they work rather like adjectives. Remember that they always come before the noun they describe. Here are the ones you have met so far, with a couple of extras thrown in:

비싼	(pissan)	*expensive*
싼	(ssan)	*cheap*
그런	(kŭrŏn)	*such a, that* (kind of)
매운	(maeun)	*spicy*
좋은	(choŭn)	*good*
나쁜	(nappŭn)	*bad*

You'll notice that they all end in **n**, and in a later lesson you will learn how they can be formed from their associated verbs.

One very common construction in Korean is to find these words before the noun 것(**kŏt**), which means *thing* (and sometimes also *fact* or *object*). This noun 것(**kŏt**) itself needs a little explanation, as it commonly occurs in several different forms. On its own the word is pronounced [걷](**kŏt**), but written 것 (**kŏs**) (remember your pronunciation rules!). It is sometimes abbreviated to 거(**kŏ**). With the topic particle its form is 것은 (**kŏs-un**) or, in casual speech, 건(**kŏn**). With the subject particle its form is 것이(**kŏsh-i**)(pronunciation rules!), but it is often shortened to 게(**ke**).

An example of the noun 것(kŏt) with an adjective would be: 싼 게 (ssan ke) or 싼 것이(ssan kŏsh-i), which mean *the cheap thing*, or, more commonly, *the cheap one*. You might put these into sentences as follows:

저는 비싼 거 좋아해요	(chŏ-nŭn pissan kŏ choa haeyo)	*I like expensive things*
그런 거 못 먹어요	(kŭrŏn kŏ mon mŏgŏyo)	*I can't eat that (kind of) thing*

Insight

Adjectives are made from verbs, but have the ending −ㄴ (−n) or −은 (−ŭn), if the verb ends in a consonant. 비싸요 (Pissayo) means *it is expensive;* 비싼 (pissan) is the adjective *expensive*.

5 Superlatives

You can easily make superlatives in Korean (e.g. the most expensive, the most pretty, the best, the fastest) by putting the word 제일(cheil) before the adjective/modifier:

제일 매운 음식	(cheil maeun ŭmshik)	*the most spicy food, the spiciest food*
제일 비싼 게	(cheil pissan ke)	*the most expensive (thing)* [subject]
제일 좋은 사람	(cheil choŭn saram)	*the best person*

6 Linking words

In continuous speech, Korean likes to show the way that sentences relate to each other by using linking words to begin consecutive sentences. In English we are encouraged not to begin sentences with 'but', 'and' and similar words, but Korean does this sort of thing a lot and it is good style.

It makes your Korean sound natural. Here are the most common examples:

그러나	(kǔrǒna)	*but* (*whereas*)
그렇지만	(kǔrǒch'iman)	*but*
그리고	(kǔrigo)	*and*
그런데	(kǔrǒnde)	*however, but*
그러니까	(kǔrǒnikka)	*therefore, that being so*
그럼	(kǔrǒm)	*so, therefore* (more colloquial)

Insight

The three linking words that are really crucial are: 그렇지만 (**kǔrǒch'iman**), *but*; 그런데 (**kǔrǒnde**), *however, but*; and 그리고 (**kǔrigo**), *and*.

7 Saying goodbye

You will see from the dialogue that Korean has two ways for saying goodbye. 안녕히 가세요(**annyǒnghi kaseyo**) is used to say goodbye to someone who is leaving (i.e. about to walk or go away) and 안녕히 계세요(**annyǒnghi kyeseyo**) is used to say goodbye to someone who is staying when the person saying it is going. Sometimes both speakers will be going, so in that case both would say 안녕히 가세요(**annyǒnghi kaseyo**). It sounds a bit tricky at first, admittedly, but once you get used to the idea it's really quite simple. All you have to think about is who is leaving and who is staying. 안녕히(**annyǒnghi**) means *in peace*, so 안녕히 가세요 (**annyǒnghi kaseyo**) means 'go in peace' (from 가-[ka-], *go*), and 안녕히 계세요(**annyǒnghi kyeseyo**) means 'stay in peace' (made, surprisingly enough, from the honorific form of the verb 있-[iss-], *exist, stay*).

Chinese characters

In the days before the Korean alphabet was invented, all writing in Korea was done in Chinese characters and then only by an elite that knew how. Even many years after King Sejong's great invention, Chinese characters still remained the most common way of writing for the educated, and it was not until the end of the 19th century that the Korean script began to grow in popularity.

Chinese characters are very complex and there are thousands of different ones, all of which have to be learned. Fortunately you do not need to do this for your studies in Korean. However, many Korean newspapers use some Chinese characters interspersed within the Korean text and educated Koreans are expected to know around 1,800 characters which are recommended by the Korean education authorities. Unless you wish to be a scholar in Oriental studies, you can survive perfectly well with no knowledge of characters and should you wish to read a Korean newspaper you can buy one which does not use them. It is then only academic and technical books that will be off-limits to you.

Out of interest, the following shows an extract from an academic book which uses both the Korean script and Chinese characters.

그러나, 이러한 부정적인 경향의 평가만으로 廉想
涉의 후기 소설의 서술방법상의 두드러진 특징들을
다 설명했다고 할 수는 없다. 비록 후기소설에 대한

총체적 평가가 부정적인 쪽으로 쏠려버렸다 해도 그의 한 편의 소설 혹은 여러 편의 소설에 주목할 만하고 본뜰 만한 긍정적 서술방법이 숨어 있을 가능성을 외면할 수는 없기 때문이다.

우선, 앞서 인용한 바 있는 단문 <나와 自然主義>에서 廉想涉이 후진들에게 「말과 글을 배울 것」을 권고했던 것을 상기해 둘 필요가 있다. 여기에다 「寫實主義를 研究할 것」이라는 권고를 덧붙인 것을 보면, 그는 후진들에게 자신 있고 능력 있다고 생각하는 내용을 권장한것임이 분명해진다. 우선, 廉想涉은 한 편의 소설을 만들어가는 과정에 있어서 최소한 「문장」에는 자신감을 가졌다. 廉想涉의 후기소설의 경우, 문제는 이렇듯 자신감에 넘친 문장력이 날카로우면서도 깊이있는 주제의식과 잘 어울릴 기회를 갖지 못한 데 있다. 문장력은 작가로서의 관록과 비례되는 것이나, 사상이니 주제의식이니 하는 것은 그렇지 않다.

Finding the way

🔊 **CD 1, TR 5, 04:20**

Mr Pak needs to find a bank to get some money changed, but he has a few problems finding what he is looking for.

박선생	실례합니다. 이 근처에 은행이 어디 있어요?
은행원 A	저 우체국에서 왼쪽으로 가면 상업은행이 있어요.
박선생	고맙습니다.

At the counter in Sangŏp bank.

박선생	영국 돈을 한국 돈으로 좀 바꾸고 싶어요.
은행원 B	우리 은행은 외환 업무를 안해요. 한국 외환 은행으로 가세요.
박선생	한국 외환 은행이 어디 있어요?
은행원 B	종로 쪽으로 가세요. 종로 사 거리에서 오른쪽으로 가면 한국 외환 은행 지점이 있어요.
박선생	여기서 멀어요?
은행원 B	아니요. 걸어서 오 분 정도 걸려요

Mr Pak	Shillye hamnida. I-kŭnch'ŏ-e ŭnhaeng-i ŏdi issŏyo?
Unhaengwon A	Chŏ uch'egug-esŏ oencchog-ŭro ka-myŏn Sangŏp unhaeng-i issŏyo.
Mr Pak	Komapsumnida.

At the counter in Sangŏp bank.

Mr Pak	Yŏngguk ton-ŭl hanguk ton-ŭro chom pakku-go ship'ŏyo.
Unhaengwon B	Uri ŭnhaeng-ŭn oehwan ŏmmu-rŭl an haeyo. Hanguk oehwan ŭnhaeng-ŭro kaseyo.
Mr Pak	Hanguk oehwan ŭnhaeng-i ŏdi issŏyo?
Unhaengwon B	Chongno cchog-ŭro kaseyo. Chongno sagŏri-esŏ orŭn cchog-ŭro ka-myŏn Hanguk oehwan ŭnhaeng chijŏm-i issŏyo.
Mr Pak	Yŏgi-sŏ mŏrŏyo?
Unhaengwon B	Aniyo. Kŏrŏsŏ o pun chŏngdo kŏllyŏyo.

1 Where is the Sangŏp bank?
2 What service is required?
3 What is the problem?
4 Where is the other bank located?

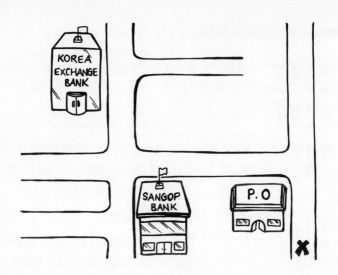

i-	이-	*this one* (+ noun), *this* (noun)
kŭnch'ŏ	근처	*district, area, vicinity*
ŭnhaeng	은행	*bank*
ŭnhaengwon	은행원	*bank clerk*
chŏ-	저-	*that one* (a long way away, old English 'yon')
kŭ-	그-	*that one* (nearer than **chŏ**)
uch'eguk	우체국	*post office*
-esŏ	-에서	location particle (place in which something happens); *from*
oen	왼	*left*
(***verb***)**-myŏn**	-면	*if* (verb) (clause ending)
sangŏp	상업	*trade*
sangŏp ŭnhaeng	상업은행	*Commercial Bank* (lit: *trade bank*)
ch'anggu	창구	*window, cashier window*
ton	돈	*money*
-(r)ŭl	-을/를	(direct object particle)
oehwan	외환	*exchange*

QUICK VOCAB

78

ŏmmu	업무	business, service
an	안	not (used to make verbs negative)
(hangwuk) oehwan ŭnhaeng	외환은행	Korea Exchange Bank
Chongno	종로	Chongno (one of the main streets in Seoul, north of the Han river)
sagŏri	사거리	crossroads
orŭn	오른	right
chijŏm	지점	branch
yŏgi-sŏ	여기서	from here (abbrev of yŏgi-eso)
mŏrŏyo	멀어요	is far (polite style, irregular stem)
aniyo	아니요	no
kŏrŏsŏ	걸어서	on foot
pun	분	minute
chŏngdo	정도	extent, about (approximately)
kŏlli-	걸리-	takes (time duration)
kŏllyŏyo	걸려요	it takes (polite style)

Grammar 8

1 Directions

The particle –(으)로(-[ŭ]ro) is used to indicate direction towards. It won't surprise you to learn that the form –으로(-ŭro) is added to nouns that end with consonants and –로(-ro) to nouns that end with a vowel. The meaning, then, is *towards, in the direction of*, and therefore it usually occurs with verbs of going and coming.

Another meaning is *into* (another shape or form), and the most important use for that is the one you meet in the dialogue, changing money from one currency *into* another one.

2 Saying 'from', and saying where something happens

The particle –에서(-esŏ) on the end of nouns means *from* (a place). It could be used in the following circumstances, for example:

From the bank (-에서[-esŏ]) to the post office (-까지[-kkaji]) takes 10 minutes
I've come from the embassy (esŏ): 대사관에서 왔어요(taesagwan-esŏ wassŏyo)

There is another important (and slightly more complicated) use of –에서(-esŏ), in addition to this meaning. When you are describing where an activity is taking place, you mark the place noun with –에서(-esŏ). For example, if you want to say that you are doing your homework in the study, you put the particle –에서(-esŏ) onto the word for study. –에서(-esŏ) thus marks the place where an activity is happening. If you want to say that you are doing some drawing in your bedroom, you put the particle –에서(-esŏ) onto the word bedroom, since that is where the activity of drawing is taking place.

Note that –에서(-esŏ) is not used to say where something exists (that is, with 있어요[issŏyo] and 없어요[ŏpsŏyo]). In those cases, you simply mark the place noun with –에[-e]. Neither is it used to say where you are going to (motion towards is marked by 에[-e], e.g. 학교에 가요[hakkyo-e kayo], as you have already learned). Observe the following examples carefully:

가게에 책 있어요/많아요(Kage-e ch'aek issŏyo/manayo)
There are books in the shop/There are many books in the shop (existence once again)

가게에서 책을 사요(Kage-esŏ ch'aek-ŭl sayo)
I am buying a book in the shop (the activity of buying)

식당에서 만납시다(**Shiktang-esŏ mannapshida**)
Let's meet in the restaurant (the activity of meeting)

식당에 가요(**Shiktang-e kayo**)
I'm going to the restaurant (motion towards the restaurant,
   going or coming)

Thus, -에(**-e**) is used with verbs of motion towards (coming and
going), and to speak about the existence or non-existence of
something in a particular place. –에서(**-eso**) is used to say where an
activity is taking place, or to mean *from*.

3 'If' clauses

The verb ending –(으)면(**-[ŭ]myŏn**) (-으면[**-ŭmyŏn**] after verb stems
ending in consonants, otherwise –면[**-myŏn**]) can be added to the
stem of any verb to make an if clause. The half of the sentence that
comes before the –면(**-myŏn**) is the part that is governed by the 'if'.
This is best illustrated by examples:

종로 쪽으로 가면 은행이 있어요(**Chongno cchog-ŭro
ka-myŏn ŭnhaeng-i issŏyo**)
If you go in the direction of Chongno, there is a bank

선생님이 맥주 주문하면 나도 맥주 주문해요
(**Sŏnsaengnim-i maekchu chumun ha-myŏn, na-do maekchu
chumun haeyo**)
If you (sir) order a beer, I'll order one too

김 선생님 찾으면 저쪽으로 가세요(**Kim sŏnsaengnim
ch'aj-ŭmyŏn chŏ-cchog-ŭro kaseyo**)
If you're looking for Mr Kim, go that way

4 The object particle

The direct object of a sentence is the bit of the sentence that gets something done to it by the subject or the actor in the sentence. This is best understood by examples. In the following sentences the objects are in bold type:

I want to drink **a beer** (what you, the subject, want to drink, the object, a beer)
He's playing **cricket** (what he, the subject, wants to play, the object, cricket)
Don't watch **television** all the time! (what you, the implied subject, want to watch, the object, TV)

Korean often marks the objects in its sentences by adding the object particle to the noun which is the object of the sentence.

The object particle is –를(-rŭl) after a vowel, and –을(-ŭl) after a consonant. Here are examples:

책을 삽시다(**Ch'aeg-ŭl sapshida**)
Let's buy a book

돈을 바꾸고 싶어요(**Ton-ŭl pakku-go ship'ŏyo**)
I want to change some money

(**NB** 한국돈을 영국돈으로 바꾸고 싶어요[**hanguk ton-ŭl yŏngguk ton-ŭro pakku-go ship'ŏyo**])

맥주 두 가지 종류를 사요(**maekchu tu kaji jongnyu-rŭl sayo**)?
Are you going to buy two (different) kinds of beer?

Please note that the verbs 있어요(**issŏyo**) and 없어요(**ŏpsŏyo**) always take subjects, and not objects, so you will not find them in conjunction with nouns that have the object particle. This means that you will always see sentences of the form 나는 책이 있어요(**na-nŭn ch'aeg-i issŏyo**); you would never see a sentence like *나는 책을 있어요(**na-nŭn ch'aeg-ŭl issŏyo**), since 있어요

(**issŏyo**) and 없어요(**ŏpsŏyo**) always take subjects. The same
thing applies to verbs of quantity like 많-(**manh-**), since that verb
and others like it are stating how much of something exists. They
are thus similar to the verbs 있어요(**issŏyo**) and 없어요(**ŏpsŏyo**).

Insight

Trouble with –에 (**-e**). The particle –에 (**-e**) is used to say
where you are going to (가게에 가요 [**kage-e kayo**] - *I'm
going to the shop*). If you're saying what you're going to be
doing at the shop then you would use the particle –에서
(**-esŏ**) instead. –에서 (**-esŏ**) can also have the meaning *from*.

5 *Saying you're not doing something*

In the last unit you learned the little word 못(**mot**) to say that
you couldn't do something. Now it's time to learn how to say
you do not, are not doing or are not going to do something
(usually by choice). In other words, it is your decision, not
circumstances beyond your control, which mean you are not
doing whatever it is.

You use the little word 안(**an**) immediately before the verb, like this:

나는 맥주 안 마셔요(**Na-nŭn maekchu an mashyŏyo**)
I'm not drinking beer/I don't drink beer (it's your choice)

재민은 시내에 안 가요(**Jaemin-ŭn shinae-e an kayo**)
Jaemin's not going into town (he doesn't want to, chooses not to, etc.)

Compare: 재민은 시내에 못 가요(**Jaemin-ŭn shinae-e mot
kayo**) (he can't, he has something else on, etc.) Sometimes,
however, the word 안(**an**) simply means 'not':

음식이 안 좋아요(**Ŭmshik-i an choayo**)
The food is not good (it's the food's fault – 못(**mot**) would be
 inappropriate)

6 Verb stems ending in -i

You have now learned several verb stems which end in **-i**.
They include 마시-(**mashi-**), 걸리-(**kŏlli-**), and 기다리-(**kidari-**).
These verbs change slightly when you add the polite particle
–요(**-yo**). The last **i** changes to **yŏ**, to give you the polite style forms:
마셔요(**mashyŏyo**), 걸려요(**kŏllyŏyo**) and 기다려요(**kidaryŏyo**).

Banking and finance

Banking is simple enough in Korea and the use of credit cards is
widespread. There are one or two peculiarities, however, including
the fact that Korea does not use cheques. The online system is highly
developed, and you can send money electronically very easily and at a
much cheaper cost than is usually possible in the West.

Cash is still the most common method of payment, however, and in
addition to the coins there are 1,000 won, 5,000 won and 10,000 won
notes (천원[**ch'ŏn won**], 오천원[**och'ŏn won**] and 만원 [**man won**]).
There is also a 50,000 won note (오만원[**oman won**]), which was first
issued in 2009.

Practice

Here is additional vocabulary for these exercises.

chan	잔	*cup*
ilk-	읽–	*read*
p'yo	표	*ticket*
pyŏng	병	*bottle*
tarŭn	다른	*another, different* (modifier/adjective)

QUICK VOCAB

1 Complete the following sentences with the words taken from the
box at the bottom.

a 우리 은행은 ___ 업무를 안 해요. ___ 은행에 ___.
Our bank does not do that (kind of business). Please go to another bank.

b 이쪽으로 ___ 식당이 있어요.
If you go this way there is a restaurant.

c 실례 ___ 한영 ___ 있어요?
Excuse me, but do you have a Korean–English dictionary?

d ___ 멀어요? 걸어서 ___ 걸려요.
Is it far from here? On foot it takes 50 minutes.

e ___ 한국 외환은행 ___ ___ 이에요.
I'm a bank clerk from the Korea Exchange Bank.

f 저 ___ 에서 ___ 쪽으로 가면 외환 ___ 이 있어요.
If you go right at the post office there is an exchange bank.

g 맥주 두 가지 ___ 있어요.
We have two kinds of beer.

h ___ 팔만원이에요. 영수증 ___?
Altogether it's 80,000 won. Would you like a receipt?

i 오래간만 ___. 요즘 ___ 은 어때요?
Long time no see! How's business nowadays?

j 제일 ___ 술 마시고 ___.
I want to drink the most expensive alcohol.

사전	은행원	여기서	종류가	다른
비싼	모두	-지만	가면	이에요
우체국	그런	싫어요	드릴까요	오른
있어요	가세요	저는	오십분	사업
의	은행			

2 In the following English sentences, which nouns are direct objects and would thus be marked with –를/을(-[r]ŭl) if they were to be translated into Korean? Note that some sentences may have more than one object, and some may not have any.

a *I want to watch a movie tonight.*
b *What are you going to do when you see him?*
c *How many cars does your family have?*
d *He just said a bad word.*
e *Can I eat some bread? No, but there are some crackers.*

3 Think up appropriate Korean questions to go with the following answers.

a 죄송하지만, 여기는 그런 사람이 없어요(Choesong ha-jiman, yŏgi-nŭn kŭrŏn saram-i ŏpsŏyo).
b *I'm sorry, I don't have time.*
c 아니요. 잘못 거셨어요(Aniyo. Chal mot kŏshyŏssŏyo).
d *Pleased to meet you. I've heard a lot about you!*
e 잠깐 기다리세요. 여기 있어요(Chamkkan kidariseyo. Yŏgi issŏyo).
f *No, I don't like Korean food.*
g *I don't particularly want to drink beer right now.*

4 Here are a number of items, and the price per item. Make up a sentence which says in Korean what the cost per item is and then say what the total cost is. For example, if you see a picture of six glasses, and the cost per glass is 500 won, you would write something like 한 잔에 오 백원 씩이에요(han-jan-e obaek won-ssig-ieyo). 그러니까 모두 삼천원이에요(kŭrŏnikka modu samch'ŏn won-ieyo).

5 The following sentences have no particles in them. Put them in!

   a 여기＿＿ 왼쪽＿＿ 가면 상업 은행 지점＿＿
        있어요.
   b 시간＿＿ 있으면 열시＿＿ 호텔 앞＿＿
        만납시다.
   c 중국 돈＿＿ 영국 돈＿＿ 좀 바꾸고 싶어요.
   d 우리 은행＿＿ 외환 업무＿＿ 안 해요.
   e 저＿＿ 매운 음식＿＿ 못 먹어요. 갈비＿＿
        먹고 싶어요.
   f 여기＿＿ 그런 사람＿＿ 없어요.
   g 그런 것＿＿ 못 마시면, 물＿＿ 마십시다.
   h 영한사전 두 가지 종류＿＿ 있어요.
   i 한 권＿＿ 이만원＿＿, 그러니까 모두
        삼만원이에요.

6 Practise counting the following things out loud.

   a *3 books, 8 books, 22 books*
   b *1 day, 3 days, 67 days*
   c *1 person, 7 people, 34 people*

d *3 octopus, 9 octopus, 14 octopus*
e *2 bottles, 10 bottles*
f *9 dogs, 1 dog (dog = 개[kae])*
g *1,000 won, 10,000 won*

7 Make up five Korean sentences based around the following verbs. Each of your sentences should put the verb in the negative, with the word 안(**an**).

a 주문하-(**chumun ha-**) **d** 기다리-(**kidari-**)
b 걸리-(**kŏlli-**) **e** 읽-(**ilk-**)
c 드세요(**tŭseyo**)

Which of your sentences would still make sense if you replaced 안(**an**) with 못(**mot**)? What would be the difference in meaning?

8 Translate the following sentences into Korean.

a *Excuse me, is there a restaurant in this area?*
b *I can't eat naengmyŏn. I can't eat kalbi either.*
c *How much is it? One plate is 2,000 won, so it's 6,000 won altogether.*
d *Go left here. If you go five minutes, you'll see (= there is) Chongno crossroads. Go left. The bank is on your right.*
e *How much is the cheapest one?*
f *It takes about 10 minutes on foot.*
g *There's no branch of the Korea Exchange Bank in this area.*
h *I want to change some money. I have about 50,000 won.*
i *In Korea there are 10 kinds of kimch'i. In England there are none.*
j *Would you like a Korean language dictionary?*
k *What type would you like?*
l *Please give me the cheapest.*
m *Is Mr Kim a bad man?*
n *You're going to the post office? Okay, goodbye!*

9 Make up a dialogue between a shopkeeper and a child going shopping. Here is the shopping list (**NB** *milk* = 우유 [**uyu**]; *bottle* = 병 [**pyŏng**]).

SHOPPING LIST

2 bottles milk	Meat
Bread	10 beers
Kimch'i	Apples

TEN THINGS TO REMEMBER

1 How to respond if someone asks **mwol ch'ajŭseyo?**

2 Asking how much something is

3 The difference between the two Korean numbering systems

4 Prices and the numbers used with the Korean **won** currency

5 How to say *I understand; okay; fine*

6 Two ways of saying goodbye and the difference between them

7 How to say *I've made a mistake*

8 Making *if ... then* sentences

9 How to ask the way somewhere

10 Recognizing the object particle and how it is used

5

Is this the bus for Tongdaemun
market?/This fruit doesn't look
too good!

In this unit you will learn
- *how to catch buses in Korea and make sure you have got to the right place*
- *how to shop for food at the market*
- *how to express surprise or exclamation*
- *comparisons*
- *how to join two sentences together to make one*

Is this the bus for Tongdaemun market?

◀》 **CD 1, TR 6**

Mr Kim is a stranger in Seoul who wants to find his way to Tongdaemun market. He ends up being persuaded to go to Namdaemun market instead.

김선생	실례지만 여기 동대문 시장 가는 버스가 있어요?
이선생	저도 서울 사람이 아니라서 잘 모르겠어요.

To Mrs O, another passer-by.

김선생	이 정류장에 동대문 시장 가는 버스가 서요?
오선생	아니요. 이 정류장에는 동대문 시장 가는 버스가 없어요. 이십 번 버스를 타면 남대문 시장에 가요.
김선생	남대문 시장이요? 남대문 시장에는 뭐가 있어요?
오선생	뭐가 있느냐고요? 남대문 시장에는 안 파는 게 없어요.
김선생	동대문 시장보다 물건이 더 많아요?
오선생	제 생각에는, 남대문 시장이 동대문 시장보다 물건도 더 많고 재미 있어요. 그렇지만 남대문 시장에서 원숭이는 안 팔아요. 동대문 시장에서는 팔지만....
김선생	정말이에요? 그런데 저는 원숭이는 필요 없어요.
오선생	그럼 이십번 버스를 타세요.
김선생	어디서 타요?
오선생	바로 길 건너편 정류장에서 타세요.
김선생	버스 요금이 얼마에요?
오선생	정말 촌사람이시군요! 구백원이에요.
김선생	고맙습니다.
오선생	빨리 가세요. 저기 버스가 와요.

Mr Kim	Shillye-jiman, yŏgi Tongdaemun shijang kanŭn bŏsŭ-ga issŏyo?
Mr Lee	Chŏ-do Sŏul saram-i ani-rasŏ chal morŭgessŏyo.

To Mrs O, another passer-by.

Mr Kim	I chŏngnyujang-e Tongdaemun shijang kanŭn bŏsŭ-ga sŏyo?
Mrs O	Aniyo. I chŏngnyujang-e-nŭn Tongdaemun shijang ganŭn bŏsŭ-ga ŏpsŏyo. Iship pŏn bŏsŭ-rŭl t'a-myŏn Namdaemun shijang-e kayo.
Mr Kim	Namdaemun shijang-iyo? Namdaemun shijang-e-nŭn mwo-ga issŏyo?
Mrs O	Mwo-ga innŭnyagoyo? Namdaemun shijang-enŭn an p'anŭn ke ŏpsŏyo.
Mr Kim	Tongdaemun shijang-poda mulgŏn-i tŏ manayo?
Mrs O	Che saenggag-enŭn, Namdaemun shijang-i Tongdaemun shijang-poda mulgŏn-do tŏ man-k'o chaemi issŏyo. Kŭrŏch'iman Namdaemun shijang-esŏ wonsungi-nŭn an p'arayo. Tongdaemun shijang-esŏ-nŭn p'aljiman ...
Mr Kim	Chŏngmal-ieyo? Kŭrŏnde, chŏ-nŭn wonsungi-nŭn p'iryo ŏpsŏyo.
Mrs O	Kŭrŏm iship pŏn bŏsu-rŭl t'aseyo.
Mr Kim	Ŏdi-sŏ t'ayo?
Mrs O	Paro kil kŏnnŏp'yŏn chŏngnyujang-esŏ t'aseyo.
Mr Kim	Bŏsŭ yogŭm-i ŏlma-eyo?
Mrs O	Chŏngmal ch'onsaram-ishigunyo! kubaek won-ieyo.
Mr Kim	Komapsŭmnida.
Mrs O	Ppalli kaseyo. Chŏgi bŏsŭ-ga wayo.

1 Why can't the first person help?
2 What happens if you take bus number 20?
3 What is the choice like at Namdaemun?
4 Which market is preferred?
5 Is there anything you can't get at Namdaemun?
6 Where should you catch the bus?
7 Why is there surprise at the last question?
8 Why the hurry?

Phrases and expressions

(chal) morŭgessŏyo	*I don't know (at all)*
an p'anŭn ke ŏpsŏyo	*there's nothing which is not sold (you can buy everything)*
mwoga innŭnyagoyo?	*you're asking what there is? (you mean you don't know?) (based on* **iss-**, *there is, exists)*
che saenggag-enŭn	*in my opinion*

Insight

'**Don't know**'. One of the most important expressions you will learn: 모르겠어요 (**morŭgessŏyo**), *I don't know*.

Tongdaemun	동대문	*Great East Gate (in Seoul), Tongdaemun*
shijang	시장	*market*
kanŭn	가는	*going to, bound for*
bŏsŭ	버스	*bus*
Sŏul	서울	*Seoul*
(noun)-ani-rasŏ	–아니라서	*since it is not (noun) (here: since I am not …)*
tarŭn	다른	*another, different*
-ege	에게	*to*
chŏngnyujang	정류장	*bus stop*
sŏ-	서–	*stop (stem)*
pŏn	번	*number*
t'a-	타–	*take (transport), travel on (transport)*
Namdaemun	남대문	*Great South Gate (in Seoul), Namdaemun*
-iyo	–이요	*(see note 3: used to check information, e.g. 'you mean?')*
p'anŭn ke	파는 게	*item for sale, items sold*
an p'anŭn ke	안 파는 게	*something which is not sold, not available*

-poda	-보다	*more than*
mulgŏn	물건	*goods*
man(h)-	많-	*is many/is a lot* (**h** is not pronounced; polite style: manayo) (**NB h + k = k'**; therefore **manh- + -ko = mank'o**)
che	제	*my* (humble form)
saenggak	생각	*thought*
-ko	-고	*and* (to join clauses)
chaemi iss-	재미 있-	*is interesting, is fun*
wonsungi	원숭이	*monkey*
p'arayo	팔아요	*sell* (polite style form, stem is irregular)
p'aljiman	팔지만	*they sell, but …* (i.e. *they do sell …, however*)
chŏngmal	정말	*really*
p'iryo ŏps-	필요 없-	*is not necessary, is not needed, has no need of*
p'iryo iss-	필요 있-	*is necessary, is needed*
paro	바로	*directly*
kil	길	*road, route*
kŏnnŏp'yŏn	건너편	*opposite side*
yogŭm	요금	*fee, fare*
ch'onsaram	촌사람	*country bumpkin, yokel*
-ishigunyo	-이시군요	(see note 7: based on copula)
ppalli	빨리	*quickly*
chŏgi	저기	*over there, over yonder*
kŏgi	거기	*over there* (nearer than **chŏgi**)
wayo	와요	*come* (polite style form)
o-	오-	*come* (stem)
pi-ga o-	비가 오-	*rains, is raining* (polite style: **pi-ga wayo**)

QUICK VOCAB (cont.)

Grammar 9

1 -이라서 (-irasŏ), -아니라서 (-anirasŏ)

In the dialogue you will find the phrase 서울 사람이 아니라서 (sŏul saram-i ani-rasŏ). This is related to the negative copula 아니에요 (anieyo) and you will see that both forms include the part 아니- (ani-). 아니라서 (anirasŏ) is a different form of 아니에요 (anieyo), and it means *since (it) is not a* (noun). The -라서 (-rasŏ) bit means *because* or *since*. The sentence in the dialogue therefore means *since I am not a Seoul person ..., since I'm not from Seoul...*

To say the opposite of this, that is, *since something is something else*, you use the form -이라서 (-irasŏ) instead of 아니라서 (anirasŏ). Thus, you could say *since I'm a Korean* with the words: 한국 사람이라서... (hanguk saram-irasŏ ...)

Here are examples of both constructions, and you should also study the example in the dialogue:

한국 사람이 아니라서 한국말 잘 못해요
(**Hanguk saram-i anirasŏ hangungmal chal mot haeyo**)
Since I'm not a Korean I can't speak Korean very well

영국 사람이라서 술 잘 마셔요
(**Yŏngguk saram-irasŏ sul chal mashyŏyo**)
Since I'm an English person I'm a good drinker

2 Particle order

You will have noticed that sometimes Korean allows you to
put more than one particle onto the end of a word, as in the
example 남대문 시장에는 뭐가 있어요(**Namdaemun shijang-
e-nŭn mwoga issŏyo**)? This makes a topic out of the phrase
'at Namdaemun market'. You have to be careful that the
particles are put into the correct order, however. For example,
you can say 한국에도 있어요(**hanguk-e-do issŏyo**) (*they have
it in Korea, too*), but *한국도에 있어요(**hanguk-do-e issŏyo**)
is wrong. You can learn the correct orders by observing
the example sentences in this course. There are some rules,
however, which you will find useful.

Many particles cannot occur together because their meanings
would be contradictory (the same noun cannot be both subject
and object, for example), so it is best to stick to only using
combinations that you have seen.

However, the particles -도(**-do**) and -은/-는(**-ŭn/-nŭn**) (*too,
also* and topic) can be added after most other particles (but **not**
the subject or object particles), both giving extra emphasis to the
noun and particle to which they are added. Possible examples are
-에서는(**-esŏnŭn**), -에서도(**-esŏdo**), and so on. You might like
to study the following two examples which illustrate the use of
combined particles:

김 선생님은 한국에도 일본에도 가요
(**Kim sŏnsaengnim-ŭn hanguk-edo ilbon-edo kayo**)
*Mr Kim goes **both** to Korea **and** to Japan*

서울에는 식당 많아요
(Sŏul-enŭn shiktang manayo)
In Seoul (topic) *there are many restaurants*

> **Insight**
> **Particles.** You've now learned several important particles:
> the subject particle -이/-가 (**-i/-ka**) and the topic particle
> -는/은 (**- [n] ŭn**), which are used to indicate either the subject
> of your sentence, or what it is you're talking about. The
> object particle -를/을 (**- [r] ŭl**) is used to indicate the object
> of the sentence (the thing that gets something done to it).
> All of these particles are optional, though you'll sound more
> authentic if you can use them.

> **Insight**
> **Particle order.** Particles like the topic particle and the
> particle -도 (**–do**), also, can be stacked onto the end of
> other particles, but always come at the end of the chain.
> For example, 가게에도 (**kage-e-do**) means *to the shops as
> well* (shops-to-also).

3 Checking on something

The particle -요(**-yo**) (or -이요[**-iyo**] after consonants) can
be added to any noun to check what has been said, to clarify
something or to show surprise. In the dialogue one speaker
asks which bus goes to Namdaemun market, and the other says
남대문 시장이요(**Namdaemun shijang-iyo**)? This translates as
*Namdaemun market? You said Namdaemun market, right? You
want Namdaemun market?* or something similar. If a shopkeeper
told you that an apple cost 10,000 won (a ridiculously high price),
you might say 만원이요(**Manwon-iyo**)? (*10,000 won? You must
be joking!*). Depending on the intonation it can express surprise or
incredulity or can simply be used to check whether what you heard
was correct.

4 Comparing things

You can compare one thing with another quite simply in Korean. Let's take an example sentence. To say that English beer is better than Korean beer, the pattern is as follows (first with the English words to show how the construction works, then with Korean):

English beer (subject or topic) Korean beer-**poda** is more good

영국 맥주는 한국 맥주보다 더 좋아요
(**Yŏngguk maekju-nŭn Hanguk maekju-poda tŏ choayo**)

You can even omit the word 더(**tŏ**) if you want to. Here is another example in which something is claimed to be more tasty than something else:

제 생각에는 한국 음식이 중국 음식보다 (더) 맛이 있어요
(**Che saenggag-enŭn hanguk umshig-i chungguk umshik-poda [tŏ] mashi issŏyo**).
In my opinion, Korean food is tastier than Chinese food

How many other examples can you spot in the dialogue?

Insight

Comparisons. The particle -보다 (**-poda**) is added to the second noun of two that you might want to compare. A B-보다 커요 (**-poda k'ŏyo**), *A is taller than B.*

---

5 Many and few, big and small

Korean uses the word 많아요(**manayo**) to say that there are many of something. It uses another word 크-(**k'ŭ-**) to say that something is big (polite style 커요[**k'ŏyo**]). The stem for the verb 많아요

(manayo) is 많-(manh-). The **h** is still there in Korean writing in the polite form 많아요(manayo), but is silent in pronunciation.

To say something is small you use the verb 작-(chak-), polite form 작아요(chagayo); to say there is or are few of something use the verb 적-(chŏk-), polite form 적어요(chŏgŏyo). Here are some examples:

영국에는 영국 사람이 많아요
(Yŏnggug-enŭn yŏngguk saram-i manayo)
In England there are many English people

영국에는 한국 사람이 적어요
(Yŏngguk-enŭn hanguk saram-i chŏgŏyo)
In England there are few Koreans

이 책은 크고 저 책은 작아요
(I-chaeg-ŭn k'ŭ-go chŏ-chaeg-ŭn chagayo)
This book is big and that one is small

6 Joining sentences together

You have learned the word 그리고(kŭrigo) which can be used to begin a second sentence with the meaning '*and …*' Take the example sentences:

한국 음식 좋아요. 그리고 일본 음식도 좋아요
(Hanguk ŭmshik choayo. Kŭrigo ilbon ŭmshik-do choayo)
Korean food is good. And Japanese food is good too

These two sentences can be joined into one by taking the verb stem of the first (좋-[choh-] from 좋아요[choayo]), and adding the ending -고(-ko) to it:

한국 음식 좋고 일본 음식도 좋아요
(Hanguk umshik choh-ko ilbon ŭmshik-do choayo)

NB h + k = k', therefore 좋고(choh-ko) **is pronounced** [조코] (cho-k'o).

This verb ending 고(-ko) is common in Korean, and it can be used with all verbs. Here is another example:

김 선생님은 책을 읽고 장 선생님은 텔레비 봐요
(**Kim sŏnsaengnim-ŭn ch'aeg-ŭl ilk-ko Chang sŏnsaengnim-ŭn t'ellebi pwayo**)
Mr Kim reads books and Mr Chang watches TV

Insight

The particle 고 (-ko) is one of the most useful and simple ways of joining two sentences together. Just add the particle right onto the end of the verb stem of the first sentence, then say the second sentence!

7 Exclamations

The verb ending 군요(-kunyo) can be added to verb stems in order to express surprise. Look at the example in the dialogue, where you will find it with the copula. It is particularly common with the copula, often in the honorific form 이시군요(-ishi-gunyo), and it is this form that you have met:

김 선생님이시군요! 반갑습니다
(**Kim sŏnsaengnim-ishi-gunyo! Pangapsŭmnida**)
Ah, so you're Mr Kim (surprise, surprise!)! Pleased to meet you!

You do not need to use this form yourself, but you need to be able to recognize it if a Korean uses it. Here is an example of its use with the normal (non-honorific) copula:

김 선생님 아들이군요! 지금 어디 가요?
(**Kim sŏnsaengnim adŭl-i-gunyo! Chigŭm ŏdi kayo?**)
So you're Mr Kim's son! Where are you going now?

Markets

Seoul has several famous and fascinating markets, particularly **Tongdaemun** and **Namdaemun** which you have learned something about in this lesson. Namdaemun is more compact, perhaps more pleasant to look round and has more tourists. Tongdaemun sprawls right on all the way down **Ch'ŏngyech'ŏn** (parallel to **Chongno**), and is cheaper for some goods. It depends a bit on what you want to buy as to which is best. Tongdaemun has a better selection of shoes and boots, for example, but both of them are well worth a visit.

Both Tongdaemun and Namdaemun are also night markets, and the best time to go is between one and six in the morning. The night markets can be good, but they can also sometimes be disappointing. If you're in Seoul for a while it's probably something which is worth trying once.

There are other markets too. **Chegi shijang** is much less well known (and therefore less touristy) and is great for food, Chinese herbs and medicines, and for ginseng products. **Itaewon** is well known for having hordes of foreigners and lots of Koreans who can speak English. But it's not the cheapest place to shop by any means. Cities out of Seoul also have good markets of course, and the fish market (much of it raw) at Pusan is a case in point. Korean markets are something you'll probably grow to love or hate!

This fruit doesn't look too good!

◄) CD 1, TR 6, 02:15

In this dialogue, a Korean girl, Minja, goes to the market to buy some boxes of apples. She has some trouble, but eventually manages to strike a good deal.

민자	여기 사과 얼마에요?
점원 A	한 상자에 삼만 원이에요.
민자	너무 비싸네요. 좀 깎아주세요.
점원 A	그럼 한 상자에 이만 팔천 원에 가져 가세요.
민자	그래도 비싸요.
점원 A	그럼 다른 데 가보세요. *(to himself)* 오늘 아침부터 재수없네!

Minja goes to another grocer.

민자	이 사과가 싱싱해 보이지 않네요. 어떤 건 좀 썩었어요.
점원 B	그래요? 그럼 좀 깎아드릴게요.
민자	얼마나요?
점원 B	한 상자에 삼만 천 원만 주세요.
민자	뭐라고요?! 옆 가게보다 더 비싸네요.
점원 B	좋아요. 그럼 이만 칠천 원만 주세요.
민자	좀 더 깎아주세요.
점원 B	좋아요. 한 상자에 이만 오천 원 내세요.
민자	고맙습니다. 세 상자 주세요.

Minja	Yŏgi sagwa ŏlma-eyo?
Chŏmwon A	Han sangja-e samman won-ieyo.
Minja	Nŏmu pissa-neyo. Chom kkakka-juseyo.
Chŏmwon A	Kŭrŏm han sangja-e iman-p'alch'ŏn won-e kajyŏ-gaseyo.
Minja	Kŭraedo pissayo.
Chŏmwon A	Kŭrŏm tarŭn te ka-boseyo. *(to himself)* Onŭl ach'im-put'ŏ chaesu ŏmne!

Minja goes to another grocer.

Minja	I-sagwa-ga shingshing haepoiji anneyo. Ŏttŏn gŏn chom ssŏgŏssŏyo.
Chŏmwon B	Kŭraeyo? Kŭrŏm chom kkakka-dŭrilgeyo.
Minja	Ŏlma-na-yo?
Chŏmwon B	Han sangja-e samman-ch'ŏn won-man chuseyo.
Minja	Mworaguyo?! Yŏp kage-poda tŏ pissaneyo.
Chŏmwon B	Choayo. Kurŏm iman-ch'ilch'ŏn won-man chuseyo.
Minja	Chom tŏ kkakka-juseyo.
Chŏmwon B	Choayo. Han sangja-e iman-och'ŏn won naeseyo.
Minja	Komapsŭmnida. Se sangja chuseyo.

1 How much reduction does the first vendor give on a box?
2 What is the response?
3 What is the problem at the second stall?
4 What is the cause for surprise?
5 What is the final price?

Phrases and expressions

chom kkakka-juseyo	*please cut the price a bit for me*
(onŭl ach'im-put'ŏ) chaesu ŏmne	*I've had no luck (all morning); I'm unlucky*
shingshing hae poiji anneyo	*they don't look fresh*
mworaguyo?	*what did you say?*

QUICK VOCAB

sagwa	사과	*apple*
sangja	상자	*box*
-e	-에	*each, per*
nŏmu	너무	*too (much)*

-neyo	–네요	*mild surprise sentence ending*
kkakka-ju-	깎아주–	*cut the price (for someone's benefit)*
kajyŏga-	가져가–	*take*
kŭraedo	그래도	*however, nevertheless, but still*
te	데	*place*
kabo-	가보–	*go and see, visit (a place)*
ach'im	아침	*morning*
-put'ŏ	–부터	*from*
chaesu	재수	*luck*
shingshing ha-	싱싱하–	*is fresh*
ŏttŏn	어떤	*certain, some (as a question word = which?)*
ssŏgŏssŏyo	썩었어요	*has gone bad, has gone off (polite style, past tense)*
kkakka- durilgeyo	깎아드릴게요	*I'll cut the price for you (polite style)*
-na	–나	*approx, about (derived from the meaning 'or' you have learned)*
-man	–만	*only*
yŏp'	옆	*next door*
nae-	내–	*pay*

Grammar 10

1 *Only*

The particle –만(**-man**) means *only*, so that 삼만원만(**samman won-man**) means *only 30,000 won*, and 책만 주세요(**chaek-man chuseyo**) means *please give me the book only* or *please just give me the book*. 나만 왔어요(**Na-man wassŏyo**) means *only I have come*. –만(**-man**) can be added to any noun in this way.

2 More surprises

The verb ending –네요(-neyo) can be added to any verb stem, and it indicates surprise, although usually of a milder form than –군요 (-kunyo). This is perhaps a more useful pattern to learn to use for yourself. Look carefully at the examples from the dialogues:

비가 오네요
(Pi-ga o-neyo)!
Oh no, it's raining!

애기가 책을 읽네요
(Aegi-ga ch'aeg-ŭl ing-neyo)! (spelt ilk-neyo)
Wow, the baby is reading a book!

그럼, 그 사람은 한국 사람이네요
(Kŭrŏm, kŭ-saram-ŭn hanguk saram-ineyo)!
So he's the Korean person, then! Or, so that person is a Korean, then! (depending on the intonation)

3 Months of the year

◆» CD 1, TR 6, 04:00

The months of the year in Korean are as follows (note carefully June and October in which the number loses the last letter):

일월	(il-wol)	*January*
이월	(i-wol)	*February*
삼월	(sam-wol)	*March*
사월	(sa-wol)	*April*
오월	(o-wol)	*May*
유월	(yu-wol)	*June*
칠월	(ch'il-wol)	*July*
팔월	(p'al-wol)	*August*

구월	(ku-wol)	*September*
시월	(shi-wol)	*October*
십일월	(shibil-wol)	*November*
십이월	(shibi-wol)	*December*

4 To and from (with people)

When you want to say *to* a person (write *to* a person, speak *to* a person, give *to* a person), you use the particle –한테(**-hant'e**) or the particle –에게(**-ege**). The particle –께(**-kke**) can be used when the person is honorific. For example:

어머니에게 편지 써요	(Ŏmŏni-ege p'yŏnji ssŏyo)	*I'm writing a letter to Mum*
재민한테 주고 싶어요	(Jaemin-hant'e chu-go ship'ŏyo)	*I want to give it to Jaemin*
아버지에게 이야기해요	(Abŏji-ege iyagi haeyo)	*I'm speaking to Father*
어머니한테 보내요	(Ŏmŏni-hant'e ponaeyo)	*I'm sending it to Mother*

'From a person' is said with the particle –한테서(**-hant'esŏ**) or –에게서(**-egesŏ**):

친구한테서 돈 받아요	(Ch'ingu-hant'esŏ ton padayo)	*I receive money from my friend*
월요일날에 어머니에게서 편지 받아요	(Wolyoil-lar-e ŏmŏni-egesŏ p'yŏnji padayo)	*I receive a letter from my mum on Mondays*
아버지한테서 전화 왔어요	(Abŏji-hant'esŏ chŏnhwa wassŏyo)	*I got a phone call from Dad (a call came)*

Cutting the price

There is plenty of bargaining to be done at Korean markets. The best advice is to go shopping with a Korean or someone who has been in Korea a long time and who knows how to get a good deal. Some shopkeepers already give the lowest price, and you must be aware that it is not fair to expect such dealers to cut. Others will give quite an inflated price when they see you are a foreigner. In general, however, Korea is a much safer place for not getting ripped off than somewhere like India or Thailand. In general, the places where there are fewer foreigners are more likely to offer the best deals (and less likely to speak English!).

Practice

1 Answer the following questions in Korean, based on the dialogues in this lesson. Make sure to use full sentences in your answers.

a 동대문 시장이 남대문 시장보다 더 재미있어요?
b 동대문 시장에서 뭘 안 팔아요?
c 이십 번 버스를 타면 어디 가요?

d 남대문 시장에는 물건이 많아요?

e 이십 번 버스를 어디서 타요?

2 Make up answers or appropriate responses to the following questions.

a 동대문 시장에 가고 싶어요. 같이 가요?
(Tongdaemun shijang-e ka-go ship'ŏyo. Kach'i kayo?)

b 오늘 아침에 뭘 하세요? (Onŭl ach'im-e mwol haseyo?)

c 이 과일이 안 싱싱해요 (I kwail-i an shingshing haeyo.)

d 버스 요금이 얼마에요? (Bŏsŭ yogŭm-i ŏlma-eyo?)

e 한국 좋아해요? (Hanguk choa haeyo?)
한국말 재미있어요? (Hangungmal chaemi issŏyo?)

3 Imagine that you suddenly recognize or are surprised by seeing the following people or things. This exercise is intended to practise the -군요(-kunyo) form with the copula. Don't forget to use the honorific form of the copula when appropriate.

a *Mr Kim's dog*
b *Mr O's wife*
c *a Japanese book*
d *the Korea Exchange Bank*
e Hyŏngjun
f *the Chinese teacher*

4 Make up sentences comparing the following sets of information. For the first set you would make up a sentence to say that Korean food is more tasty than Japanese food.

a *Korean food*	*Japanese food*	*tasty*
b *Here*	*there*	*more of them*
c *Train*	*bus*	*faster* (빨라요[ppallayo])
d *Mr Kim*	*Mr Pak*	*more luck*
e *Namdaemun*	*Tongdaemun*	*more expensive*

5 Write a dialogue between a Korean in Paris who wants to get a bus to the Louvre and a Japanese, who the Korean mistakenly thinks is a Korean. Fortunately, the Japanese can also speak

Korean so, after explaining that he is Japanese not Korean, he tells him that the Louvre is nearby (not far). He doesn't need to take a bus and it only takes seven minutes to walk.

6 Translate the following sentences into English.

a 여기 비싸네요(Yŏgi pissaneyo). 옆 가게에 가봅시다 (Yŏp kage-e ka-bopshida).

b 여기서 팔지만 다른 데에 가면 더 싸요 (Yŏgi-sŏ p'al-jiman tarŭn te-e ka-myŏn tŏ ssayo).

c 서울 시내에 가는 버스를 어디서 타요 (Sŏul shinae-e kanŭn bosŭ-rŭl ŏdi-sŏ t'ayo)?

d 오늘 아침부터 재수없네요 (Onŭl ach'im-put'ŏ chaesu ŏmneyo)!

e 일본은 한국보다 더 비싸요(Ilbon-ŭn hanguk-poda tŏ pissayo). 그래도 한국도 비싸요(Kŭraedo hanguk-do pissayo).

f 제 생각보다 한국에 영국 사람이 많아요 (Che saenggak-poda hangug-e yŏngguk saram-i manayo).

g 깎아드릴게요(Kkakka-dŭrilgeyo). 한 상자에 만 삼천원에 가져 가세요(Han sangja-e mansamch'ŏnwon-e kajyŏ-gaseyo).

h 주문하시겠어요(Chumun hashigessŏyo)?

i 여기가 한국 아니라서 김치를 파는 데 적어요 (Yŏgi-ga hanguk-anirasŏ kimch'i-rŭl p'anŭn te chŏgŏyo).

j 원숭이 있느냐구요(Wonsungi innŭnyaguyo)? 동대문 시장에 가보세요(Tongdaemun shijang-e ka-boseyo).

7 Which of the following particle sequences are acceptable and which are not?

a 시간에는 (shigan = *time*)
b 음식을은
c 어머니에게도
d 길에서는

e 버스에가
f 국이를 (kuk = *soup*)
g 아침부터를
h 밤부터는

8 Translate the following sentences and put them into the −네요 (-neyo) mild surprise form.

a *My, these dictionaries are expensive!*
b *Taegyu is coming!*
c *What are you doing? (surprise!)*
d *This newspaper's really interesting.*

9 Join the following pairs of sentences, with the −고(-ko) clause ending.

a 이 사람이 박 선생님이에요. 저 사람이 강 선생님이에요.
b 어머니는 책 읽어요. 아버지는 텔레비를 봐요.
c 고기 못 먹어요. 사과도 못 먹어요.
d 십일 번 버스가 남대문 시장에 가요. 이십 번 버스는 동대문 시장에 가요.
e 상준도 버스 타요. 명택도 버스타요.

10 어느 버스가 학교에 가는 버스에요(Ŏnŭ bŏsŭ-ga hakkyo-e kanŭn bŏsŭ-eyo)? 십팔번 버스가 어디 가요(Shipp'al pŏn bŏsŭ-ga ŏdi kayo)?

TEN THINGS TO REMEMBER

1 How to say you don't know

2 How to ask *Is this the bus for Tongdaemun market?*

3 Expressing that something is your opinion

4 The phrase to say something is or isn't necessary or that you do or don't need something

5 Making comparisons with **-poda**

6 Saying there are many or few

7 Saying something is expensive or cheap

8 How to ask for a discount

9 Counting the months (revising the numbers!)

10 Using the particle for *only*

6

Off to the mountains/I've got a nasty headache!

In this unit you will learn
- *how to talk about short-term plans*
- *how to suggest and discuss activities*
- *how to express your aches and pains, say that you are ill and get sympathy*
- *the probable future (what you expect to do or what is most probable)*
- *how to make suggestions and tell others what you are thinking of doing*

Off to the mountains

◆) CD 1, TR 7

Mr Kim wants to take Tony mountain climbing, but with Tony's busy schedule they have some difficulty finding a convenient date.

김선생	요즘 날씨가 아주 좋아요.
토니	네. 한국은 영국보다 날씨가 좋아요.
김선생	내일 뭐 할 거에요? 별일 없으면 등산이나 갈까요?

토니	가고 싶지만 내일은 집사람하고 동대문
	시장에서 쇼핑 하기로 했어요.
김선생	그럼 다음 일요일은 어때요?
토니	다음 일요일에는 대학 동창들하고
	불국사에 갈까 해요.
김선생	그럼 다음 일요일도 안 되겠네요. 언제가
	좋을까요?
토니	그 다음 일요일은 아마 괜찮을
	거에요.
김선생	좋아요. 그럼 그 다음 일요일에
	갑시다.
토니	저도 등산을 좋아해요.
	그런데 영국에는 산이 많지 않아서
	등산을 많이 못 했어요.
	그런데 어느 산에 갈까요?
김선생	도봉산이 편할 거에요.
토니	그럼 도봉산 입구에서 만날까요?

Mr Kim	Yojŭm nalssi-ga aju choayo.
Tony	Ne. Hanguk-ŭn yŏngguk-poda nalssi-ga choayo.
Mr Kim	Naeil mwo ha-lkŏeyo? Pyŏlil ŏps-ŭmyŏn tŭngsan-ina
	ka-lkkayo?
Tony	Ka-go ship'-jiman naeil-ŭn chipsaram-hago
	Tongdaemun shijang-esŏ shyop'ing ha-giro
	haessŏyo.
Mr Kim	Kŭrŏm taŭm iryoir-ŭn ŏttaeyo?
Tony	Taŭm iryoil-enun taehak tongch'ang-hago
	pulguksa-e ka-lkka haeyo.
Mr Kim	Kŭrŏm taŭm iryoil-do an toe-genneyo. Ŏnje-ga
	cho-ŭlkkayo?
Tony	Kŭ taŭm iryoir-ŭn ama kwaench'an-ŭlkŏeyo.
Mr Kim	Choayo. Kŭrŏm kŭ taŭm iryoil-e kapshida.

Tony	Chŏ-do tŭngsan-ŭl choa haeyo. Kŭrŏnde yŏngguk-enŭn san-i manch'i anasŏ tŭngsan-ŭl mani mot haessŏyo. Kŭrŏnde ŏnŭ san-e ka-lkkayo?
Mr Kim	Tobongsan-i p'yŏn ha-lkŏeyo.
Tony	Kŭrŏm Tobongsan ipku-esŏ manna-lkkayo?

1 How does English weather compare with Korean?
2 What does Mr Kim suggest and under what circumstances?
3 What plans does Tony have for tomorrow?
4 With whom has he made plans for the following Sunday?
5 What is resolved?
6 What do you know about Tony's opinion regarding the experience of mountain climbing?

Phrases and expressions

naeil mwo hal kŏeyo?	*what are you going to do tomorrow?*
pyŏlil ŏpsŭmyŏn . . .	*if you don't have anything special on . . .*
an twoegenneyo	*it won't be any good, then (unfortunately)*
ama kwaench'anŭlkŏeyo	*it will probably turn out (be) okay*

nalssi	날씨	*weather*
naeil	내일	*tomorrow*
-(ŭ)l kŏeyo	–(으)ㄹ 거에요	(used to give verbs a future meaning, see note 3)
pyŏlil	별일	*a special matter, something particular*
tŭngsan	등산	*mountain climbing*
-(ŭ)lkkayo	–(으)ㄹ까요	(verb ending meaning *shall we?*, see note 6)

QUICK VOCAB

shyop'ing (ha-)	쇼핑(하-)	*shopping (do/go shopping)*
-kiro haessŏyo	-기로 했어요	*decided to*
iryoil	일요일	*Sunday*
iryoillal	일요일날	*Sunday (longer form)*
taehak	대학	*university*
tongch'ang	동창	*colleague (fellow student* in this case)
pulguksa	불국사	*Pulguksa* (Korean Buddhist temple, the largest in Korea, near Kyŏngju)
-(ŭ)lkka haeyo	-(으)ㄹ까 해요	*am thinking of doing*
ŏnje	언제	*when*
san	산	*mountain*
man-ch'i anasŏ	많지 않아서	*since there aren't many* (written **manh-ji anh-asŏ**)
haessŏyo	했어요	*did (past tense form of* **ha-** *do)*
ŏnŭ	어느	*which one*
Tobongsan	도봉산	*Tobongsan* (mountain in Seoul)
p'yŏn ha-	편하-	*is comfortable, is convenient*
ipku	입구	*entrance*

Grammar 11

1 *Verb stems ending in i*

This unit contains several verbs whose stems end in **i**, for example: 움직이-(**umjigi-**) (*move*), 놀리-(**nolli-**) (*tease*), and you have previously met 마시-(**mashi-**) (*drink*), 기다리-(**kidari-**) (*wait*) and 걸리-(**kŏlli-**) (*lasts, takes (time)*). All these verbs change the last **i** to **yo** and add **yo** in order to form the present polite style. This gives the polite style forms 움직여요(**umjigyŏyo**), 놀려요 (**nollyŏyo**), 마셔요(**mashyŏyo**), 기다려요(**kidaryŏyo**), 걸려요 (**kŏllyŏyo**).

2 Days of the week

◀) CD 1, TR 7, 01:45

The following are the days of the week in Korean:

월요일	(wolyoil)	*Monday*
화요일	(hwayoil)	*Tuesday*
수요일	(suyoil)	*Wednesday*
목요일	(mokyoil)	*Thursday*
금요일	(kŭmyoil)	*Friday*
토요일	(t'oyoil)	*Saturday*
일요일	(iryoil)	*Sunday*

Insight

Time. In the last couple of units we've learned both the days of the week and the months of the year. The months use one of the normal numbering systems, but the days of the week have their own terms. Make sure you have them both written down.

3 Probable future

The most common way to give a sentence a future meaning in Korean is to add -(으)ㄹ 거에요(**-[ŭ]lkŏeyo**) to the stem of the main verb. As you would expect, you add -ㄹ 거에요(**-l kŏeyo**) if the stem ends in a vowel, and -을 거에요(**-ŭlkŏeyo**) if the stem ends in a consonant. Thus 만나-(**manna-**) becomes 만날 거에요

(manna-l kŏeyo) (*I will meet*), and 앉-(anj-) becomes 앉을 거에요 (anj-ŭlkŏeyo) (*I will sit*).

We have called the form the probable future, because there are other ways of expressing the future tense in Korean – there is a definite future, for example, which you might use if there is scarcely any doubt that you will do something, or if you want to stress your intention to do it. The probable future is the most common, and is used in most everyday situations when you want to say that you are going to do something:

내일 중국 대사관에 갈 거에요
(Naeil chungguk taesagwan-e ka-l kŏeyo)
I will (probably) go to the Chinese embassy tomorrow

내년에 차를 살 거에요
(Naenyŏn-e ch'a-rŭl sa-l kŏeyo)
I'm going to buy a car next year (**naenyŏn**, *next year*)

The same form has another meaning, in addition to the future. It can also mean something like *is probably* (verb)*ing*.

비가 올 거에요
(Pi-ga o-l kŏeyo)
It is probably raining

Insight

There are several different ways of expressing the future in Korean, but the − (으)ㄹ 거에요 (-[ŭ]l kŏeyo) form you learn in this unit is one of the simplest and most common – so make sure you master it.

4 Making decisions

To say that you have decided to do something, simply add -기로 했어요(-kiro haessŏyo) onto the verb stem of the verb you have decided to do. To say that you have decided to eat with Mr Kim, for example, you would say: 김 선생님하고 점심을 먹기로 했어요(Kim sonsaengnim-hago chŏmshim-ŭl mŏk-kiro haessŏyo):

대학 동창하고 등산하기로 했어요
(Taehak tongch'ang-hago tŭngsan ha-giro haessŏyo)
*I've decided to go mountain climbing with my friend(s) from
  university*

5 Thinking about it

Sometimes when you still haven't made definite plans, you want to say that you are thinking about doing something. You might say, for example, *I am thinking about going away for the weekend*. Korean provides an easy way of allowing you to do this. Simply add the ending –ㄹ까 해요(-lkka haeyo) to a verb stem ending in a vowel, or –을까 해요(-ŭlkka haeyo) to a verb stem ending in a consonant. That's all there is to it. To take one example, suppose you were thinking of going to 설악산 (Sŏrak mountain) on Sunday, you simply say, 일요일에 설악산에 갈까 해요(iryoir-e sŏraksan-e ka-lkka haeyo). Can you work out the meaning of the following example? 점심에 비빔밥을 먹을까 해요(chŏmshim-e pibimpab-ŭl mŏg-ŭlkka haeyo).

Insight
Verbs with 하– (ha-). In this unit you learn a number of new constructions where you take a verb stem, and add on another form, finishing the whole thing with the verb 하– (ha-), *do*. Two such constructions are –기로 했어요 (-kiro haessŏyo), *I/we decided to ...*, and – (으)ㄹ까 해요 (- [ŭ]lkka haeyo), *I'm thinking of ...*

6 Shall we?

To say to someone 'shall we do something or other?', you add a verb ending very like the one you have just learned.

Add −ㄹ까요(-lkkayo)? to a verb stem ending in a vowel, and −을까요(-ŭlkkayo)? to a verb stem ending in a consonant. To say to someone 'shall we sit here?' you would therefore say 여기 앉을까요(yŏgi anj-ŭlkkayo)?, and to say 'shall we have a beer?' you would say 맥주 마실까요(maekchu mashi-lkkayo)?

Korean pastimes

Koreans are very fond of mountain climbing and if you go to virtually any Korean mountain on a weekend or public holiday, you will be sure to find hordes of Koreans all dressed up in hiking gear, proceeding with great enthusiasm. For most Koreans mountain climbing means a strenuous hike rather than scaling rock faces, but that in no way diminishes the fun (or the steepness of the mountains!).

Sport is very popular, too, and nowadays the most popular sports are the American imports: baseball (야구[**yagu**], verb: 야구하-[**yagu ha-**]) and basketball (농구-[**nonggu**]). Football (축구[**ch'ukku**]) is also popular and, for the wealthy, golf has great status (골프[**golp'ŭ**]).

Other pastimes include the 노래방(**noraebang**) and *karaoke*; Koreans also love to drink, and sometimes break into song as they do so. Board and card games are also popular among some, the most common ones being 바둑(**paduk**) (*go* is the Japanese equivalent, and is somewhat known in the West), and 화투(**hwat'u**).

———————————————— — ————————————————

I've got a nasty headache!

◄) CD 1, TR 7, 02:40

Yongtae is sick – everything seems to be hurting and his friend Jaehoon isn't very sympathetic. When Yongtae wants his friend Jaehoon to get him some medicine, Jaehoon has another suggestion. But Yongtae is not impressed.

재훈	저 시내에 가는데 같이 갈까요?
용태	글쎄요 . . . 저는 몸이 좀 좋지 않아요.
재훈	또 몸이 좋지 않아요? 용태씨는 항상 꾀병을 부리지요!
용태	아니요. 그렇지 않아요. 오늘은 정말 아파요.
재훈	오늘은 어디가 아파요?
용태	두통이 있어요. 머리가 좀 아파요.
재훈	그게 다에요? 걱정하지 마세요. 아마 날씨가 더워서 그럴 거에요.
용태	아닌 것 같아요. 배도 아파요.
재훈	많이 아파요?
용태	그래요. 많이 아파요.
재훈	그럼 약을 사러 약국에 갑시다.
용태	저는 못 가요. 힘이 없어요. 게다가 다리도 좀 아파요.
재훈	다리도요? 전신이 다 아프군요. 안 아픈 데가 있어요?
용태	시끄러워요! 놀리지 마세요. 약을 먹어야겠어요.
재훈	여기 만병통치약 술이 있어요! 사실 약보다 술이 더 좋아요.
용태	농담하지 마세요. 술 못 마셔요. 정말 병원에 가야겠어요.

Jaehoon	Chŏ shinae-e ka-nŭnde, gach'i ka-lkkayo?
Yongtae	Kŭlsseyo . . . chŏ-nŭn mom-i chom choch'i anayo.
Jaehoon	Tto mom-i choch'i anayo? Yongtae-sshi-nŭn hangsang kkoebyŏng-ŭl purijiyo!
Yongtae	Aniyo. Kŭrŏch'i anayo. Onŭl-ŭn chŏngmal ap'ayo.
Jaehoon	Onŭr-ŭn ŏdi-ga ap'ayo?
Yongtae	Tut'ong-i issŏyo. Mŏri-ga chom ap'ayo.

Jaehoon	Kŭ-ge ta-eyo? Kŏkjŏng ha-ji maseyo. Ama nalssi-ga tŏwosŏ kŭrŏlkŏ-eyo.
Yongtae	Anin kŏt kat'ayo. Pae-do ap'ayo.
Jaehoon	Mani ap'ayo?
Yongtae	Kŭraeyo. Mani ap'ayo.
Jaehoon	Kŭrŏm yag-ŭl sa-rŏ yakkug-e kapshida.
Yongtae	Chŏ-nŭn mot kayo. Him-i ŏpsŏyo. Kedaga tari-do chom ap'ayo.
Jaehoon	Tari-doyo? Chŏnshin-i ta ap'ŭ-gunyo. An ap'ŭn de-ga issŏyo?
Yongtae	Shikkŭrŏwoyo! Nolli-ji maseyo. Yag-ŭl mŏgŏ-yagessŏyo.
Jaehoon	Yŏgi manbyŏngt'ongch'iyak, sur-i issŏyo! Sashil yak-poda sur-i tŏ choayo.
Yongtae	Nongdam ha-ji maseyo. Sul mot mashyŏyo. Chŏngmal pyŏngwon-e ka-yagessŏyo.

1 Why is there little sympathy at first?
2 What are the symptoms?
3 What is the suggested reason for the illness?
4 Why can't they both go for the medicine?
5 What cure-all is suggested?

Phrases and expressions

chŏ-nŭn mom-i chom choh-ch'i anhayo	*I don't feel very well*
kŭrŏhch'i anayo	*of course not*
kkoebyŏng-ŭl purijiyo	*you're making it up! (feigning an illness)*
kŏkchŏng ha-ji maseyo	*don't worry! (colloquial form:* **kokjong maseyo**)
anin kŏt gat'ayo	*I don't think so; it doesn't seem like it*
chŏnshin-i ta ap'ŭgunyo!	*your whole body must be hurting!*
shikkŭrŏwoyo!	*shut up!, be quiet! (lit: 'it's noisy')*
nolli-ji maseyo	*don't joke, don't kid me, don't tease*
yag-ŭl mŏgŏyagessŏyo	*I'll have to take some medicine*

-nǔnde	–는데	(verb ending for clauses, see note 4)
kǔlsseyo	글쎄요	*I dunno, I'm not sure, who knows?*
mom	몸	*body*
cho-ch'i anh-	좋지 않–	*is not good* (from **choh-**)
tto	또	*again; moreover, also, furthermore*
hangsang	항상	*always*
kkwoebyǒng	꾀병	*a feigned illness*
ap'ǔ-	아프–	*hurts* (stem)
ap'ayo	아파요	*hurts* (polite style)
tut'ong	두통	*headache*
mǒri	머리	*head*
kǒkchǒng	걱정	*worry, concern*
kǒkchǒng ha-	걱정하–	*be worried*
-ji maseyo	–지 마세요	*please don't*
ama	아마	*perhaps, probably*
tǒwosǒ	더워서	*because it is hot* (can also mean *because you're hot*, but here subject is weather)
kǔrǒlkǒeyo	그럴 거에요	*it will probably be like that*
kat'-	같–	*seems like*
pae	배	*stomach*
yak	약	*medicine*
yakkuk	약국	*chemists, drugstore*
him	힘	*strength, energy*
kedaga	게다가	*on top of that*
tari	다리	*leg*
chǒnshin	전신	*the whole body*
ap'ǔn	아픈	*hurting, painful* (adjective)

nolli-	놀리-	*make fun of*
manbyŏngt'ongch'iyak	만병통치약	*cure-all medicine, miracle cure, panacea*
-yagessŏyo	-야겠어요	*will have to*
sashil	사실	*fact (the fact is . . .)*
nongdam	농담	*joke (noun)*
nongdam ha-	농담하-	*jokes (verb)*
pyŏngwon	병원	*hospital*

Grammar 12

1 *To hurt*

The verb stem 아프-(**ap'ŭ-**) (*hurt*) belongs to another group of verbs all ending in -으(-**ŭ**). These delete the **ŭ** and add instead 아(**a**) or 어(**ŏ**), followed by 요(**yo**) to form the polite style. Thus 아프-(**ap'ŭ-**) in the polite style is 아파요(**ap'ayo**).

How do you know whether the last vowel before the 요(**yo**) will be an 아(**a**) or an 어(**ŏ**)? Simply remember this rule: if the preceding vowel is an 아(**a**) (as in 아프-[**ap'ŭ-**]) or 오(**o**) (as in 고프- [**kop'ŭ-**]), then the 으(**ŭ**) becomes 아(**a**), otherwise it is 어(**ŏ**).

2 *Don't do it!*

When you want to tell someone not to do something, take the stem of the verb you want to tell them not to do and add -지 마세요 (-**ji maseyo**) to it. Thus, 맥주를 마시지 마세요(**maekju-rŭl mashi-ji maseyo**) means *please don't drink beer*. The two phrases in this dialogue, 걱정하지 마세요(**kŏkchŏng ha-ji maseyo**) and 놀리지 마세요(**nolli-ji maseyo**) are quite common. The first means *don't worry!*, and the second means *don't tease me!*. What other useful examples can you think of? How would you say 'please don't wait here' and 'don't do the shopping'?

3 *Long negatives*

You have learned how to make negative sentences in Korean with 못(mot) and 안(an), by putting them immediately in front of the verb. There is another way also, which is known as the long negative. There is no particularly significant difference between the two, though there are some circumstances in which you are more likely to find the long form than the shorter one you have learned already. To spell out these distinctions would be rather long winded and would also make the difference seem more important than it really is. The best advice is to look carefully at the dialogues in this book, and to imitate Korean speakers whenever you can. You will then pick up a feel for which to use. Generally, short negatives are better in short, simple sentences; long negatives should be used in more complex sentences.

Here is how to make the long negative. Instead of adding something before the verb you wish to negate, take the stem of that verb and add -지 않아요(-ji an[h]ayo) or -지 못해요 (-ji mot haeyo), depending on whether you want to give the sense of the Korean word 안(an) (*won't or isn't going to*) or 못(mot) (*can't*).

Therefore, 못 가요(mot kayo) in the long negative form would be 가지 못해요(kaji mot haeyo), and 안 먹어요(an mŏgŏyo) in the long negative form would be 먹지 않아요(mŏk-ji an(h)ayo). Here is an example of each:

아버지는 농담하지 않아요
(Abŏji-nŭn nongdam ha-ji anayo)
Dad doesn't tell jokes

윤 선생님은 등산을 좋아하지만, 윤 선생님 부인은
등산을 하지 못해요
(Yun sŏnsaengnim-ŭn tŭngsan-ŭl choa ha-jiman, Yun sŏnsaengnim
 puin-ŭn tŭngsan-ŭl ha-ji mot haeyo)

Mr Yun likes mountain climbing, but his wife can't do it

Insight

Two ways of making negatives. The particle –지 (-ji) added
to a verb stem enables you to make the verb negative. But
there are a couple of ways of doing this, depending on what
you put after the –지 (-ji). 하지 않아요 (haji anayo) means
I'm not doing it or *I won't do it*, wheras 하지 못해요 (haji
mot haeyo) means *I can't do it*. A subtle, but important
difference!

4 *Imminent elaboration*

This sounds rather forbidding, but it isn't really all that difficult!
Korean has a very common way of linking two clauses together
to show that the first one is not all that you have got to say and
that there is more coming in the second clause which relates to it.
For example, look at the first sentence in the dialogue: 저 시내에
가는데(chŏ shinae-e ka-nŭnde). That is the end of the first clause.
The meaning is straightforward enough, *I'm going into town*, but
the –는데(-nŭnde) added on to the end of 가-(ka-) indicates that
the speaker still has more to say which relates to what he has just
said. It is a clue to the listener not to reply yet, but to wait until
the rest has been said. The statement is not complete; there is
more to come. In this case, the second clause is 같이 갈까요(kach'i
kalkkayo)? (*shall we go together?*). Koreans use this pattern all
the time to show that they have something more to say about
what has just been said (in this case an invitation), and from now
on you will meet the –는데(-nŭnde) pattern frequently in the unit
dialogues.

The formation of the pattern is easy: take any verb which expresses an action (that is, not an adjectival verb) and add 는데(-nŭnde) to the stem. Note that you can also use 는데(-nŭnde) with the verbs 있-(iss-) and 없-(ŏps-), giving you the forms 있는데(innnŭnde) and 없는데(ŏmnŭnde).

Verbs which describe things (e.g. is green, is hot, is foolish etc.) take the form -(으)ㄴ데(-[ŭ]nde) instead (-은데[ŭnde] after consonant stems, -ㄴ데[nde] after vowels). The copula also takes this form, -ㄴ데(-nde):

저는 박재민인데 김 선생님 만나러 왔어요
(Chŏ-nŭn Pak Jaemin-i-nde Kim sŏnsaengnim manna-rŏ wassŏyo)
I'm Pak Jaemin (and I've got more to say): I've come to meet Mr Kim

You have not learned the past tense yet, but you might like to keep in the back of your mind the fact that 는데(-nŭnde) is added to the past stem of all verbs, whether they describe an action or are adjectival. In other words, it doesn't make the distinction that the present tense does.

5 Descriptive verbs and processive verbs

Korean has two basic kinds of verbs – descriptive and processive. Processive verbs describe a process, the doing of something, an action. Thus, 먹-(mŏk-), 앉-(anj-), 가-(ka-), 하-(ha-), 만나-(manna-) are all processive verbs. Descriptive verbs describe something, so 좋-(choh-) is an example, because it describes something as good. 좋아하-(cho[h]a ha-), by contrast, is processive, because it describes the process or action of the speaker liking something. Descriptive verbs function like adjectives in English. They are adjectival verbs.

We tell you all this because some verb endings will only work with one of the two kinds of verbs. What we have just said about 는데

(-**nŭnde**), for example, could have been said much more compactly by saying that -는데(-**nŭnde**) can only be added to processive verbs, and that -(으)ㄴ데(-**[ŭ]nde**) is added to descriptive verbs and the copula. In the future we shall be making use of these two terms when we describe verb endings.

Insight

The terms *descriptive verbs* and *processive verbs* are a bit of a mouthful, but it's important to understand the distinction – and in essence, it's a fairly straightforward concept. A descriptive verb describes how something is, whereas a processive verb recounts a process, an action. It's important to differentiate between them, because some particles and verb endings will only go on one or other of the two types.

The two verbs 있-(**iss-**) and 없-(**ŏps-**) can be either processive or descriptive depending on their use, and we will tell you about whether or not they can be used with particular verb endings as we go along.

There is one other verb, the copula, which is in a class of its own. We will tell you about this also on a case-by-case basis, as we did with -는데(-**nŭnde**).

6 *What you will have to do*

This unit introduces you to one final pattern – how to say that you will have to do something.

To form the construction, take off the -요(-**yo**) of the polite style form of the verb and add -야겠어요(-**yagessŏyo**). Take the verb 먹-(**mŏk-**) as an example. The polite style is 먹어요 (**mŏgŏyo**), so taking off the -요(-**yo**) and adding the -야겠어요 (-**yagesŏyo**) ending, we have 먹어야겠어요(**mŏgŏ-yagessŏyo**). This can then be used in a sentence: 지금 먹어야겠어요 (**chigŭm mŏgŏ-yagessŏyo**) (*I am going to have to eat now [I'm obliged to]*).

The dialogue had two examples of the pattern: 약을 먹어야겠어요 (yag-ŭl mŏgŏ -yagessŏyo) and 병원에 가야겠어요(pyŏngwon-e ka-yagessŏyo). Can you remember what they mean?

Doctors and chemists

Most medicines can be bought over the counter without prescription at the 약국(yakkuk) (*pharmacy*). Doctors are available at hospitals and generally speaking there is no equivalent of going to a doctor independent of the hospital. Koreans are enthusiastic takers of medicines for headache, tiredness, flu and so forth, and many frequently take tonics and health drinks to stay healthy.

Chinese medicine is also very popular in Korea and there are markets which concentrate on selling the herbs and potions which it prescribes.

Practice

1 Here is an exercise about putting verbs into different forms. We give you some sentences with the verb stem, you write out the sentences in full, putting the verb into the correct form.

Future

a 양주 마시면 내일 머리가 아프- (**Yangju mashi-myŏn naeil mŏri-ga ap'ŭ-**)

b 이따가 점심을 먹- (**Ittaga chŏmshim-ŭl mŏk-**)

c 한국 사람 만나면 한자 사전 필요없- (**Hanguk saram manna-myŏn hanja sajŏn p'iryo ŏps-**)

Decided

d 병원에 가- (**Pyŏngwŏn-e ka-**)

e 원숭이를 사- (**Wonsungi-rŭl sa-**)

f 오늘은 음식을 안 먹- (**Onŭl-ŭn ŭmshig-ŭl an mŏk-**)

Thinking of

g 저는 'Star Wars' 보- (Chŏ-nŭn 'Star Wars'(!) po-)

h 오늘 아침 쇼핑하- (Onŭl ach'im shyop'ing ha-)

i 일요일에 불국사에 가- (Iryoir-e pulguksa-e ka-)

Shall we

j 언제 등산 가- (Ŏnje tŭngsan ka-)?

k 김 선생님을 어디서 만나- (Kim sŏnsaengnim-ŭl ŏdi-sŏ manna-)?

l 우체국 앞에서 버스를 타- (Uch'eguk ap'-esŏ bŏsŭ-rŭl t'a-)?

2 The following dialogue concerns a boy who wants to go mountain climbing with Jisoo, a reluctant girl who keeps making up reasons why she can't go with him. Can you fill in the missing parts, giving reasons why she can't go? (NB 안녕 [annyŏng] is a way of saying hello to a close friend, or someone younger than you.)

Boy	지수, 안녕(Jisoo, annyŏng)! 내일 시간이 있어요 (Naeil shigan-i issŏyo)?
Girl	(*State another plan*)
Boy	그럼 일요일에 별일 없으면 같이 등산 갈까요(Kŭrŏm ilyoil-e pyŏlil ŏps-umyŏn kach'i tungsan kalkkayo)?
Girl	(*Too busy doing something else*)
Boy	다음 일요일은 어때요(Taum iryoir-ŭn ŏttaeyo)?
Girl	(*Another plan*)
Boy	언제 시간이 있어요, 그럼(Ŏnje shigan-i issŏyo, kŭrŏm)? 나를 안 좋아해요(Na-rŭl an choa haeyo)?
Girl	(*Doesn't like mountain climbing*)
Boy	그럼, 안 되겠데요(Kŭrŏm, an twoegennneyo).

3 Can you write a simple conversation between two friends, one who has a headache and the other who thinks she doesn't have any medicine and suddenly realizes that she does?

4 Here are some situations in which you might use one of the following idiomatic expressions. See if you can match them up. In some cases, more than one expression will fit, so be sure to find all the possibilities and then choose the most likely.

a *Your friend is making fun of you.*
b *You want to go out tonight with your friend, but she can't make it.*
c *You're in awful pain, and every part of your body seems to hurt.*
d *Someone has just said something really stupid.*
e *You're trying to concentrate, but someone is making too much noise.*
f *You've made a mistake.*
g *Your junior colleague has just said something you disagree with.*
h *Your boss has just said something you disagree with.*
i *Your mother is panicking about your health.*
j *You didn't hear properly what your younger brother just said.*

착각했어요   전신이 다 아프군요
놀리지 마세요   그렇지 않아요
시끄러워요   아닌 것 같아요

걱정하지 마세요   재수 없네요
뭐라구요?   안되겠네요

5 This exercise is designed to help you practise the 一는데(-**nŭnde**)
pattern. For each question we give you one of two clauses in
which the first one always ends in 一는데(-**nŭnde**). Your task is to
make up an appropriate clause which fits with the one we have
given you to make a complete sentence.

   a 버스가 오는데(**Bŏsŭ-ga o-nŭnde**) _____
   b _____ -(느) ㄴ데 안 가요(**-[nŭ]nde an kayo**).
   c 이 옷이 비싼데(**I-osh-i pissa-nde**) _____ (옷 [**os**]: *clothes*)
   d 영국 대사관에 가는데(**Yŏngguk taesagwan-e ka-nŭnde**)
      _____
   e 그 사람 좋은데(**Kŭ-saram cho[h]-ŭnde**) _____

6 Choose the best word from those given here to fit in the gaps in
the sentences. More than one might be possible, so choose the
best option.

그렇지만 (**kŭrŏch'iman**) 게다가 (**kedaga**)   그런데 (**kŭrŏnde**)
그런 (**kŭrŏn**)   글쎄요 (**kŭlsseyo**) 그리고 (**kŭrigo**)

   a 힘이 하나도 없어요(**Him-i hana-do ŏpsŏyo**). _____
      전신이 다 아파요(**chŏnshin-i ta ap'ayo**).
   b 같이 쇼핑 갈까요(**Kach'i shyop'ing ka-lkkayo**)? _____.
      다른 데에 가기로 했는데요(**Tarŭn te-e ka-giro
      haennnŭndeyo**).
   c 상민씨는 농담 많이 해요(**Sangmin-ssi-nŭn nongdam
      mani haeyo**). _____ 재미 없어요(**chaemi ŏpsŏyo**).
   d 불국사에 가기로 했어요(**Pulguksa-e ka-giro haessŏyo**).
      _____ 못 가요(**mot kayo**).
   e 박 선생님 학교에 가세요(**Pak sŏnsaengnim hakkyo-e
      kaseyo**). _____ 김 선생님도 가세요(**Kim sŏnsaengnim-do
      kaseyo**).

7 Put the following sentences into the long negative form.

   a 고기를 좋아해요.   **d** 이 사과가 싱싱해요.
   b 지금 못 가요.   **e** 버스 못 타요.
   c 주문해요.

8 Sangmin is in bed sick, with the following symptoms. Can you describe them?

TEN THINGS TO REMEMBER

1 Commenting on the weather (when it's good; when it's bad)

2 Making a suggestion (*shall we go to the mountains?*)

3 Another way of making suggestions (*let's go to the mountains!*)

4 How to ask what someone is going to do tomorrow

5 The future tense

6 Saying that you're thinking of doing something

7 How to say you're not feeling well

8 Telling someone not to worry

9 The days of the week

10 How to tell someone not to do something (*don't go to the shops!*)

7

Review

Introduction

This unit is designed to give you the opportunity to soak
up all the things you have learned already and to give you
more practice both with practical language use, and with the
grammar patterns. In addition, the unit has another important
section which you must work through carefully – it describes all
the common types of Korean verb stems and the way in which
the endings are put on them. It is very important to master this,
as you need to be comfortable putting different verb endings
onto the different types of verb stem in order to progress
quickly with your Korean studies. You should use this section
to work through the grammar points, as you normally would,
but you will also probably want to keep coming back to it for
reference.

The unit is a further opportunity for you to revise both the
practical topics we've gone through so far (finding your way,
ordering food, and so on), and to check you are happy with all the
major grammar points. If you find there are some topics which you
are not so comfortable with, make sure you go back to the relevant
lesson and cover them again.

Topic revision

Here is a list of the topics you have covered so far. Make sure that you know the basic words and phrases that you would need for each of them.

1 meeting, identifying and introducing people
2 finding out what other people are up to: where they are going and why
3 buying drinks and going out for entertainment
4 making simple phone calls and arranging to meet people
5 discussing food and ordering food and drink in a restaurant
6 shopping and money
7 finding your way around
8 catching the right bus
9 planning your free time
10 feeling ill

Korean verbs

You have been learning the stems of Korean verbs and you have learned about the way in which endings are put onto these stems to give particular meanings. You have learned about vowel stems to which the particle –요(-yo) is added to give the polite style; you have learned about consonant stems to which you add either –어요(-ŏyo) or –아요(-ayo) to give the polite style. However, each of these two types of verb stem – consonant and vowel – can be broken down into further categories (one of these you have seen already – stems that end in –이[-i]). Each of these sub-categories has certain peculiarities which affect the way in which verb endings are added. We are now going to take you through each of the main types of verb stem in Korean, to show you how the endings are added. Some of this will be revision, but much will be new. Many of the verb stems we teach you are also new, and these may occur in the exercises from now on. They are all common verbs, and you should learn them.

Consonant stems

- Most stems which end in consonants take the polite style endings −어요(-ŏyo) or −아요(-ayo), depending on whether or not the last vowel of the stem was an 오(o) or an 아(a). Verb endings like −고(-ko) and −지만(-jiman) attach straight to the consonant base. Endings like −(으)ㄹ까요(-[ŭ]lkkayo) and −(으)ㅂ시다(-[ŭ]pshida) attach the longer form (with the 으[ŭ]) to the verb stem. Here are some examples:

먹–		먹어요	먹지만	먹을까요
(mŏk-)	eat	(mŏgŏyo)	(mŏk-jiman)	(mŏg-ŭlkkayo)
앉–		앉아요	앉지만	앉을까요
(anj-)	sit	(anjayo)	(ant-jiman)	(anj-ŭlkkayo)
받–		받아요	받지만	받을까요
(pat-)	receive	(padayo)	(pat-jiman)	(pad-ŭlkkayo)
좋–		좋아요	좋지만	좋을까요
(cho(h)-)	is good	(choayo)	(cho-ch'iman)	(cho-ŭlkkayo)
읽–		읽어요	읽지만	읽을까요
(ilk-)	read	(ilgŏyo)	(ilk-jiman)	(ilg-ŭlkkayo)

- Certain Korean verb stems which end in ㄹ(l) change the ㄹ(l) to a ㄷ(t) before endings that begin with a consonant (like −고[-ko] and −지만[-jiman]). The only very common verb that does this is:

들- 들어요 듣지만 들을까요

(tŭl-) *listen, hear* **(tŭrŏyo)** **(tŭt-jiman)** **(tŭr-ŭlkkayo)**

- Some verbs whose stem ends in ㅂ(**p**) change the ㅂ(**p**) to a 우(**u**) before adding the polite ending −어요(**-ŏyo**). The ㅂ(**p**) remains in endings which begin with consonants (−고[**-ko**] and −지만[**-jiman**]), but changes to the letter 우(**u**) before endings with two forms like −(으)ㄹ까요(**-[ŭ]lkkayo**) and −(으)ㅂ시다(**-[ŭ]pshida**). The shorter form (without the −으 [**-ŭ-**]) is then added:

덥–	더워요	덥고	더울까요
(tŏp-) *is hot*	**(tŏwoyo)**	**(tŏp-ko)**	**(tŏu-lkkayo)**

어렵–	어려워요	어렵고	어려울까요
(ŏryŏp-) *is difficult*	**(ŏryŏwoyo)**	**(ŏryŏp-ko)**	**(ŏryŏu-lkkayo)**

춥–	추워요	춥고	추울까요
(ch'up-) *is cold*	**(ch'uwoyo)**	**(ch'up-ko)**	**(ch'uu-lkkayo)**

가깝–	가까워요	가깝고	가까울까요
(kakkap-) *is near*	**(kakkawoyo)**	**(kakkap-ko)**	**(kakkau-lkkayo)**

맵–	매워요	맵고	매울까요
(maep-) *is spicy*	**(maewoyo)**	**(maep-ko)**	**(maeu-lkkayo)**

- Perhaps the most confusing category is the last, the ㄹ (**l**)-irregular verbs. These all end in ㄹ(**l**), but the ㄹ(**l**) disappears before all endings that have two forms: −(으) ㅂ시다(**-[ŭ]pshida**), −(으)ㄹ까요(**-[ŭ]lkkayo**) and so on, that is, the last column of our table. The shorter endings (without the −으[**-ŭ**]) are then added.

살-		살아요	살고	살까요
(sal-)	*live*	(sarayo)	(sal-go)	(sa-lkkayo)

놀-	*have fun,*	놀아요	놀고	놀까요
(nol-)	*play*	(norayo)	(nol-go)	(no-lkkayo)

알-		알아요	알고	알까요
(al-)	*know*	(arayo)	(al-go)	(a-lkkayo)

팔-		팔아요	팔고	팔까요
(p'al-)	*sell*	(p'arayo)	(p'al-go)	(p'a-lkkayo)

멀-		멀어요	멀고	멀까요
(mŏl-)	*is far*	(mŏrŏyo)	(mŏl-go)	(mŏ-lkkayo)

Vowel stems

You will find that all the vowel bases are regular in the final two columns. The only difficulty is in the formation of the polite style.

- Most vowel bases add the ending -요(**-yo**) directly to the stem to form the polite style. Endings like -고(**-ko**) and -지만(**-jiman**) are added straight to the stem; endings with two forms (-을까요 [**-ŭlkkayo**] and -ㄹ까요[**-lkkayo**]; -읍시다[**-ŭpshida**] and -ㅂ시다[**-pshida**]) add the shorter form straight to the stem since the stem ends in a vowel (note 하-[**ha-**] has an irregular polite style form):

가- (ka-)	go	가요 (kayo)	가고 (ka-go)	갈까요 (ka-lkkayo)
자- (cha-)	sleep	자요 (chayo)	자고 (cha-go)	잘까요 (cha-lkkayo)
떠나- (ttŏna-)	leave	떠나요 (ttŏnayo)	떠나고 (ttŏna-go)	떠날까요 (ttŏna-lkkayo)
일어나- (irŏna-)	get up	일어나요 (irŏnayo)	일어나고 (irŏna-go)	일어날까요 (irŏna-lkkayo)
구경 (kugyŏng)	view	구경 (kugyŏng)	구경 (kugyŏng)	구경 (kugyŏng)
하- (ha-)	sight-see	해요 (haeyo)	하고 (ha-go)	할까요 (ha-lkkayo)
공부 (kongbu)	study	공부 (kongbu)	공부 (kongbu)	공부 (kongbu)
하- (ha-)		해요 (haeyo)	하고 (ha-go)	할까요 (ha-lkkayo)

The verbs 오-(o-) (*come*) and 보-(po-) (*look or watch*) are regular apart from their polite forms 와요(wayo) and 봐요 (pwayo). The stem 되-(toe-) (*become, is all right*) also has an irregular polite style 돼요(twaeyo).

- Stems that end in −이(-i) change the 이(i) to 여(yŏ) before the polite style 요(yo) is added. Everything else is as you would expect. Do remember, however, that some verb ending patterns are based on the polite style minus the −요 (-yo) ending. For example, there is an ending −서(-sŏ) which attaches to the polite style minus the 요(yo). In this case, the stem 마시−(mashi-) would be 마셔서(mashyŏsŏ), since it is based on the polite style 마셔요(mashyŏyo) minus the 요(yo), plus 서(sŏ):

마시−		마셔요	마시고	마실까요
(mashi-)	*drink*	(mashyŏyo)	(mashi-go)	(mashi-lkkayo)

가르치−		가르쳐요	가르치고	가르칠까요
(karŭch'i-)	*teach*	(karŭch'yŏyo)	(karŭch'i-go)	(karŭch'i-lkkayo)

- Stems that end in the vowel 으(ŭ) delete this 으(ŭ) before adding the polite style ending as you would for a consonant base (either −어요[-ŏyo] or −아요[-ayo]):

쓰−		써요	쓰고	쓸까요
(ssŭ-)	*use; write*	(ssŏyo)	(ssŭ-go)	(ssŭ-lkkayo)

아프−		아파요	아프고	아플까요
(ap'ŭ-)	*hurt*	(ap'ayo)	(ap'ŭ-go)	(ap'ŭ-lkkayo)

바쁘−		바빠요	바쁘고	바쁠까요
(pappŭ-)	*is busy*	(pappayo)	(pappŭ-go)	(pappŭ-lkkayo)

Note, however, that verb stems which end in 르(lŭ) not only delete the 으(ŭ), but add another 르(l) before the polite style ending −어요(-ŏyo) or −아요(-ayo). Everything else is regular:

빠르–		빨라요	빠르고	빠를까요
(pparŭ-)	*is fast*	(ppallayo)	(pparŭ-go)	(pparŭ-lkkayo)

모르–		몰라요	모르고	모를까요
(morŭ-)	*not know*	(mollayo)	(morŭ-go)	(morŭ-lkkayo)

부르–		불러요	부르고	부를까요
(purŭ-)	*sing, call*	(pullŏyo)	(purŭ-go)	(purŭ-lkkayo)

- Bases that end in 우(u) change the 우(u) to 워(wo) before the polite style –요(-yo) is added. 주–(chu-) may generally not be shortened like this, however, and has the polite form 주어요 (chuŏyo) or 줘요(chwoyo):

배우–		배워요	배우고	배울까요
(paeu-)	*learn*	(paewoyo)	(paeu-go)	(paeu-lkkayo)

피우–		피워요	피우고	피울까요
(p'iu-)	*smoke*	(p'iwoyo)	(p'iu-go)	(p'iu-lkkayo)

주–		주어요	주고	줄까요
(chu-)	*give*	(chuŏyo)	(chu-go)	(chu-lkkayo) (or 줘요[chwoyo])

Practice

1 Translate the following sentences into English. Most of them should look familiar, as they are based closely on sentences you have met in the dialogues of units 1 to 6.

a 그럼, 같이 가요 (kŭrŏm, kach'i kayo).

b 오늘 점심에 시간이 있어요(onŭl chŏmshim-e shigan-i issŏyo)?

c 진짜 오래간만이에요(chinccha oraeganman-ieyo).

d 저는 일본말 선생님이 아니에요(chŏ-nŭn ilbonmal sŏnsaengnim-i anieyo).

e 죄송합니다(choesong hamnida). 착각했어요(chakkak haessŏyo).

f 다음 월요일은 아마 괜찮을 거에요(taŭm woryoir-ŭn ama kwanch'an-ŭl wakŏeyo).

g 저도 서울 사람이 아니라서 잘 모르겠어요(chŏ-do sŏwul saram-i ani-rasŏ chal morugessŏyo).

h 전신이 다 아프군요(chŏnshin-i ta ap'ŭ-gunyo). 안 아픈 데가 있어요(an ap'ŭn te-ga issŏyo)?

i 영국 돈을 중국 돈으로 바꾸고 싶어요(yŏngguk ton-ŭl chungguk ton-ŭro pakku-go ship'ŏyo).

j 그리고 저는 냉면도 먹고 싶어요(kŭrigo chŏ-nŭn naengmyŏn-do mŏk-ko ship'ŏyo).

k 마른 안주하고 파전 주세요(marŭn anju-hago p'ajŏn chuseyo).

l 한 상자에 이만원에 가져 가세요(han sangja-e iman won-e kajyŏ-gaseyo).

2 Telling the time in Korean is easy. To ask what time it is, you say 몇 시에요(myŏt-shi-eyo)? Literally this means *how many hours is it*? To ask at what time something happens you would say either 몇 시에 학교에 가요(myŏt-shi-e hakkyo-e kayo)? or 언제 학교에 가요(ŏnje hakkyo-e kayo)?

The hours are counted by the pure Korean numbers, and the minutes by Sino-Korean numbers. *9 o'clock* is 아홉시(ahop-shi); *2 o'clock* is 두시(tu-shi); *3.35* is 세시 삼십오분(se-shi samshibo-bun); *12.02* is 열두시 이분(yŏldu-shi i-bun). You can say *at* a certain time with the particle −에 (**-e**). Thus, *at 2.40* is 두시 사십분에 (**tu-shi saship-pun-e**) and so on. You can say *half past* with the word 반 (**pan**). *Half past one is* 한시 반 (**han-shi pan**).

Answer the question 몇 시에요 (**myŏt-shi-eyo**)? for each of the following.

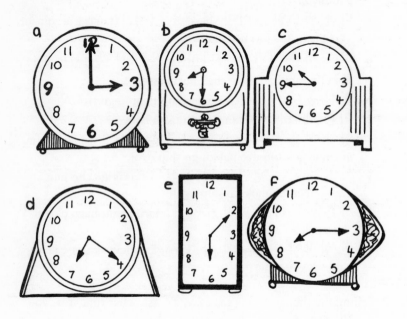

3 Give the polite style, the −고 (**-ko**) form and the −읍시다 (**-ŭpshida**) form of the following verbs.

   a 하−(**ha-**)   **d** 바쁘−(**pappǔ-**)

   b 닫−(**tat-**) *(shut)*   **e** 움직이−(**umjigi-**) *(move)*

   c 팔−(**p'al-**)

Check your answers carefully with the information about verbs that we have given you.

4 You are planning a trip away with your friend. Make up responses to his questions.

a 어디 갈까요(ŏdi ka-lkkayo)?
b 뭐 하러 거기 가요(mwo ha-rŏ kŏgi kayo)?
c 언제 갈까요(ŏnje ka-lkkayo)?
d 몇 시에 만날까요(myŏt-shi-e manna-lkkayo)?
e 어디서 만날까요(ŏdi-sŏ manna-lkkayo)?

5 You go to a restaurant with your two friends. One of you wants to eat 불고기(pulgogi), another 갈비(kalbi), and a third 냉면 (naengmyŏn). Write a dialogue which includes the following questions from the waiter and your answers to them. (You decide to have a beer each).

Can I help you?
Can you eat spicy food? (literally, do you eat well spicy food?)
Would you like anything to drink?
물도 드릴까요(mul-do tŭrilkkayo)?

6 Make up five short dialogues based on the following information. The dialogue pattern is like this:

a *Where are you going?*
b *(answer)*

a *What are you going to buy/do/drink/eat there?*
b *(answer)*

Here is the information you need for the answers:

a 가게(kage)　　오징어(ojingŏ) **d** 집(chip)　　차(cha)
b 학교(hakkyo)　야구(yagu)　　**e** 시장(shijang) 과일(kwail)
c 식당(shiktang) 불고기(pulkogi)

7 Here is a typical day for Mr Pak. Answer the questions that follow.

7.30	*get up*
9.00	*shopping*
10.00	*meet Mr Lee's wife at Hilton Hotel*
1.00	*lunch at Chinese restaurant*
2.00	*doctor's appointment*
6.00	*home for meal*
7.30	*cinema*
11.00	*bed*

a 박선생님은 몇 시에 일어나요?
b 10시에는 뭐 해요?
c 점심 때는 뭘 먹어요?
d 밤에는 어디 가요?
e 몇시에 자요?

8 Read the following questions and answer each one negatively with a full sentence (*no, I'm not* or *no, I don't*). Try to use the long negative pattern for one or two of the questions. Then make up another sentence saying what you do instead.

a 축구 좋아해요 (ch'ukku choa haeyo)?
b 매운 거 잘 먹어요 (maeun kŏ chal mŏgŏyo)?
c 텔레비젼을 많이 봐요 (tellebijyŏn-ŭl mani pwayo)?

d 노래를 잘 불러요 (norae-rŭl chal pullŏyo)?

e 중국말 배워요 (chunggungmal paewŏyo)?

9 Look at the following street plan and answer the questions with full Korean sentences.

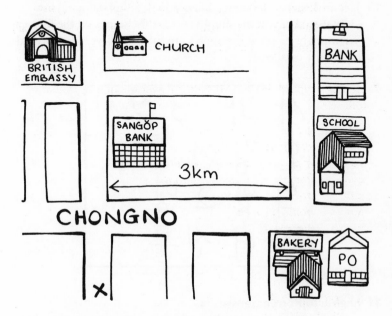

a 교회에서 영국 대사관은 멀어요 (kyohoe-esŏ yŏngguk taesagwan-ŭn mŏrŏyo)?

b 이 근처에 한국 외환은행이 있어요 (i-kŭnch'ŏ-e hanguk oehwan ŭnhaeng-i issŏyo)?

c 학교가 어디에요 (hakkyo-ga ŏdi-eyo)?

d 학교가 가까워요 (hakkyo-ga kakkawŏyo)?

e 우체국은 대사관보다 더 멀어요 (uchegug-ŭn taesagwan-poda tŏ mŏrŏyo)?

f 학교에 가면 시간 많이 걸려요 (hakkyo-e ka-myŏn shigan mani kŏllyŏyo)?

g 우체국이 어디에요 (uchegug-i ŏdi-eyo)?

교회	(kyohoe)	*church*
학교	(hakkyo)	*school*
제과	(chegwa)	*bakery*

10 Jaemin has gone shopping. Have a look at his shopping list. How would he ask the shopkeeper for the things on the list? What might he say if the apples are too expensive? How would he ask the total cost?

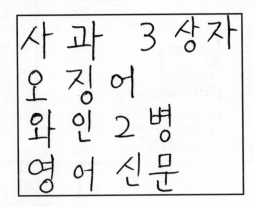

11 English to Korean translation.

  a *I'm going to school to study English too.*
  b *Let's meet outside the shop. See you later!*
  c *Enjoy your meal.*
  d *I'll really have to go to hospital.*
  e *Just pay 15,000 won, then.*
  f *It takes about 15 minutes.*
  g *How's business these days?*
  h *Give me the cheapest one, please.*
  i *The weather is good nowadays.*
  j *I came to meet Mr Pak from the Korean embassy.*
  k *I can't eat spicy things.*
  l *Does the bus for the post office stop at this stop?*

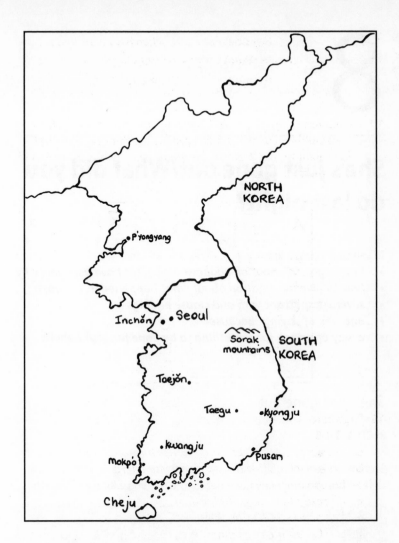

NORTH
KOREA

• P'yongyang

Inchŏn • • Seoul

Sorak
mountains

SOUTH
KOREA

Taejŏn •

Taegu •   • Kyongju

• Kwangju

Mokpo •   • Pusan

Cheju

8

She's just gone out/What did you do last night?

In this unit you will learn
- *how to give information about where people have gone and why*
- *how to give information about what happened in the past*
- *several important verb and clause endings*
- *one way of saying 'because'*
- *a way of asking for something to be done for your benefit*

She's just gone out

◄)) CD 1, TR 8

Jaemok rings up his girlfriend Chŏngmin to cancel a date with her, only to find that she'd already gone out for the evening with someone else!

윤선생	여보세요?
재목	여보세요. 정민씨 좀 바꿔주세요.
윤선생	네. 잠깐만 기다리세요.

A little while later.

윤선생	미안합니다. 조금 전까지 있었는데, 방금 나갔어요.

재목	혹시 어디 갔는지 아세요?
윤선생	잘 모르겠어요.
	잠깐만 기다려 보세요. 우리 집사람이
	아마 알고 있을 거에요.
부인	정민씨 오늘 남자 친구랑 영화 보러
	나갔어요.
재목	그래요? 이상하네. 오늘 저녁에
	나하고 만나기로 했는데.
부인	저런, 정민씨는 다른 남자랑 데이트
	하러 갔는데 … 아마 밤 늦게까지 안
	들어올거에요.
재목	그럼 잘 됐네요. 오늘 저녁 약속을
	취소하려고 전화했거든요.
	오늘 저한테 바쁜 일이 생겼어요.
부인	아, 그래요. 잘 됐네요.
	정민씨한데 전할 말이 있으세요?
재목	아니요, 없어요. 안녕히 계세요.

Mr Yun	Yŏboseyo?
Jaemok	Yŏboseyo. Chŏngmin-ssi chom pakkwo-juseyo.
Mr Yun	Ne. Chamkkan-man kidariseyo.

A little while later.

Mr Yun	Mian hamnida. chogŭm chŏn-kkaji issŏn-nŭnde,
	panggŭm nagassŏyo.
Jaemok	Hokshi ŏdi kannŭnji aseyo?
Mr Yun	Chal morŭgessŏyo.
	Chamkkan-man kidaryŏ-boseyo. Uri chipsaram-i
	ama al-go iss-ŭl kŏeyo.
Mrs Yun	Chŏngmin-ssi onŭl namja ch'ingu-rang yŏnghwa
	po-rŏ nagassŏyo.
Jaemok	Kŭraeyo? Isang ha-ne. Onŭl chŏnyŏg-e na-hago
	manna-giro haennŭnde …

Mrs Yun	Chŏrŏn, Chŏngmin-ssi-nŭn tarŭn namja-rang deit'ŭ ha-rŏ kannŭnde ....
	Ama pam nŭtke-kkaji an torao-l kŏeyo.
Jaemok	Kŭrŏm chal toenneyo. Onŭl chŏnyŏk yaksog-ŭl chwiso ha-ryŏgo chŏnhwa haet-kŏdŭnyo.
	Onŭl chŏ-hant'e pappŭn ir-i saenggyŏssŏyo.
Mrs Yun	A, kŭraeyo. Chal toenneyo.
	Chŏngmin-ssi-hant'e chŏn hal mar-i issŭseyo?
Jaemok	Aniyo, ŏpsŏyo.
	Annyŏnghi kyeseyo.

Phrases and expressions

ŏdi kannŭnji aseyo?	*do you know where (she) has gone?*
ama al-go issŭ-l kŏeyo	*will perhaps know*
isang ha-ne	*(it is) strange!*
chŏrŏn	*oh dear!, oh no!*
chal twoenneyo	*it's turned out well, it's all for the better*
... hant'e chŏn hal mar-i issŭseyo?	*do you have a message for ...?*

pakku-	바꾸–	*change*
chogŭm chŏn	조금 전	*a little while ago*
chogŭm	조금	*a little, a bit*
chŏn	전	*before*
chŏn-e	전에	*previously*
-kkaji	–까지	*until*
-(ŏ)ss-	–었	*(used to form the past tense, see note 4)*
panggŭm	방금	*just now*
naga-	나가–	*go out*
hokshi	혹시	*maybe, perhaps, possibly*
onŭl	오늘	*today*

namja ch'ingu	남자 친구	*boyfriend*
-(i)rang	–(이)랑	*with* (**-irang** after consonants)
yŏnghwa	영화	*film, movie*
isang ha-	이상하–	*is strange, bizarre*
chŏnyŏk	저녁	*evening, supper*
deit'ŭ ha-	데이트하–	*to date*
pam	밤	*night*
nŭkke	늦게	*late*
torao-	돌아오–	*come back, return*
yaksok	약속	*appointment*
chwiso ha-	취소하–	*cancel*
-ryŏgo	–려고	*with the intention of* (see note 5)
chŏnhwa ha-	전화하–	*telephone* (verb stem)
pappŭn	바쁜	*busy*
-kŏdŭnyo	–거든요	(see note 6)
saenggi-	생기–	*to occur, happen, take place*
chŏn ha-	전하–	*communicate*

Grammar 13

1 *Continuous states*

In English we have a present continuous tense, used in sentences like *I am going, he is sitting*. This continuous tense is indicated by the ending -*ing*. In English we use the continuous tense fairly frequently, whereas in Korean the continuous form is used only for special emphasis, to stress that something is going on continuously. This means that when in English you meet a verb form that ends in -*ing*, you must not automatically assume that you should translate it by a Korean continuous form; in most cases you should probably not do so.

Let's take an example to illustrate this. In English it is quite common to say a sentence like *I'm going home.* This uses the continuous tense. It would be very unusual to translate this by the Korean continuous tense, and you would only do so if you particularly wanted to stress the process or the ongoing action of your going home. You would be far more likely to use the normal Korean present tense form 나는 집에 가요(**na-nǔn chib-e kayo**).

There are certain circumstances in which the Korean continuous form is used, however, and you should note these. It is often used with the verb *to know.* The phrase 알고 있어요(**al-go issŏyo**) literally means *I am knowing,* and the Korean emphasis is *I am in a state of knowing that,* and sometimes has the force *I already know that (you didn't need to tell me).* You meet that form in this unit.

Other common uses are to stress what you are in the process of doing right now. Thus, as answers to the question 뭘 해요(**mwol haeyo**)? *(what are you doing?)*, you might say:

책 읽어요(**chaek ilg-ŏyo**)
책 읽고 있어요(**chaek ilk-ko issŏyo**)

They both mean *I'm reading a book*, but the second one stresses that you are in the process of reading the book even as you speak, that is what you are busy with and in the middle of doing.

Generally you should only use the present continuous tense when you are sure that you want to stress that particular meaning of continuous action.

To make the form, take the verb stem and add ‒고 있‒(**-ko iss-**), for example, in the polite style, ‒고 있어요(**-ko issŏyo**). You will not normally find negatives in the continuous pattern; you would simply use a normal verb form, for example 안 읽어요(**an ilgŏyo**) *(I'm not reading).*

Insight

Emphasizing the continuity of an action is very easy in
Korean. Simply add –고 있어요 (**–ko issŏyo**) to the stem of
the verb in question. 먹고 있어요 (**mŏk-ko issŏyo**), *I am
eating* (and it's an ongoing action – I'm still doing it!).

2 Probabilities

You will remember that we said in the last unit that the probable
future form –을 거에요(**-ŭl kŏeyo**) can also be used simply to
mean 'probably'. You have an example in this dialogue in the
phrase 아마 알고 있을 거에요(**ama al-go issŭl kŏeyo**) (*my wife
will probably know, perhaps my wife will know*). Notice that
this isn't a proper future tense; it is just a way of expressing
probability.

3 Having a go at ...

You have already learned the verb 가보–(**kabo-**), which we told
you meant 'go and see'. It is not really one verb at all, however, but
a compound of the verb 가–(**ka-**) (*go*) and the verb 보–(**po-**) (*see*).
You can make other compound verbs by adding the verb 보–(**po-**)
to another verb. You must take the other verb in the polite style
–요(**-yo**) form, knock off the –요(**-yo**), and then add on the verb
보–(**po-**). Here are some examples:

stem	polite	minus –요 (-yo)	plus 보-(po-)	meaning
가–	가요	가–	가보–	go and see
먹–	먹어요	먹어–	먹어보–	eat and see have a go at eating
기다리–	기다려요	기다려–	기다려보–	wait and see try waiting

The two most common uses for this pattern are as follows:

- It is often used in the polite honorific style to mean *please have a go at* (verb) *and see, please try out* (verb)*ing*. For example, 기다려보세요(**kidaryŏ-boseyo**) in this lesson means *please wait and see, please try waiting, please have a go at waiting*.

- In the past tense it means *have you tried* (verb)*ing?, have you had a go at* (verb)*ing?*, e.g. 테니스를 해봤어요(**t'enisŭ-rŭl** (*tennis*) **hae-bwassŏyo**)? (*have you ever played tennis? have you ever tried playing tennis?*) (how to make the past tense is in the following point).

Insight

If you want to say you'll have a go at something, or you'll try and see, take the regular polite style of the verb, take off the –요 (**–yo**) ending, and replace it with the verb 보– (**po-**), *see*. You can put any verb ending you want onto 보– (**po-**), depending on what you want to say. So 먹어요 (**mŏgŏyo**) would become 먹어봅시다 (**mŏgŏ-popshida**), 먹어봐요 (**mŏgŏ-pwayo**), or 먹어봤어요 (**mŏgŏ-pwassŏyo**) – *Let's try (eating it) and see, I'm trying it (= tasting it, giving it a go), I tried eating it.*

4 The past tense

The past tense in Korean is used very similarly to the past tense in English to say what someone did or was doing in the past. You just need to learn how to form it and, fortunately, that is fairly easy too. Take the verb you want in the polite style (e.g. 먹어요[**mŏgŏyo**], 알아요[**arayo**], 기다려요[**kidaryŏyo**], 앉아요[**anjayo**]), take the –요 (**-yo**) off the end and add –ㅆ(**-ss**). What you now have is the past stem (previously you have been learning the present stem of verbs). This past stem can then be made into a verb form in the normal way, by adding, for example, the polite style ending –어요(**-ŏyo**):

stem	polite	minus –요 (-yo)	plus –ㅆ (-ss)	polite past
먹–	먹어요	먹어	먹었–	먹었어요
알–	알아요	알아	알았–	알았어요
기다리–	기다려요	기다려	기다렸–	기다렸어요
앉–	앉아요	앉아	앉았–	앉았어요

Remember that you can put all sorts of endings on the past base, just as you can on the normal verb bases that you have learned previously. Sometimes the forms you make will look a bit odd because of the rules of sound change – the –ㅆ(-ss) might disappear into another sound, but it will still be there in Korean writing. For example, with the past base 먹었-(mŏgŏss-) you could make: 먹었어요(mŏgŏssŏyo), 먹었구나(mŏgŏt-kuna) (먹었[mŏgŏss-] + 구나[-kuna]), 먹었고(mŏgŏt-ko) (먹었 [mŏgŏss-] + 고[ko]), 먹었네요(mŏgŏn-neyo) (먹었[mŏgŏss-] + 네요[neyo]), etc.

Remember that the forms 했는데(haennŭnde) and 갔는데 (kannŭnde) are also past tense forms in which the –ㅆ(-ss-) of the past tense has become ㄴ(n) by the rules of sound change. These two forms are thus the past bases 했-(haess-) and 갔-(kass-) with the imminent elaboration –는데(-nŭnde) added to them. This past tense –는데(-nŭnde) form is very common in Korean.

To make honorific past forms, take the present verb base, and add –셨-(-shyŏss-) to give you the honorific past base (if the stem ends in a vowel), or –으셨-(-ŭshyŏss-) (if the stem ends in a consonant). This can then be made into, for example, 앉으셨어요 (anjŭshyŏssŏyo) (you [honorific] sat down), from the honorific past base 앉으셨-(anjŭshyŏss-).

It looks difficult at first, but with the practice in the exercises, you should soon crack it. Everything is regular, you just have to remember the right rules and apply them.

5 With the intention of ...

Very early in this course you learned how to say sentences such as
빵 사러 시내에 가요 (ppang sa-rŏ shinae-e kayo) (*I'm going to the
city centre to buy bread*). The constructions were made by adding
–러 (-rŏ) to the verb in the first clause, to mean *in order to*. That
construction can only be used with the two verbs *go* and *come*
at the end of the sentence, however. This lesson introduces you
to a way to say a similar thing, *in order to, with the intention of,*
which can be used with other verbs as well. You add –(으)려고 (-[ŭ]
ryŏgo) to the stem of the verb of the first clause (–으려고 [-ŭryŏgo]
if the stem ends in a consonant. Here is a reminder of the example
of the construction which you saw in the dialogue: 취소하려고
전화했어요 (ch'wiso ha-ryŏgo chŏnhwa haessŏyo) *I'm calling*
(literally, *I have called*) *with the intention of cancelling (in order to
cancel*).

Here are some more examples:

영어 배우려고 영어 책 샀어요 (yŏngŏ paeu-ryŏgo yŏngŏ
ch'aek sassŏyo)
*(I) bought an English language book with the intention of learning
English*

책 읽으려고 도서관에 가요 (ch'aek ilg-ŭryŏgo tosŏgwan-e
kayo)
(I) am going to the library in order to read books

결혼하려고 돈을 벌었어요 (kyŏr[h]on ha-ryŏgo ton-ŭl
pŏrŏssŏyo)
I earned some money with the intention of getting married

yŏngŏ	영어	*English language*
hangugŏ	한국어	*Korean language*
-ŏ	-어	*language*
kyŏrhon ha-	결혼하-	*get married*
pŏ-l-	벌-	*earn*

6 –거든요 (-kŏdǔnyo)

The verb ending –거든요 (-kŏdǔnyo) is a common form in colloquial speech, although it is a bit difficult to pin down precisely what it means in English.

The pattern is used when you are adding an explanation to something that you have already said. Look carefully at the last sentence of Jaemok in the dialogue. He has just said 'it's turned out well then', and then he goes on to say another sentence which ends in –거든요 (-kŏdǔnyo). This sentence explains why he has just said that it turned out well – because he was ringing to cancel the date in any case. In a way, therefore, –거든요 means something like *it's because ..., you see*, when you add an explanation to something. But you must have already said something else which the –거든요 phrase is an explanation of! Work through the questions in the exercise carefully, thinking through why the –거든요 form has been used in each case. If you can, try to mimic Koreans in the way they use this pattern. That's the best way to make sure you are using it properly.

The ending –거든요 is added simply to the verb stem, either a present or a past stem, although the past is probably a bit more common.

If you are able to use it correctly, Koreans will be very impressed as it really does make your speech sound colloquial.

7 Saying 'and then' and 'because'

Along with the past tense, this grammar note is probably the most crucial part of this unit. It introduces you to a form which is used all the time in spoken and written Korean.

First, we will look at how to form it, and afterwards at what it means. It is used to end the first clause of a two-clause construction, and you take off the –요(-yo) of the polite-style present of the verb and add –서(-sŏ). For example:

stem	polite	minus –요(-yo)	–서(-so) form
먹–	먹어요	먹어	먹어서
마시–	마셔요	마셔	마셔서

The –서(-sŏ) pattern has two meanings. In both cases, imagine a sentence of the form (clause A)-sŏ (clause B).

- It can mean 'after having done A, then B', or 'A and then B', where there is a close sequential link between the two clauses (usually a link of time: *after A, then B*). An example would be: 학교에 가서 공부할 거예요(hakkyo-e ka-sŏ kongbu hal kŏeyo), which could be translated as follows:

  I'll go to school and then study
  After going to school, I will study

Here are some more examples:

친구를 만나서 술집에 가요(ch'ingu-rŭl manna-sŏ sulchib-e kayo)
I meet (my) friend and then (we) go to the pub

한국에 가서 한국 친구를 만났어요(Hangug-e ka-sŏ hanguk ch'ingu-rŭl mannassŏyo)
I went to Korea, and then I met a Korean friend

- It can mean 'because A, then B', and this is perhaps the meaning which you will use (and meet) most frequently. A good example would be:

비가 와서 학교에 못 가요(Pi-ga wa-sǒ hakkyo-e mot kayo)
It's raining, so I can't go to school
I can't go to school because it's raining

Here are some more examples:

오늘 바쁜 일이 생겨서 약속을 못 지켜요
(Onǔl pappǔn ir-i saenggyǒ-sǒ yaksog-ǔl mot chik'yǒyo)
Something has come up today, so I cannot keep the appointment
(lit. *a busy matter has come up*)

머리가 아파서 술을 못 마셔요(Mǒri-ga ap'a-sǒ sur-ǔl mot masyǒyo)
My head hurts, so I cannot drink

Insight

Connecting sentences with −서 (-sǒ). This is the third pattern in this unit which is formed by stripping off the −요 (-yo) of the regular polite style and replacing it with a different ending, in this case −서 (-sǒ). It means *because of* or *since* and you then add a second clause or sentence which explains what the consequences of the first clause or sentence are.

What did you do last night?

🔊 **CD 1, TR 8, 01:55**

Yongtae has a new girlfriend, and his friend Taegyu appears rather inquisitive – what's her name, where does she work, how did they meet, what do they do together?

용태	태규씨 안녕하세요?
태규	안녕하세요.
	요즘 재미가 어떠세요?
용태	요즘 바빠요.
	여자 친구가 생겨서 더 바빠요.
태규	그런 줄 알았어요.
	여자 친구 이름이 뭐에요?
용태	김정민이에요.
	작년에 서울대학교를 졸업하고 지금은 현대자동차에서 일하고 있어요.
태규	어떻게 만났어요?
용태	친구가 소개해 주었어요.
	처음에는 그렇게 마음에 들지 않았는데, 한달 후에 파티에서 우연히 다시 만났어요.
	그때부터 자주 만나기 시작했어요.
태규	지금은 거의 매일 만나서 데이트 하지요?
용태	그런 편이에요.
태규	어제 밤에도 내가 전화했는데 없었어요. 어제 밤에 어디 갔었어요?
용태	어제 밤이요?
	기억이 안 나요. 아마 어딘가 갔을 거에요.
태규	기억이 안 나요? 그렇게 술을 많이 마셨어요?
용태	누가 술을 마셔요?
	태규씨가 오히려 매일 술만 마시잖아요?
태규	어쨌든 어제 어디 갔었어요?

용태	노래방에 갔었어요. 내 여자 친구는 노래방을 아주 좋아해요.
태규	노래방에서 나와서 어디 갔었어요?
용태	탁구를 좀 쳤어요.
태규	그게 다에요? 솔직히 말해보세요.
용태	정말이에요. 아무 일도 없었어요.

Yongtae	Taegyu-ssi annyŏng haseyo?
Taegyu	Annyŏng haseyo. Yojŭm chaemi-ga ŏttŏseyo?
Yongtae	Yojŭm pappayo. Yŏja ch'ingu-ga saenggyŏ-sŏ tŏ pappayo.
Taegyu	Kurŏn-jul arassŏyo. Yŏja ch'ingu irŭm-i mwo- eyo?
Yongtae	Kim Chŏngmin-ieyo. Changnyŏn-e sŏul taehakkyo-rŭl chorŏpha-go chigŭm-ŭn Hyŏndae chadongch'a-esŏ ilha-go issŏyo.
Taegyu	Ŏttŏk'e mannassŏyo?
Yongtae	Ch'ingu-ga sogae hae-juŏssŏyo. Ch'ŏŭm-enŭn kurŏk'e maŭm-e tŭl-ji anannŭnde, han tal hu-e p'at'i-esŏ uyŏnhi tashi mannassŏyo. Kŭ-ttae-but'ŏ chaju manna-gi shijak haessŏyo.
Taegyu	Chigŭm-ŭn kŏŭy maeil manna-sŏ deit'ŭ hajiyo?
Yongtae	Kŭrŏn p'yŏn-ieyo.
Taegyu	Ŏje pam-edo nae-ga chŏnhwa haennŭnde ŏpsŏssŏyo. Ŏje pam-e ŏdi kassŏssŏyo?
Yongtae	Ŏje pam-iyo? Kiŏg-i an nayo. Ama ŏdinga kassul kŏeyo.
Taegyu	Kiŏg-i an nayo? Kŭrŏk'e sur-ŭl mani mashyŏssŏyo?
Yongtae	Nuga sur-ŭl mashyŏyo? Taegyu-ssi-ga ohiryŏ maeil sul-man mashijanayo?
Taegyu	Ŏcchaettŭn ŏje ŏdi kassŏssŏyo?

Yongtae	Noraebang-e kassŏssŏyo.
	Nae yŏja ch'ingu-nŭn noraebang-ŭl aju choa
	haeyo.
Taegyu	Noraebang-esŏ nawa-sŏ ŏdi kassŏssŏyo?
Yongtae	T'akku-rŭl chom ch'yŏssŏyo.
Taegyu	Kŭ-ge ta-eyo? Solchikhi mal hae-boseyo.
Yongtae	Chŏngmal-ieyo. Amu il-do ŏpsŏssŏyo.

Phrases and expressions

yojŭm chaemi-ga ŏttŏseyo?	*how are you doing? how are things these days?*
kŭrŏn-jul arassŏyo	*I thought so*
maŭm-e tŭl-ji anayo	*I don't like (her)* (**maum-e an tŭroyŏ**)
... maŭm-e tŭ-l-	*(I) like ...*
kŭrŏn p'yŏn-ieyo	*(we) tend to be so/do so (it's usually like that, etc.)*
kiŏg-i an nayo	*I don't remember*
ama ŏdinga kassŭl kŏeyo	*I expect (we) went somewhere or other; maybe ...*
solchikhi mal hae-boseyo	*tell me the truth!*

yojŭm	요즘	*nowadays*
pappŭ-	바쁘–	*is busy*
yŏja ch'ingu	여자 친구	*girlfriend*
irŭm	이름	*name*
changnyŏn	작년	*last year*
taehakkyo	대학교	*university*
chorŏpha-	졸업하–	*graduate* (verb stem)
Hyŏndae chadongch'a	현대자동차	*Hyundai car* (company)
chadongch'a	자동차	*car*
ch'a	차	*car* (short form)

il ha-	일하–	*work* (verb stem)
sogaeha-	소개하–	*to introduce*
ŏttŏk'e	어떻게	*how?*
ch'ŏŭm	처음	*at first*
kŭrŏk'e	그렇게	*like that* (here: *particularly*)
irŏk'e	이렇게	*like this*
maŭm	마음	*mind, heart*
tal	달	*month*
hu	후	*after*
p'at'i	파티	*party*
uyŏnhi	우연히	*by chance, coincidentally*
tashi	다시	*again*
ttae	때	*time*
-put'ŏ	–부터	*from*
chaju	자주	*often, frequently*
shijak ha-	시작하–	*begin, start*
kŏŭy	거의	*nearly, almost*
maeil	매일	*everyday*
kiŏk	기억	*memory*
ŏdinga	어딘가	*somewhere or other*
nuga	누가	*who?* (subject form)
ohiryŏ	오히려	*rather, on the contrary*
ŏcchaettŭn	어쨌든	*anyway*
noraebang	노래방	*'karaoke' singing room*
nae	내	*my*
che	제	*my* (humble form)
t'akku	탁구	*table tennis*
ch'i-	치–	*to play* (tennis, table tennis etc.)
solchikhi	솔직히	*frankly, honestly*

Grammar 14

1 *For my benefit*

You have learned how to ask people to do things by using polite requests ending in −세요(-seyo). The construction you are about to learn enables you to make such requests even more polite, and to stress that they are for your benefit. Suppose you want to say 'please do it for me, please do it (for my benefit)'. Previously you would have said 하세요(haseyo). Instead, take the polite style of the verb (해요[haeyo]), knock off the −요(-yo) (해−[hae-]), and add the verb stem 주−(chu-) (*give*) and then add the verb ending you want. Usually you will still want to use the polite request ending, so you would make the form 해 주세요(hae + chu + seyo, hae-juseyo) (*please do it for me*). The literal meaning of the construction is *please do it and give* and you can see how the verbs make this meaning when they are put together, and imply that you are asking for something to be done for your benefit.

This is quite a common pattern. Here are a couple of examples:

오늘 점심 좀 사주세요 (onǔl chǒmshim chom sa-juseyo)?
Please will you buy my lunch for me today?

이 우산 좀 빌려 주세요 (i-usan chom pillyǒ-juseyo)
Please lend me your (this) umbrella

한국말 너무 어려워요(hangung mal nǒmu ǒryǒwoyo). 쉽게 가르쳐 주세요(shwipke karǔch'yǒ-juseyo)

Korean is so difficult (or *too difficult*). *Please teach it simply for me*

usan	우산	*umbrella*
pilli-	빌리−	*borrow*
pillyǒ-ju-	빌려주−	*lend*
shwipke	쉽게	*easily*

2 Beginning to do things

You can say that someone is beginning to do something in Korean by adding −기 시작하−(-ki shijak ha-) to a processive verb stem (a verb of doing). Here are two good examples:

학교에서 일본말을 공부하기 시작해요(Hakkyo-esŏ ilbon mar-ŭl kongbu ha-gi shijak haeyo)
(We) are beginning to study Japanese at school

요즘 어떤 영국 사람이 한국말을 배우기 시작했어요(yojŭm ŏttŏn yŏngguk saram-i hangung mar-ul paeu-gi shijak haessŏyo)
Nowadays some English people have begun to learn the Korean language

3 Sentence endings with −지요(-jiyo)

You can end sentences with the form −지요(-jiyo) added to any stem. As you can see, it is a bit like the polite style (since it ends in −요[-yo]). It means something like *I suppose, you know, I guess,* etc., and it gives your sentences a bit more flavour than the polite style. However, the exact meaning of −지요 corresponds to a number of English meanings, depending on whether they occur in statements, yes–no questions, or suggestions. It is used when the speaker wants to draw the hearer in to what is being said. The following examples illustrate some of the ways it can be used:

한국 사람이지요 (hangguk saram-ijiyo)?	*I suppose you are Korean, aren't you?*
점심 벌써 먹었지요 (chŏmshim pŏlssŏ mŏgŏt-jiyo)?	*You've eaten lunch already, haven't you?*
지금 점심 먹지요 (chigŭm chŏmshim mŏk-jiyo)	*Let's have lunch now (I suggest we have lunch now)*
술을 좋아하지요 (sur-ŭl choaha-jiyo)?	*I guess you like alchohol, don't you?*

4 The double past

Korean has what is known as a double past construction, which is a past tense of a verb formed in the normal way, with an additional -었-(-ŏss-) added. Thus, 먹었었-(mŏgŏssŏss-) would be the double past base of 먹-(mŏk-).

The precise meaning of the form is a bit more difficult to define and is beyond the scope of this book. It emphasizes the remoteness of a past event and shows that an event occurred and *was completed* in the distant past. What you do need to know about it, however, concerns its use with the two verbs 가-(ka-) and 오-(o-), 'go' and 'come.' Compare the following two sentences:

어제 밤 여기 왔어요 (ŏje pam yŏgi wassŏyo)	*I came here yesterday*
어제 밤 여기 왔었어요 (ŏje pam yŏgi wassŏssŏyo)	*I came here yesterday*

The implication of the first of these might well be that you are still here, you came and you remain. However, the implication of the second is that the action is over, that is, that you came, and that you went again and that it all took place in the past. The same would be true of 갔어요(kassŏyo) and 갔었어요(kassŏssŏyo).

This rule is something of a simplification, but it will explain most of the occurrences of the double past that you are likely to need to know about for the time being. Take a close look at the example in the dialogue to see that emphasis: *we came to this restaurant last night* (and, by implication, we left again afterwards). The act of our coming (and going) all took place last night.

Insight
You'll recognize the double past by its two uses of a double 's' (e.g., 먹었었어요 [mŏgŏssŏssŏyo]). It tends to locate an action in the distant past, but while it's useful to be able to recognize it, you're probably unlikely to need to reproduce it yourself.

Practice

1 Put the following sentences into the past tense.

  a 학교에 가요.
  b 맥주 많이 마셔요.
  c 약속을 못 지켜요.
  d 친구를 만나요.
  e 영화를 보고 싶어요.
  f 도봉산에 갈까 해요.

2 Make the following into polite requests (asking someone to do something for your benefit).

  a 하세요.
  b *Please go shopping for me.*
  c 점심 사세요.
  d *Can you phone Mr Kim for me?*
  e *Please buy me some medicine.*
  f 시작하세요.

3 Complete the following by filling in the blanks.

오늘 ___ 친구를 만나 ___. ___ 바쁜 일이 ___ 못
만났어요. ___ 취소 ___ 전화 ___. 약속 못 ___.

했어요	그렇지만	하려고	아침에
지켰어요	기로 했어요	생겨서	그러니까

4 Write out the following sentences, and in each case add a second sentence along the lines suggested in the brackets to explain what has just been said in the first sentence. This is practice for the −거든요 pattern, and you might want to look

back at the lesson notes for that pattern before you do the
exercise.

a 오늘 학교에 못 가요   (*head aches*)
b 일요일날에 시내에 못 가요   (*another appointment*)
c 오늘밤 탁구 못 쳐요   (*arm* [팔(**p'al**)] *has begin to hurt*)

d 노래방에 가요? 나는 안 가요   (*don't like* **noraebangs**)
e 재민씨 못 가요? 그럼 잘   (*I can't go either*)
   됐네요

5 Read the following page from someone's diary and then answer
the questions.

6월 (June)		6월 (June)	
월 6	토니와 점심 약속	월 13	不
화 7		화 14	대구 출장
수 8	회의	수 15	↓
목 9	회의	목 16	
금 10	김 선생 생일 파티	금 17	휴가 시작
토 11	대학 동창회	토 18	집 청소
일 12	집사람하고 쇼핑	일 19	도봉산 등산

휴가	*holiday*
출장	*business trip*
동창회	*alumni meeting*

오늘은 6 월 7 일 화요일이에요.

a 이번 토요일에 무슨 약속이 있어요?
b 언제가 김선생의 생일이에요?

c 이번 일요일에 무엇을 하려고 해요?
d 다음 일요일에는 어디가려고 해요?
e 언제부터 휴가예요?
f 어제는 누구하고 점심을 먹었어요?

6 Translate the following (using verb compounds with 보- for the English to Korean examples).

a 탕 먹어보세요! (탕: *spicy soup*)
b *You should visit Pulguksa one time* (lit: *Please visit …!*)
c 바쁘지만 가보세요.
d 탁구를 못 쳐봤어요? 그럼 한번 해보세요.
e *Jaemin hasn't come yet? Please (try) waiting a little longer.*

7 Use the following pairs of information to make up Korean sentences, each with two clauses linked by -sŏ. The first three have the sense of 'because A, B', the last three are sequential, 'and then'.

a *busy matter has come up*	*can't go*
b *no food in house*	*go to restaurant*
c *business is not good*	*no money*
d *let's go outside*	*and wait*
e *go to Sangmin's*	*what shall we do?*
f *go to city*	*buy some fruit*

8 Translate the following into Korean.

a *I'm ringing to cancel my appointment. Something came up (you see).*
b *Sangmin has just gone out to play table tennis.*
c *At first I didn't particularly like kimch'i, but I got used to it.* (*get used to*: 익숙해지-[**iksuk haeji-**])
d *When did you graduate?*
e *We met by chance in a bar.*
f *That's strange! Chris has come back already.*
g *What did you do last night? Tell me the truth.*

9 Ask your friend if they have tried doing the following things. Make up appropriate answers.

TEN THINGS TO REMEMBER

1 How to say *Please wait a moment!*

2 The past tense

3 Asking someone if they know where someone has gone

4 Saying someone went out to do something (*she went out to watch a movie*)

5 How to ask someone if they want to leave a message for someone

6 Sentences describing continuous states

7 Asking someone how things have been going/whether anything interesting has happened

8 How to say you don't like someone

9 How to say you don't remember

10 The difference between **wassŏyo** and **wassŏssŏyo**, or between **kassŏyo** and **kassŏssŏyo**

9

···

We bought him that last year!/ I'm sorry, I really didn't know!

In this unit you will learn
- *how to disagree and to apologize*
- *about buying presents and traffic offences*
- *another way of saying that you can and can't do something*
- *more about honorifics*
- *modifier form of verbs*

We bought him that last year!

◀) **CD 1, TR 9**

A husband and wife are deciding what to buy Grandfather for his birthday. However, the task is not as easy as it sounds!

부인	내일이 할아버지 생신이에요.
남편	뭐? 벌써?
부인	그래요. 무엇을 사드릴까 결정해야겠어요.
남편	당신이 정할 수 없어요? 나는 바빠요.
부인	항상 내가 결정하잖아요. 이번에는 좀 도와주세요.
남편	좋아요. 잠바를 사드릴까요?

부인	잠바는 벌써 열 벌이나 갖고 계세요.
	잠바는 더 이상 필요 없어요.
남편	그러면 셔츠는 어떨까요?
부인	셔츠도 더 이상 필요 없어요.
남편	그럼, 책은요?
부인	할아버지는 독서를 싫어하시잖아요?
남편	할머니는 독서를 좋아하시니까 대신
	읽으시면 되잖아요.
부인	농담하지 마세요.
	좀 더 좋은 생각을 말해보세요.
남편	우산은 어떨까요?
부인	할아버지는 비 올 때 나가지
	않으시잖아요.
남편	그럼 양말은?
부인	작년에 사드렸잖아요.
남편	그럼 새 전기 면도기는 어떨까요?
부인	그건 재작년에 사 드렸잖아요.
	그리고 할아버지는 면도를 잘 안
	하세요.
남편	그것 보라구!
	당신은 내 의견을 좋아하지 않잖아요.
	내가 처음 말한대로 당신 혼자
	결정하면 되잖아요.

Puin	Naeir-i harabŏji saengshin-ieyo.
Namp'yŏn	Mwo? Pŏlssŏ?
Puin	Kŭraeyo. Muŏs-ŭl sa-dŭrilkka kyŏlchŏng hae-yagessŏyo.
Namp'yŏn	Tangshin-i chŏng ha-l su ŏpsŏyo? Na-nŭn pappayo.
Puin	Hangsang nae-ga kyŏlchŏng ha-janayo. I-bŏn-enŭn chom towa-juseyo.
Namp'yŏn	Choayo. Chamba-rŭl sa-dŭrilkkayo?

Puin	Chamba-nŭn pŏlssŏ yŏl pŏl-ina kat-ko kyeseyo.
	Chamba-nŭn tŏ isang p'iryo ŏpsŏyo.
Namp'yŏn	Kŭrŏmyŏn shyŏch'ŭ-nŭn ŏttŏlkkayo?
Puin	Shyŏch'ŭ-do tŏ isang p'iryo ŏpsŏyo.
Namp'yŏn	Kŭrŏm, ch'aeg-ŭn-yo?
Puin	Halabŏji-nŭn toksŏ-rŭl shirŏ hashi-janayo?
Namp'yŏn	Halmŏni-nŭn toksŏ-rŭl choa hashi-nikka
	taeshin ilgushi-myŏn toe-janayo.
Puin	Nongdam ha-ji maseyo.
	Chom tŏ cho-ŭn saenggag-ŭl mal hae-boseyo.
Namp'yŏn	Usan-ŭn ŏttŏlkkayo?
Puin	Harabŏji-nŭn pi o-l ttae naga-ji anŭshi-janayo.
Namp'yŏn	Kŭrŏm yangmal-ŭn?
Puin	Changnyŏn-e sa tŭryŏt-janayo.
Namp'yŏn	Kŭrŏm sae chŏnggi myŏndogi-nŭn ŏttŏlkkayo?
Puin	Kŭ-gŏn chaejangnyŏn-e sa tŭryŏt-janayo.
	Kŭrigo harabŏji-nŭn myŏndo-rŭl chal an haseyo.
Namp'yŏn	Kŭ-gŏt poragu!
	Tangshin-ŭn nae ŭygyŏn-ŭl choaha-ji anch'anayo.
	Nae-ga ch'ŏŭm-e mal han daero tangshin honja
	kyŏlchŏngha-myŏn toe-janayo!

Phrases and expressions

-nŭn ŏttŏlkkayo?	*how about …?, what do you think about …?*
kŭ-gŏt poragu!	*you see?!*
tangshin-ŭn nae ŭygyŏn-ŭl choaha-ji anch'anayo	*you don't like my suggestions, you see!*
mal han daero	*as (I) said, like (I) said*

namp'yŏn	남편	*husband*
harabŏji	할아버지	*grandfather*
saengshin	생신	*birthday (honorific form)*
saengil	생일	*birthday (normal form)*

muŏs	무엇	*what* (full form of **mwo**)
kyŏljŏng ha-	결정하–	*decide*
tangshin	당신	*you* (often used between husband and wife)
chŏng ha-	정하–	*decide*
towa-ju-	도와주–	*to help*
-(ŭ) su iss-/ŏps-	–(으)ㄹ 수 있/없–	(see note 4: *can/can't*)
pŏn	번	*time* (as in *first time, second time, many times*)
i-bŏn	이번	*this time*
chamba	잠바	*jacket (jumper)*
pŏl	벌	(counter for clothes)
katko kyeshi-	갖고 계시–	*have, possess* (for honorific person; polite style: **katko kyeseyo**)
kyeshi-	계시–	*exist* (honorific of **iss-** in its existential *there is/are* meaning)
issŭshi-	있으시–	*have* (honorific of **iss-** in its meaning of possession)
tŏ isang	더이상	*any more*
p'iryo ŏpsŏyo	필요 없어요	*is not needed*
p'iryo ha-	필요하–	*is needed* (**p'iryo iss-** also exists but is less common)
shyŏch'ŭ	셔츠	*shirt*
toksŏ	독서	*reading*
shirŏ ha-	싫어하–	*to dislike*
halmŏni	할머니	*grandma*
-(ŭ)nikka	–(으)니까	*because* (clause ending, added to verb stems)
taeshin	대신	*instead, on behalf of*
saenggak	생각	*idea*

QUICK VOCAB (cont.)

usan	우산	umbrella
-(ŭ)l ttae	-(으)ㄹ 때	when
yangmal	양말	socks
chŏnggi myŏndogi	전기 면도기	electric shaver
kŭ-gŏn	그건	that thing (topic)
chaejangnyŏn	재작년	the year before last year
myŏndo(-rŭl) ha-	면도(를) 하-	shave
ŭygyŏn	의견	suggestion, opinion
honja	혼자	alone, on one's own

Grammar 15

NB The verb endings to some of the sentences in this unit (the ones with **-sh-** and **-s-** in them) are new, but we won't explain them until after the second dialogue.

> ### Insight
> Adding to what you've said. Remember the –거든요 (**-kŏdŭnyo**) ending from Unit 8? This is a really useful way of adding an extra bit of information, extending or explaining what you've just said. And it makes you sound like a native! If you've forgotten, check it out again back in Unit 8.

1 *Doing something for someone else*

We learned in the last unit how to ask someone to do something for your benefit by combining verbs with the verb 주-(**chu-**) (*give*), as in 사 주세요(**sa-juseyo**) (*please buy it for me*). Now we are going to expand on this to look at how to talk about doing things for other people's benefit, for the benefit of someone else. The dialogue you have just looked at is all about buying presents for

Grandad, and there is an implied for 'Grandad's benefit' in many of the sentences. Once more you can make a compound verb which means literally 'buy and give', but which in practice means 'buy for him', 'buy for his benefit'.

There are two ways of doing this, and it depends on whether the person for whose benefit you are doing something is esteemed (honorific) or not. Grandad is definitely honorific and this means that instead of making the compound with the verb 주-(chu-) as you would expect, Korean uses a special verb 드리-(tǔri-) which means *give (to someone honorific)*. Compare the following two sentences: the first one means that you will have to decide what to buy for someone honorific, the second means you will have to decide what to buy for someone of your own or lower status (for example, your child):

무엇을 사드릴까 결정해야겠어요(muǒs-ǔl sa-dǔri-lkka kyǒljǒng hae-yagessǒyo)
무엇을 사줄까 결정해야겠어요(muǒs-ǔl sa-ju-lkka kyǒljǒng hae-yagessǒyo)

As you can see, Korean has two different verbs for *give*, depending on who you are giving to.

Here are some more examples using the two verbs for *give*:
할아버지에게 책을 읽어 드렸어요(harabǒji-ege ch'aeg-ǔl ilgǒ-dǔryǒssǒyo)
(I) read a book for my grandfather

친구에게 책을 읽어 주었어요(ch'ingu-ege ch'aeg-ǔl ilgǒ-juǒssǒyo)
(I) read a book for my friend

김 선생님을 기다려 드렸어요(kim sǒnsaengnim-ǔl kidaryǒ-dǔryǒssǒyo)
I waited for Mr Kim

친구를 기다려주었어요(ch'ingu-rŭl kidaryŏ-juŏssŏyo)
I waited for my friend

Insight

Who are you talking to? There are a number of occasions where Korean has two different verbs for the same concept, one which is used to talk to or about people of equal or lesser status and the other to talk to people who are esteemed or of higher status. This unit introduces you to two verbs for *give* based on just that distinction.

2 Wondering, worrying and deciding

In English we make quite a few constructions with the word 'whether', e.g. *I'm wondering whether, I'm worrying whether (or, that), I'm trying to decide whether …* Korean makes these kind of sentences by adding −ㄹ까(-lkka) or −을까(-ŭlkka) to the base of the verb (this is the same ending as −(으)ㄹ까요(-[ŭ]lkkayo)? (*shall we?*) without the −요(-yo); you met it also in −(으)ㄹ까 해요(-[ŭ] lkka haeyo) (*I'm thinking of*). The −을까 pattern is used in the following construction: 김 선생님 갈까(Kim sŏnsaengnim ka-lkka). This would form part of a sentence and it means *whether Mr Kim will go*. It could be used with any of the following verbs: 걱정하−(kŏkjŏng ha-) (*worry*), 궁금하−(kunggum ha-) (*wonder*), 결정하−(kyŏljŏng ha-) (*decide*). Here are a couple of example sentences:

여자 친구가 약속을 지킬까 궁금해요(yŏja ch'ingu-ga yaksog-ŭl chik'i-lkka kunggŭmhaeyo)
I wonder whether my girlfriend will keep the appointment

운전수가 술을 많이 마실까 걱정했어요(unjŏnsu-ga sur-ŭl mani mashi-lkka kŏkjŏnghaessŏyo)
I was worried that the driver would drink a lot

This basic −을까 pattern is also found in a few common variations.

Sometimes –을까 is followed in colloquial speech by another word, 말까(**malkka**), to mean *whether* or *not*, as in the following example:

갈까 말까 걱정해요(**kalkka malkka kŏkchŏng haeyo**)
I'm worrying whether to go or not

This form with 말까(**malkka**) can only be used with verbs in which a person is wondering whether or not they themselves will do something. You could not use 말까 in a sentence to mean *I'm wondering whether it will rain or not*, since there is no decision to be taken about whether or not to actually do something.

Insight

Adding –ㄹ– (**-l-**) to verbs. You've already met a number of patterns that add – (으)ㄹ (**-[ŭ]l**) to a verb stem, and this unit introduces you to several more. The particle expresses the idea of possibility or uncertainty, of something that *may* be, but is not yet the case. Think of its use in the ending – (으) ㄹ까해요 (**-[ŭ]lkka haeyo**), for instance, where the meaning is *I'm thinking of…*. You haven't actually done it yet, but you might.

Often when Koreans are saying that they are worried that something might happen, they use a slightly longer form of the pattern: –을까봐(**-ŭlkka bwa**):

비가 올까봐 걱정해요(**pi-ga o-lkka-bwa kŏkchŏng haeyo**)
I'm worried that it might rain

여자 친구가 나를 버릴까봐 걱정해요(**Yŏja ch'ingu-ga na- rŭl pŏri- lkka-bwa kŏkchŏng haeyo**)
I am worried that my girlfriend might dump me

| pŏri- | 버리– | throw away |

QV

The other form is simply a contraction of this longer version.

Insight

The verb ending – (으)ㄹ까 (-[ǔ]lkka) is used to express
questioning or wondering, and has the basic meaning
whether. The unit notes introduce you to several different
expressions and contexts in which the form may
be used.

3 *Things you'll have to do*

This unit should remind you of the way to say that you are going
to have to do something (often the context concerns something
that you'd really rather not have to do). The pattern is –야겠어요
(-yagessǒyo), and it is added onto any processive verb base. The
form literally means something like 'only if I do such and such will
it do'; –야(-ya) is a particle which means 'only if'.

내일까지 이 일을 끝내야겠어요(naeil-kkaji i-ir-ǔl kkǔnnae-
  yagessǒyo)
I'll have to finish the work by tomorrow

내년에는 꼭 결혼해야겠어요(naenyǒn-enǔn kkok
  kyǒlhonhae-yagessǒyo)
I'll have to marry next year

kkǔnnae-	끝내–	finish (verb stem, *to finish something*)
kkok	꼭	*without fail, definitely*

4 *You can and you can't*

Korean has a very common way of saying that you can or can't
do something (in the sense of being able to carry it out, rather

than knowing how to). Take a processive verb stem (a verb of doing), add the ending -ㄹ 수 (-l su) if the stem ends in a vowel and -을 수(-ŭl su) if it ends in a consonant, and then add either 있어요(issŏyo), to say you can do the verb, or 없어요(ŏpsŏyo), to say that you can't. For example:

먹을 수 있어요 (mŏg-ŭl su issŏyo)	*I can eat it*
먹을 수 없어요 (mŏg-ŭl su ŏpsŏyo)	*I can't eat it*
갈 수 있어요 (ka-l su issŏyo)	*I can go*
갈 수 없어요 (ka-l su ŏpsŏyo)	*I can't go*

It's as simple as that! But you must practise it until you can do it fast. The exercises should give you plenty of practice. Here are two examples:

일찍 돌아올 수 없어요(ilcchik torao-l su ŏpsŏyo)
I won't be able to get home early

저 한자를 읽을 수 있어요(chŏ hanja-rŭl ilg-ŭl su issŏyo)?
Can you read those Chinese characters over there?

ilcchik	일찍	*early*

5 *Retorting*

Sometimes people say things which are really stupid and Korean provides a nice (and not too rude) way of pointing that out and implying (just gently) that the person should have known better. This dialogue has lots of examples. The man keeps suggesting what to buy for Grandad for his birthday and the wife thinks his suggestions are a bit silly. For example, he suggests buying something they bought last year. The implication is that the man should know what they bought for Grandad last year, so he shouldn't have been so stupid as to suggest buying it again. Therefore the wife says:

작년에 샀잖아요(changnyŏn-e sat-janayo) (from 샀-[sa-ss-],
 past base of 사-)
We bought that last year!

Note the implication: you should know we bought him that last
year, stupid! What did you go and suggest it again for?

One of the very common uses of the pattern is to give an answer
when someone asks you something obvious, to which they should
really know the answer. Suppose someone met you and you
were dressed all in black and they asked you why. You could
say 'because I'm going to a funeral!' and you would put -잖아요
(-janayo) onto the stem of the main verb of the sentence. Suppose
you are going to get married and someone asked you why. You
might respond:

사랑하잖아요(sarang ha-janayo)!
It's because I love them, stupid!

| sarang ha- | 사랑하- | *love* |

It's a very useful pattern, and one that makes your Korean sound
natural and colourful.

The ending -잖아요(-janayo) (spelt **-janhayo**) attaches to a present
or a past base, and to honorific bases (note the sound change **ss** to **t**
when **-janayo** is added to past bases).

6 Having one right there

You know how to say that someone has something by using the
verb 있어요(issŏyo). Korean has another verb form, which stresses
a bit more the act of possessing: 갖고 있-(katko iss-) and 갖고
계시-(katko kyeshi-) (the second one is the honorific form and

is usually found in the polite honorific form 갖고 계세요[katko kyeseyo]).

Often it has the force 'I have one right here', 'I have one with me now'. Imagine a situation in which someone wants a lighter. Someone else in the room has one and as he fumbles in his pockets, he might well say, 나는 갖고 있어요(na-nŭn katko issŏyo). This stresses that he has one with him right there.

This is a form you need to be able to recognize rather than to actually use frequently yourself.

I'm sorry, I really didn't know!

◄) **CD 1, TR 9, 02:06**

A policeman catches a driver going the wrong way up a one-way street.

경찰	실례합니다.
	면허증 좀 보여주세요.
운전수	왜요? 무슨 문제가 있나요?
경찰	정말 몰라서 그러세요?
운전수	뭘 말이에요?
경찰	여기 주차한 차들을 한 번 보세요.
	차를 다 똑같은 방향으로
	주차했잖아요.
운전수	그래서요?
경찰	그러면 저 빨간 색 일방 통행 표지를
	못 봤어요?
운전수	아! 일방통행로군요.
	미안합니다. 정말로 몰랐어요.

경찰	큰 실수를 하셨어요.
	일방통행로에 잘못 들어오면 아주
	위험하고 벌금도 많아요.
운전수	정말 표지판을 못 봤어요.
	한 번만 봐주세요.
경찰	다음부터 조심하세요.
	벌금은 오만원입니다.
운전수	고맙습니다. 수고하세요.

Kyŏngch'al	Shillye hamnida.
	Myŏnhŏcchŭng chom poyŏ-juseyo.
Wunjŏnsu	Waeyo? Musŭn munje-ga innayo?
Kyŏngch'al	Chŏngmal mollasŏ kŭrŏseyo?
Wunjŏnsu	Mwol mar-ieyo?
Kyŏngch'al	Yŏgi chuch'ahan ch'a-dŭr-ŭl han pŏn poseyo.
	Ch'a-rŭl ta ttok kat'ŭn panghyang-uro
	chuch'a haet-janayo.
Wunjŏnsu	Kŭraesŏyo?
Kyŏngch'al	Kŭrŏmyŏn chŏppalgan saek ilbang
	t'onghaeng p'yoji-rŭl mot pwassŏyo?
Wunjŏnsu	A! Ilbang t'onghaengno-gunyo.
	Mian hamnida. Chŏngmallo mollassŏyo.
Kyŏngch'al	K'ŭn shilsu-rŭl hashyŏssŏyo.
	Ilbang t'onghaengno-e chalmot turŏ o-myŏn
	aju wihŏm ha-go pŏlgŭm-do manayo.
Wunjŏnsu	Chŏngmal p'yojip'an-ŭl mot pwassŏyo.
	Hanbŏn-man pwa-juseyo.
Kyŏngch'al	Taŭm-put'ŏ choshim haseyo.
	Pŏlgŭm-ŭn oman won-imnida.
Wunjŏnsu	Komapsŭmnida. Sugo haseyo.

Phrases and expressions

mwol mar-ieyo?	*what are you talking about?*
chŏngmal molla-sŏ kŭrŏseyo?	*do you really not know (what you're doing)?*

kŭraesŏyo?	so what?
chŏngmal mollassŏyo	I really didn't know/realize
hanbŏn-man pwa-chuseyo	please let me off just this once!
sugo haseyo!	work hard! (said to someone doing their job)

아주 위험하고
벌금도 많아요!

ONE
WAY

kyŏngch'al	경찰	policeman
unjŏnsu	운전수	driver
myŏnhŏcchŭng	면허증	(driving) licence
poyŏ-ju-	보여주-	to show
waeyo	왜요?	why?
musŭn	무슨	what (kind of)
munje	문제	problem
chuch'a han	주차한	parked
chuch'a ha-	주차하-	to park
ttok	똑	exactly, precisely (often used with **kat'-**)
kat'ŭn	같은	same
kat'-	같-	be the same, be similar
panghyang	방향	direction

ppalgan	빨간	red
saek	색	colour
ilbang t'onghaeng	일방통행	one way
ilbang t'onghaengno	일방통행로	one-way street
p'yoji	표지	sign, signpost
k'ŭn	큰	big
shilsu	실수	mistake
shilsu ha-	실수하–	make a mistake
tŭrŏ o-	들어오–	to enter
wihŏm ha-	위험하–	be dangerous
pŏlgŭm	벌금	fine, penalty
p'yojip'an	표지판	signpost
choshim ha-	조심하–	be careful, be cautious

Grammar 16

1 *Questions with* -nayo

The particle –나(-**na**) is often used as a way of asking questions and when you use it in the polite style, you should also add the polite particle –요(-**yo**) to give –나요(-**nayo**). (Without the –요 it is an informal question which you could only use between friends or to ask a question of someone younger or of lower status than you.)

It is added onto the stem of any verb (either the present stem or the past stem). Here are a couple of examples:

주문했나요(**Chumun haen-nayo**)?   *Have you ordered?* (했– past base of 하–)

신문 거기 있나요(**Shinmun kŏgi innayo**)?   *Is the newspaper over there?* (from 있–)

어디 가나(Ŏdi ka-na)?　　　　　　*Where are you going?*
점심 먹었나(Chŏmshim mŏgŏn-na)?　*Did you have lunch?*
　　　　　　　　　　　　　　(먹었 – past base of 먹–)

2 Honorific forms

It's now time that we talked a bit more systematically about
honorific verbs. You have already learned that honorifics are used
in Korean to show respect to the person you are talking about
and in the present tense this is often done by using the form
which you have learned as the 'polite request form' –(으)세요(-[ŭ]
seyo). In actual fact this form is not only used to make requests, it
is also used to make statements or to ask questions about anyone
to whom you wish to show respect. It is very common in Korean,
and you will use it whenever you meet and talk to new people of
equivalent or senior status (to ask them questions, for example).

Actually, the form –(으)세요 is an abbreviation of the honorific
particle (으)시([ŭ]shi), plus the vowel –어(-ŏ), plus the polite
particle –요. This contracts to give the form you know –(으)세요.

Just as there are present and past stems, so also there are honorific
stems. The honorific present stem is the usual stem plus the
honorific particle –(으)시. The honorific past stem is the usual stem
plus –(으)셨–(-[ŭ]shyŏss-):

stem	hon stem	hon past stem
앉–	앉으시–	앉으셨–
읽–	읽으시–	읽으셨–
가–	가시–	가셨–
오–	오시–	오셨–

You can add verb endings to the present honorific stem, as you
would a normal verb with a stem ending in –이–(-i-). Everything
about the honorific stems is regular apart from the present polite
style which contracts to –(으)세요, as you have already learned:

할아버지는 은행에 가시고 할머니는 우체국에 가세요
(**harabŏji-nŭn unhaeng-e kashi-go halmŏni-nŭn uch'egug-e kaseyo**)
Grandad is going to the bank and Grandma is going to the post office

김 선생님 운전하실 수 있어요(**Kim sŏnsaengnim unjŏn hashi-l su issŏyo**)?
Can Mr Kim drive?

김 선생님 운전할 수 있으세요(**Kim sŏnsaengnim unjŏn ha-l su issŭseyo**)?
Can Mr Kim drive? (identical)

벌써 가셨구나(**Pŏlssŏ kashyŏt-kuna**)! (from 가셨-, past honorific base of 가-)	He's already gone (surprise, surprise!)
탁구를 치셨어요(**T'akku-rŭl ch'ishyŏss-ŏyo**)	He played table tennis

3 Introducing modifiers: making verbs into nouns

You now need to learn about something called modifiers, which are a kind of verb. First, we will show you how to make them, and then we will worry about what they mean. In this unit we shall just look at one of their uses and then in Unit 11 we shall look at the other uses.

How you make the modifier form of a verb depends on whether it is a processive or a descriptive verb.

Processive verbs
For processive verbs, add ―는(-**nŭn-**) to the verb stem. Thus the modifier form of 가-(**ka-**) is 가는(**kanŭn**), the modifier form of 먹-(**mŏk-**) is 먹는(**mŏngnŭn**) (written **mŏknŭn**), and so on.

You will find that when you add –는 to verb stems that end in consonants, sound changes will take place. For 먹–, therefore, the *hangul* letters will literally read 먹는(**mŏk-nŭn**), but the pronunciation (according to the rules of sound change you learned at the beginning of the book) will be [멍는](**mŏngnŭn**).

To make a past tense modifier form for processive verbs you add –(으)ㄴ(-[**ŭ**]**n**) to the stem, so that the past tense modifier forms of 먹– and 가– are 먹은(**mŏgŭn**) and 간(**kan**). You cannot do this with the verbs 있–(**iss-**) and 없–(**ŏps-**). These verbs behave like processive verbs, so that the modifier forms are 있는(**innŭn**) and 없는(**ŏmnnŭn**) in the present tense – they do not have past tense modifier forms.

Descriptive verbs

For descriptive verbs, simply add –ㄴ(**-n**) if the stem ends in a vowel, and –은(**-ŭn**) if it ends in a consonant. As you can see, this is identical to the past tense modifier form for processive verbs. There is no past tense modifier form for the descriptive verbs.

Try to memorize these rules.

We will now look at just one meaning of the modifier form of verbs. Sometimes you want to talk about the act of doing things (doing verbs), as though they were nouns. In English, for example, we say things like *I like swimming* which means *I like the act of swimming*, and of course 'swimming' comes originally from the verb 'swim'.

Korean is able to express *the act of* (verb)*ing* by using a modifier form, plus the noun 것(**kŏt**), often abbreviated to 거(**kŏ**). Here are examples:

가는 것(**kanŭn kŏt**)   *the act of going*
영화 보는 거(**yŏnghwa ponŭn kŏ**)   *the act of seeing a film*
여기 앉는 거(**yŏgi annŭn kŏ**)   *the act of sitting here*
                                      (from 앉–)

You can then simply add verbs like 좋아요(**choayo**)/좋아해요 (**choa haeyo**)/싫어해요(**shirŏ haeyo**)/안 좋아해요(**an choa**

haeyo) afterwards to say what you think about those particular activities, e.g.:

영화 보는 거 좋아해요(yŏnghwa ponŭn kŏ choa haeyo)?
Do you like seeing films?

여기 있는 거 좀 보세요(yŏgi innŭn kŏ chom poseyo)
Please look at what is here (literally, the thing that is/exists here)

편지 쓰는 거 싫어해요(p'yŏnji ssŭnŭn kŏ shirŏ haeyo)
I hate writing letters

술 마시고 운전하는 거 위험해요(sul mashi-go unjŏn hanŭn kŏ wihom haeyo)
It's dangerous to drink and drive

| p'yŏnji | 편지 | *letter* |
| ssŭ- | 쓰– | *write* |

Practice

1 Say that you are worried about the following things.

   a *That teacher will come (to a party).*
   b *That there won't be enough food.*
   c *That Mr Kim might not come.*
   d *That your girlfriend might not like you any more.*
   e *That it might rain.*

2 Make the following passage honorific where appropriate. We have told you that normally you only need one honorific verb in a sentence, but for the purposes of this exercise use as many honorifics as you can. Look out for sentences that should not have them, however!

김 선생님은 대학교 선생님이에요. 런던 대학교에서
한국말을 가르치고 일본말도 가르쳐요. 매일 아침
공원에 가서 산책해요. 개하고 같이 가요. 공원은
아주 좋아요. 김 선생님의 개는 고기를 잘 먹어요.
작년부터 부인도 가끔 산책하기 시작했어요. 부인도
가면 둘이 식당에 가서 커피 한잔 마셔요.

3 Here are some situations. Make up Korean sentences to say
what you will have to do because of them, using −야겠어요
(-yagessŏyo).

a *Your head hurts.*
b *You can't meet your boyfriend tonight.*
c *You need to use a dictionary, but you don't have one.*
d *You go out and realize you've forgotten something.*
  (You'll have to go back.)
e *You want to know what's going on at the theatre.*
  (You'll have to look at the newspaper.)

4 You're trying to decide about the following things. Say so in
Korean, using a similar pattern to the one you were using in
question 1.

a *What to buy.*
b *What to wear.* (*wear:* 입−[ip-])
c *Where to sit.*
d *What to order.*
e *Where to go at the weekend.*

5 Translate the following sentences into Korean, using the pattern
−(으)ㄹ 수 있어요/없어요(-[u]l su issŏyo/ŏpsŏyo) that you have
learned in this lesson.

a *Can I come too?*
b *Is this edible?*
c *Can you meet me tomorrow?*
d *I can't speak Japanese.*

e *I don't have any money, so I can't buy it.*
f *I can't park here.*

6 Make up retorts to the following Korean statements using the
   −잖아요(-**janayo**) pattern.

   a 왜 안 샀어요?   (*I bought it yesterday, didn't I!*)
   b 이 사람이 남자   (*No, I'm already
      친구에요?   married, stupid!*)
   c 면도 안 하세요?   (*I already did it!*)
   d 이 책을 읽어보세요.   (*I hate reading, stupid!*)
   e 이 사람이 누구세요?   (*It's my wife! You only
                            met her yesterday!*)

7 Imagine you are talking to your sister and discussing with her
   what to buy your brother for a birthday present. You make the
   following suggestions of what to buy, but she manages to find
   a reason against it until the very last suggestion. Write out your
   suggestions and the answers she makes, trying to make
   the dialogue as interesting as you can. (**NB** *jeans*, 청바지;
   CD, 씨디)

TEN THINGS TO REMEMBER

1 Saying you're busy

2 How to ask for some help

3 Saying someone dislikes something (with the verb **silh-**)

4 Suggesting ideas for gifts (*how would such-and-such be?*)

5 Telling someone not to make jokes/that it's no laughing matter

6 How to say *You don't like my suggestions!*

7 Vocabulary for items of clothing

8 The basics of honorific verb forms

9 How to say *Please let me off (just this once ...)!*

10 The concept of 'modifiers' (used to make verbs into nouns) – how to recognize them, and how they are used

10

What did you do with it?/Nasty headaches

In this unit you will learn
- *how to describe things that you have lost and say when and where you lost them*
- *how to buy medicine from a Korean yakkuk or chemist*
- *'when' clauses*
- *how to say it seems as though something or other will happen*

What did you do with it?

◀》 **CD 1, TR 10**

손님	저 실례합니다.
	저는 어제 친구들이랑 여기 왔었는데요,
	가방을 놓고 갔어요.
종업원	제가 가서 한번 찾아보지요.
	가방이 어떻게 생겼어요?
손님	네, 아주 크고, 검정색이고, 가죽으로
	만들었어요.
종업원	저기 서류 가방이 있는데, 저거에요?
손님	아니요, 서류 가방이 아니에요.

A little while later.

종업원	없는 것 같은데요.
	뭐 중요한 게 들어 있나요?
손님	예, 사실 아주 중요한 서류하고 책하고
	은행카드가 들어 있어요.
종업원	저런! 잠깐 기다려보세요.
	사장님한테 한번 물어볼께요.

The manager comes.

사장	안녕하세요? 무슨 일입니까?
손님	제 가방을 잃어버렸어요.
	어제 여기서 식사하고 놓고
	나왔어요.
사장	몇 시에 저희 식당에서 나가셨나요?
손님	한 열한 시 쯤이에요.
사장	영업 끝날 때쯤 . . .
	아, 예, 생각나요. 오늘 아침 청소할 때
	가방이 하나 있었어요.
손님	그걸 어떻게 하셨어요?
사장	경찰서에 보냈어요.
	그 사람들이 보관하고 있을 거에요.
손님	경찰서가 어디인지 좀 가르쳐주시
	겠어요?
사장	식당에서 나가서 좌회전한 다음에
	오른쪽으로 세 번째 골목에 있어요.
손님	정말 감사합니다.
	안녕히 계세요.

Sonnim	Chŏ, shillye hamnida.
	Chŏ-nŭn ŏje ch'ingu-dŭl-irang yŏgi
	wassŏnnŭndeyo, kabang-ŭl nok'o kassŏyo.
Chongŏbwon	Che-ga ka-sŏ han-pŏn ch'aja pojiyo.
	Kabang-i ŏttŏk'e saenggyŏssŏyo?
Sonnim	Ne, aju k'ŭgo, kŏmchŏng saeg-igo, kajug-ŭro
	mandŭrŏssŏyo.
Chongŏbwon	Chŏgi sŏryu kabang-i innŭnde, chŏ-gŏ-eyo?
Sonnim	Aniyo, sŏryu kabang-i anieyo.

A little while later.

Chongŏbwon	Ŏmnŭn kŏt kat'ŭndeyo.
	Mwo chungyo han ke turŏ innayo?
Sonnim	Ye, sashil aju chungyohan sŏryu-hago ch'aek-
	hago ŭnhaeng k'adŭ-ga tŭrŏ issŏyo.
Chongŏbwon	Chŏrŏn! Chamkkan kidaryŏ-boseyo.
	Sajangnim-hant'e hanbŏn murŏ-bo-lkkeyo.

The manager comes.

Sajang	Annyŏng haseyo? Musŭn ir-imnikka?
Sonnim	Che kabang-ŭl irŏbŏryŏssŏyo.
	Ŏje yŏgi-sŏ shiksa ha-go no-k'o nawassŏyo.
Sajang	Myŏt shi-e chŏhŭy shiktang-esŏ
	nagashyŏnnayo?
Sonnim	Han yŏlhan-shi cchŭm-ieyo.
Sajang	Yŏngŏp kkŭnna-l ttae cchŭm . . .
	A, ye, saenggang nayo. Onŭl ach'im ch'ŏngso
	ha-l ttae kabang-i hana issŏssŏyo.
Sonnim	Kŭ-gŏ-l ŏttŏk'e hashyŏssŏyo?
Sajang	Kyŏngch'alsŏ-e ponaessŏyo.
	Kŭ-saram-dŭr-i pogwan ha-go iss-ŭl kŏeyo.
Sonnim	Kyŏngch'alsŏ-ga ŏdi-inji chom karŭch'yŏ-
	jushigessŏyo?
Sajang	Shiktang-esŏ naga-sŏ chwahoejŏn han taŭme
	orŭn cchog-ŭro se-bŏn-cchae kolmog-e issŏyo.
Sonnim	Chŏngmal kamsahamnida. Annyŏnghi kyeseyo.

Phrases and expressions

ŏmnŭn kŏt kat'ŭndeyo	*it doesn't look as though there is anything/are any*
musŭn ir-imnikka?	*how can I help you?, what's the problem?*
ŏttŏk'e saenggyŏssŏyo?	*what does it look like?*
(... -hant'e) han-bŏn murŏ-bo-lkkeyo	*I'll just ask (such and such a person)*
kŭ-gŏ-l ŏttŏk'e hashyŏssŏyo	*what did you do with it?*
... -i/ga ŏdi-inji chom karŭch'yŏ-juseyo	*please tell me where (such and such) is*
chwahoejŏn han taŭm-e	*after doing a left turn*
uhoejŏn han taŭm-e	*after doing a right turn*

sonnim	손님	*customer*
chŏ ...	저 ...	*er ..., hmm ...*
kabang	가방	*a briefcase, a bag*
no(h)-	놓–	*put down, leave*
ch'aja po-	찾아보–	*have a look, look for*
ch'aj-	찾–	*search*
ŏttŏk'e	어떻게	*how?*
irŏk'e	이렇게	*like this*
kŭrŏk'e	그렇게	*like that*
saenggi-	생기–	*look (like)*
kŏmjŏng	검정	*black*
kajuk	가죽	*leather*
mandŭrŏssŏyo	만들었어요	*be made of (past tense of **mandul-, I** irregular verb)*
mandŭl-	만들–	*make (**I**-irregular verb like **p'al-, nol-** etc.)*
sŏryu	서류	*document*

chungyo han	중요한	*important* (modifier form, like an adjective)
chungyo ha-	중요하-	*be important*
turŏ iss-	들어 있-	*be contained, be included*
ye	예	*yes* (politer form of **ne**)
sashil	사실	*in fact*
k'adŭ	카드	*a card* (e.g. credit card)
sajang(nim)	사장(님)	*manager* (honorific form)
murŏ-bo-	물어보-	*ask*
irŏbŏri-	잃어버리-	*lose*
shiksa ha-	식사하-	*have meal*
nao-	나오-	*come out*
chŏhŭy	저희	(humble form of **wuri**, *our, my*)
han (*number/ time*) **cchŭm**	한 … 쯤	*about, around, approximately*
yŏngŏp	영업	*business*
kkŭnna-	끝나-	*finish* (as in *it finishes*)
-(u)l ttae	-(으) ㄹ 때	*when* (see note 4)
ttae	때	*time* (*when*)
saenggang na-	생각나-	*remember, it comes to mind*
ch'ŏngso ha-	청소하-	*clean up*
kyŏngch'alsŏ	경찰서	*police station*
bonae-	보내-	*send*
bogwan ha-	보관하-	*keep*
chwahoejŏn	좌회전	*left turn*
uhoejŏn	우회전	*right turn*
cchae	째	*number* (time)
kolmok	골목	*alley, small road*

Grammar 17

1 *Making plurals*

You will have noticed that a Korean noun can be either singular or plural, depending on the context. In other words, Korean does not have one word for *dog* and another word for *dogs*; it has just one word 개(**kae**) which can mean either. It is very rare that there is any ambiguity or confusion because of this, however.

There is a plural particle which can be used to show explicitly that a word is plural – it is –들(**-tŭl**). You can then add subject, object, topic (-이[**-i**], -을[**-ŭl**], -은[**-ŭn**]) or other particles, such as –도(**-do**) or –하고(**-hago**), onto the plural form. Thus you could have any of the following forms: –들도(**-dŭl-do**), –들은(**-dŭr-ŭn**), –들이(**-dŭr-i**), –들을(**-dŭr-ŭl**), –들하고(**-dŭl-hago**), –들한테 (**-dŭl-hant'e**), and so on.

2 *Ending sentences with* –는데요(**-nŭndeyo**)

We have already studied the clause ending –는데(**-nŭnde**), to indicate that you have something more to say, that you are going to elaborate on what you have just said. You can also end a sentence with –는데 by adding the polite particle –요 after it. The use is very like that for –는데, except that saying –는데요

allows you to make more of a pause than using –는데. Often –는데요 is used to explain who you are, where you have come from, or what you want to do. The following sentence would go on to give more specific information, either about what the person you are speaking to should do about it or what you would like to happen (on the basis of having explained who you are, for example!). This all sounds a bit confusing in writing, and it is perhaps best to explain by example. In the following sentences, the first could be ended in Korean with –는데요. Notice how the second sentence often makes an explicit request, or homes in to ask something:

I'm from the BBC (**nŭndeyo**)	*I'd like to do an interview*
I'd like to buy a bicycle (**nŭndeyo**)	*Can you show me your range?*
I'm the brother of your friend (**nŭndeyo**)	*Pleased to meet you! May I have a seat?*

Since –는데요 is a colloquial expression, you will sometimes find it used in other ways which do not seem to fit exactly into the system we have described here. However, for using the form yourself, if you remember the rules we have given you, you won't go wrong.

Note also that –는데요 and the related –는데 are added to the present stem of processive verbs, and on to the past stem of both processive and descriptive verbs. The form (으)ㄴ데요 and the related (으)ㄴ데 are only used for the present tense of descriptive verbs. Taking a processive verb and a descriptive verb in both past and present tenses, then, we would get the following forms:

	하- *(processive)*	좋- *(descriptive)*
present	하는데요 (**ha-nŭndeyo**)	좋은데요 (**cho-ŭndeyo**)
past	했는데요 (**haen-nŭndeyo**)	좋았는데요 (**choan-nŭndeyo**)

Remember that in the past examples the first of the two **ns** (before the hyphen) represents the double **s** of the past base which has become pronounced as an **n** through the pronunciation rules we described at the beginning of the course.

Insight

Elaborating. Both –는데 (**-nŭnde**) and –는데요 (**-nŭndeyo**) are used at the end of a clause or sentence to indicate that you have more to say which will explain or elaborate upon what you have just said. Both forms make you sound very colloquial.

3 It seems like

You can say that 'it seems like something is happening' in Korean by using modifier forms of verbs plus 것 같아요(**kŏt kat'ayo**). 같-(**kat'-**) is a verb which means *is like*, so 비가 오는 것 같아요 (**pi-ga o-nŭn kŏt kat'ayo**) means literally 'the act of raining it is like', or, in effect, *it seems like it's raining*. Remember that the modifier forms are different depending on whether the main verb is processive or descriptive.

Here are some examples:

선생님이 티비를 보시는 것 같아요	(sŏnsaengnim-i TV-rŭl poshi-nŭn kŏt kat'ayo)	*It seems like the teacher is watching TV*
민호가 빵을 먹는 것 같아요	(minho-ga ppang-ŭl mŏng-nŭn kŏt kat'ayo)	*It seems like Minho is eating bread*
영국은 날씨가 나쁜 것 같아요	(yŏnggug-ŭn nalssi-ga nappŭ-n kŏt kat'ayo)	*It seems like the weather is bad in England*
이 집이 좋은 것 같아요	(i chib-i choŭn kŏt kat'ayo)	*This house seems to be nice*

4 When something happens

You have met many times the form (으)ㄹ([ŭ]l) added to the stem
of verbs, for example in the endings: (으)ㄹ까(요)([ŭ]lkka[yo]),
(으)ㄹ까 해요([ŭ]lkka haeyo), (으)ㄹ거에요([ŭ]l kŏeyo). In actual
fact this (으)ㄹ is the future modifier. It is a modifier just like –는
and -(으)ㄴ, but it has a future meaning. This means that you can
use the pattern you have just learned (modifer + 것 같아요[kŏt
kat'ayo]) to say *it seems like something will happen*:

비가 올 것 같아요	(pi-ga o-l kŏt kat'ayo)	*It seems like it will rain*
갈 것 같아요	(ka-l kŏt kat'ayo)	*It seems as though s/he will go*

Insight

To make a *when* clause, use the future modifier – (으)ㄹ
(- [ŭ]l) followed by the noun 때 (ttae), *time*. 시간이 있을 때
(shigan-i iss-ŭl ttae) means *when I have time*.

Insight

You can use present or future modifiers with 것 (kŏt), *thing* to
make sentences which mean *it seems like*. 비가 올 것 같아요
(piga o-l kŏt gat'ayo) means *it seems like it will rain*, while 비가
오는 것 같아요 (piga o-nŭn kŏt gat'ayo) means *it seems like it's
raining*.

An even more important use of -(으)ㄹ is when it is followed by
the noun 때(ttae) which means *time*. The whole construction (verb
stem)-(으)ㄹ 때(-[ŭ]l ttae) means *when (verb) happens*. Have a
look at the examples:

학교에 갈 때	(hakkyo-e ka-l ttae)	*when I go to school*
비가 올 때	(pi-ga o-l ttae)	*when it rains*
어머니 돌아올 때	(ŏmŏni torao-l ttae)	*when Mum gets back*

Here are some examples in sentences:

방에서 나올 때 방을 청소하세요	(pang-esŏ nao-l ttae pang-ŭl ch'ŏngsoha-seyo)	*When you come out of the room, please clean it up*
한국말을 가르칠 때 학생들이 많았어요	(hanguk mar-ŭl karŭch'i-l ttae haksaeng-dŭr-i manassŏyo)?	*Were there many students when you taught Korean?*

Nasty headaches

◄⑨ **CD 1, TR 10, 02:18**

Mr Pak goes to the chemist to get some medicine for a nasty headache.

약사	어서 오세요. 무슨 약을 드릴까요?
박선생	네, 두통이 아주 심한데, 두통약 좀 주시겠어요?
약사	네, 언제부터 아프기 시작했어요?
박선생	어제부터 아프기 시작했어요. 회사에서 일을 너무 많이 하고 스트레스를 많이 받았어요. 아마 과로하고 스트레스가 원인인 것 같아요.
약사	그렇군요. 눈은 아프지 않으세요?
박선생	네, 조금 아파요.
약사	잠은 잘 주무세요?
박선생	아니요. 머리가 너무 아파서 잘 못 자요.
약사	알겠어요. 아마 스트레스하고 관련이 있는 것 같아요. 이 약을 잡쉬보세요.

박선생	하루에 몇 번씩 먹나요?
약사	두통이 심할 때는 네 시간마다 한 알씩 드시고, 좀 나아지면 식후에 한 알씩 하루 세 번 드세요.
박선생	부작용 같은 것은 없나요?
약사	이 약을 먹으면 졸음이 오니까 조심하세요. 그리고 쉽게 피로를 느껴도 놀라지 마세요.
박선생	네, 고맙습니다.

Yaksa	Ŏsŏ oseyo. Musŭn yag-ŭl tŭrilkkayo?
Mr Pak	Ne, tut'ong-i aju shim ha-nde, tut'ong yak chom chushigessŏyo?
Yaksa	Ne, ŏnje-but'ŏ ap'ŭ-gi shijak haessŏyo?
Mr Pak	Ŏje-but'ŏ ap'ŭ-gi shijak'aessŏyo. Hoesa-esŏ ir-ul nŏmu mani ha-go sŭt'ŭresŭ-rŭl mani padassŏyo. Ama kwaro-hago sŭt'ŭresŭ-ga wonin-i-n kŏt kat'ayo.
Yaksa	Kŭrŏk'unyo. Nun-ŭn ap'ŭ-ji anŭseyo?
Mr Pak	Ne, chogŭm ap'ayo.
Yaksa	Cham-ŭn chal chumuseyo?
Mr Pak	Aniyo. Mŏri-ga nŏmu ap'asŏ chal mot chayo.
Yaksa	Algessŏyo. Ama sŭt'ŭresŭ-hago kwallyŏn-i innŭn kŏt kat'ayo. I yag-ŭl chapswo-boseyo.
Mr Pak	Haru-e myŏt pŏn sshik mŏngnayo?
Yaksa	Tut'ong-i shim ha-l ttae-nŭn ne shigan-mada han al sshik tushi-go, chom naaji-myŏn, shikhu-e han al sshik haru sebŏn tŭseyo.
Mr Pak	Pujagyong kat'ŭn kŏs-ŭn ŏmnayo?

Phrases and expressions

ama sŭt'ŭresŭ-ga wonin-i-n kŏt kat'ayo	*it seems as though it's because of stress*
ne-shigan-mada han al sshik tŭseyo	*take one tablet every four hours*
shikhu-e han al sshik se-bŏn tŭseyo	*take one tablet three times a day after meals*
shwipke p'iro-rŭl nŭkkyŏ-do nolla-ji maseyo	*don't be surprised if you feel tired very easily*

yaksa	약사	*pharmacist, chemist*
shim ha-	심하-	*is serious*
ŏnje	언제	*when*
hoesa	회사	*company*
sŭt'ŭresŭ	스트레스	*stress*
pat-	받-	*receive*
kwaro	과로	*overwork*
wonin	원인	*reason, cause*
kŭrŏk'unyo	그렇군요	*ah, I see; it's like that, is it?!*
nun	눈	*an eye*
cham	잠	*sleep (noun)*
chumushi-	주무시-	*sleep (honorific equivalent of cha-)*
kwallyŏn	관련	*relation, link*
chapswo po-	잡쉬보-	*try eating (honorific form)*
chapsushi-	잡수시-	*eat (honorific equivalent of mok-)*

QUICK VOCAB

han al	한알	*one tablet*
naaji-	나아지-	*get better*
haru-e	하루에	*per day*
-mada	-마다	*each, every*
shikhu	식후	*after meals, after the meal*
pujagyong	부작용	*a side-effect*
chorŭm	졸음	*sleepiness, drowsiness*
kat'ŭn kŏt	같은 것	*(a) similar thing, something similar*
shwipke	쉽게	*easily*
p'iro	피로	*fatigue, weariness*
nŭkki-	느끼-	*to feel*
nolla-	놀라-	*to be surprised, be shocked*

Grammar 18

1 *The future marker* -kess

-겠(-kess) can be added to verbs to make future forms. An
explanation of this is given in Unit 12 and you do not need to be
concerned about it until then.

2 *Immediate future*

You have previously learned to put sentences in the future with the
form -(으)ㄹ 거에요(-[ŭ]l kŏeyo). Korean has another future form
-(으)ㄹ게요(-[ŭ]lkeyo), added to the present stem of processive
verbs which expresses a more definite (rather than probable)
future: something you will certainly do, are promising to do or
are just about to do. It is often used in circumstances where there
is no doubt about whether or not you will be able to do the thing
concerned. You can only use this form to say what you yourself

will do, since you have control over your own actions. You cannot say what someone else will do, since you have no control over their actions and there is therefore always a certain element of doubt about them.

3 Asking polite questions

Korean often uses the ending –겠어요(**-kessŏyo**) added to the honorific stem of verbs to ask polite questions. Examples are: 지금 가시겠어요(**chigŭm kashigessŏyo**)? (*are you going now?*), 주문하시겠어요(**chumun hashigessŏyo**)? (*would you like to order?*). It can also be used to express requests: 해 주시겠어요 (**hae-jushigess ŏyo**)? (*would you do it for me?*).

4 Honorific verbs

Korean has several verbs which are only used in the honorific form (the non-honorific form is a completely different verb). In this unit you meet the verb 주무시–(**chumushi-**) which is the honorific stem of the verb 자–(**cha-**) (*sleep*). Here is a list of the common honorific verbs and their non-honorific equivalents. Notice especially the verb 있어요(**issŏyo**).

non-honorific	meaning	honorific	hon polite
자–(**cha-**)	*sleep*	주무시– (**chumushi-**)	주무세요 (**chumuseyo**)
먹–(**mŏk-**)	*eat*	잡수시– (**chapsushi-**)	잡수세요 (**chapsuseyo**)
있–(**iss-**)	*exist, stay*	계시– (**kyeshi-**)	계세요 (**kyeseyo**)
있–(**iss-**)	*have*	있으시– (**issŭshi-**)	있으세요 (**issŭseyo**)

죽-(chuk-)	*die*	돌아가시- (tora-gashi-)	돌아가세요 (tora-gaseyo)
먹-(mǒk-)/ 마시-(mashi-)	*eat/drink*	드시-(tǔshi-)	드세요(tǔseyo)

Insight

Some verbs have specific honorific verbs which are entirely different from their non-honorific counterparts (see Grammar note 4 to the second dialogue). Note particularly the verbs for *eat, sleep, stay,* and *die*. It can be quite insulting to use the non-honorific form by mistake for an esteemed person, so it's worth getting these right.

Practice

1 This exercise is designed to help you practise the –(느)ㄴ데요 (-[nǔ]ndeyo) form. If we give you a Korean sentence ending in –(느)ㄴ데요, you must provide a second sentence that fits with it. If we give you the second sentence in Korean, then you are meant to make up a first sentence with –(느)ㄴ데요 along the lines of the English that we suggest.

a 영국 대사관의 토니인데요. (*Create appropriate second sentence*)

b (*I've come from England*) 거기서 한국말을 조금 공부했어요.

c (*I telephoned yesterday*) 김 선생님 좀 바꿔 주시겠어요?

d 어제 친구하고 여기 왔는데요. (*Create appropriate second sentence*)

e *(I want to buy a dictionary)* 하나 보여주시겠어요?

f 저는 김 선생님의 부인인데요. *(Where has Mr Kim gone?)*

2 Make up a sentence for each of the following verbs. Put the verb into the 'it seems like' pattern with −(느)ㄴ 것 같아요(-(nŭ)n kŏt kat'ayo).

a 비가 와요.

b 박 선생님이에요.

c 독서를 싫어해요.

d 동대문 시장에 갔어요.

e 김 선생님 오세요.

f 가방을 여기 놓았어요.

3 You have lost your jacket and the man at the lost property office asks you to describe it. *(pocket:* 주머니*)*

4 Join up the following sets of clauses, so that the meaning is 'when A, B.' Thus, the first one will be *When you eat your food, don't talk* or, in better English, *Don't talk when you're eating.*

a *When you eat food*   *don't talk*

b *When you park your car*   *take care*

c *When you are going into town*   *call me*
d *When the film's over*   *let's go to a restaurant*
e *When I arrived home*   *I had a beer*
(도착하-[**toch'ak ha-**], *arrive*)
f *When you go out*   *let's go together*

5 Translate the following sentences into English.

a 어쨌든 지금 무엇을 하기로 했어요?

b 우리 여자 친구 못 봤어요? 보면 저한테
전화하세요.

c 좀 나아지면 약을 더 이상 먹지 마세요.

d 언제 졸업할 거에요? 그 다음에 무슨 계획이
있어요?

e 이 서류가 중요해요? 중요하지요! 내
면허증이잖아요!

f 데이트를 할 때 영화 보러 자주 가요.

6 Translate the following into Korean.

◀》 CD 1, TR 10, 04:00

a *You've made a big mistake!*
b *If you go into the city late at night it's dangerous.*
c *Would you show me that dictionary? Where did you buy it?*
d *Is there a problem? Yes, I seem to have lost my medicine.*
e *I've had so much stress lately and I can't sleep at night.*
f *You've lost your bag? What was inside?*
g *You don't like my ideas!*
h *So what did you do?*

7 You have a headache and your friend, who has gone out while you were asleep, leaves you some tablets with a note about when to take them. What are his instructions?

심할 땐 네 시간마다
두 알 드세요.
좀 나아지면,
점심 때만 식전에 한 알씩
드세요

TEN THINGS TO REMEMBER

1 How to say you've lost something or left it behind

2 Describing items of lost property

3 Describing what was/is inside something (e.g. the contents of a missing bag)

4 Telling the time

5 Giving directions (revision)

6 Describing an ailment (e.g. a nasty headache)

7 Asking for medicine

8 Parts of the body

9 Understanding instructions for taking medicine

10 Formation of *when-* clauses

11

Would you like to try it on?/ Do you think it suits me?

In this unit you will learn
- *how to shop for clothes*
- *commenting on prices, quality and style*
- *comparing one thing with another*
- *informal styles of speech (used between close friends)*
- *more about modifiers and honorifics*

Would you like to try it on?

◆) **CD 1, TR 11**

Minho and Byongsoo go to Namdaemun market to buy some clothes.

입어보시겠어요?

민호	저 셔츠 좀 봐라. 정말 좋다.
병수	그래? 내 생각에는 디자인이 좀 구식 같다.
민호	아니야. 내 마음에 꼭 들어. 아가씨, 저 셔츠 얼마에요?

점원 A	팔천원이에요.
민호	와, 정말 싸다.
병수	에이, 그런데 이거 봐. 질이 별로 안 좋아.
민호	글쎄, 그럼 다른 곳에 가볼까?

Minho and Byongsoo decide to try out the department store instead.

점원 B	어서 오세요. 뭘 찾으세요?
민호	좀 활동적인 옷을 찾는데요, 좀 밝은 색으로요.
	청바지하고 같이 입을 수 있는 멋있고 질 좋은 옷이요.
점원 B	이거 어때요? 요즘 아주 유행하는 스타일이에요.
민호	재료가 뭐에요?
점원 B	백 퍼센트 면이에요. 한번 입어보시겠어요?
민호	네, 고맙습니다 . . . 나한테 어울려요?

Minho	Chŏ shyŏch'ŭ chom pwa-ra. Chŏngmal cho-t'a.
Byongsoo	Kŭrae? Nae saenggag-enŭn dijain-i chom kushik kat-ta.
Minho	Ani-ya. Nae maŭm-e kkok tŭrŏ. Agassi, chŏ-shyŏch'ŭ ŏlma-eyo?
Chŏmwon A	P'al ch'ŏn won-ieyo.
Minho	Wa, chŏngmal ssa-da.
Byongsoo	Ei, kŭrŏnde i-gŏ pwa. Chir-i pyŏllo an choa.
Minho	Kŭlsse, kŭrŏm tarŭn kos-e ka-bo-lkka?

Minho and Byongsoo decide to try out the department store instead.

Chŏmwon B	Ŏsŏ oseyo. Mwol ch'ajŭseyo?
Minho	Chom hwalttongjŏg-in os-ŭl ch'an-nŭndeyo, chom palgŭn saeg-ŭro-yo. Ch'ŏngbaji-hago kach'i ib-ŭl su in-nŭn mŏshit-ko chil choŭn osh-iyo.
Chŏmwon B	I-gŏ ŏttaeyo? Yojŭm aju yuhaeng ha-nŭn sŭt'ail-ieyo.
Byongsoo	Chaeryo-ga mwo-eyo?
Chŏmwon B	Paek p'ŏsentŭ myŏn-ieyo. Hanbŏn ibŏ-boshigessŏyo?
Minho	Ne, komapsŭmnida ... Na-hant'e ŏullyŏyo?

Phrases and expressions

nae maŭm-e kkok tŭrŏ (yo)	*I like it very much*
hanbŏn ibŏ-boshigessŏyo?	*would you like to try it on?*
wa, chŏngmal ssada	*wow, that's really cheap*
... -hant'e ŏullyŏyo?	*does it suit ...?*

For any verb endings that you do not recognize, read the grammar section after reading the dialogue.

shyŏch'ŭ	셔츠	*shirt*
dijain	디자인	*design*
kushik	구식	*old style, old fashioned*
kkok	꼭	*exactly, certainly, precisely*
wa!	와!	*wow!*
ei!	에이	*hey!*
chil	질	*quality*
pyŏllo	별로	*(not) particularly (see note 2)*
kos	곳	*place*

QUICK VOCAB

hwalttongjŏk	활동적	casual, active
hwalttongjŏg-in	활동적인	(modifier form of the above, like an adjective)
palgŭn	밝은	bright
ch'ŏngbaji	청바지	blue jeans
mŏshiss-	멋있-	be stylish, be handsome
yuhaeng ha-	유행하-	be popular, be in vogue
sŭt'ail	스타일	style
chaeryo	재료	stuff, (raw) material (also ingredients)
p'ŏsent'ŭ	퍼센트	per cent
myŏn	면	cotton
ŏulli-	어울리-	suit (a person)

Grammar 19

1 The plain style

The plain style is used between very close friends or when speaking to someone much younger than you. It can also be used when saying something to yourself out loud and it is used as a written form in notices and in books and newspapers.

Its form is very like that of the modifiers you met in Unit 9, but with some important differences. For processive verbs you add 는(-nŭn) (after a consonant stem) or ㄴ(-n) (after a vowel stem) onto the verb stem for the present tense, plus the verb ending 다 (-da). Hence: 듣는다(tŭn-nŭnda), 기다린다(kidari-nda), 먹는다 (mŏng-nŭnda), 한다(ha-nda), 마신다(mashi-nda) etc. For the past tense you simply add 다(-da) onto the past stem of the verb: 기다렸다(kidaryŏtta), 먹었다(mogŏtta), 했다(haetta), 마셨다 (mashyŏtta).

218

For descriptive verbs, you add −다(-da) to the stem of the verb, either the past stem or the present stem according to whether you want a past or present meaning.

Here are some example sentences in the plain style.

민호가 시장에 간다 (minho-ga shijang-e ka-nda)
Minho goes to the market

민호가 시장에 갔다 (minho-ga shijang-e kat-ta)
Minho went to the market

민호가 사과를 먹는다 (minho-ga sagwa-rŭl mŏng-nŭnda)
Minho eats an apple

민호가 사과를 먹었다 (minho-ga sagwa-rŭl mŏg-otta)
Minho ate an apple

오늘 날씨가 좋다 (onŭl nalssi-ga cho-t'a)
Today, the weather is good

어제 날씨가 좋았다 (ŏje nalssi-ga choat-ta)
Yesterday, the weather was good

In addition, there are two very common ways of asking questions in the plain style.

One of these you have learned already: it is the question particle −나(-na) added to any verb stem (past, present, honorific) without the particle −요(-yo) on the end. Here are some examples: 뭘 먹나 (mwol mŏng-na)? (*what are you eating?*), 뭘 하나(mwol ha-na)? (*what are you doing?*).

Another common question pattern is to add −니(-ni)? to any verb stem: 비가 오니(piga o-ni)? 어디 갔니(ŏdi gan-ni)? meaning *is it raining?* and *where did you go?* respectively.

Here are some examples of questions in the plain style:

남대문 시장이 어디니 (namdaemun shijang-i ŏdi-ni)?
Where is Namdaemun market?

오늘 아침 무슨 약을 먹었니 (onŭl ach'im musŭn yak-ŭl mŏgŏn-ni)?
What medicine did you take this morning?

You can make commands in the plain style by adding -라(-ra) to the polite style of the present tense, minus the -요(-yo). Thus, plain style commands would include: 먹어라(mŏgŏ-ra), 해라(hae-ra), 가지 마라(ka-ji ma-ra) *eat it!, do it!, don't go!* (from 하지 마세요 [ha-ji maseyo]), and so on.

Plain style suggestions can be made by adding -자(-ja) to the present stem of any processive verb: 먹자(mŏk-ja), 하자 (ha-ja), 이야기 하자(iyagi ha-ja) (*let's eat, let's do it, let's talk*) and so on.

Insight

The plain style is used among very close friends or to people who are much younger. It's also used to say things to yourself (out loud). It's okay not to use it (you'll not offend anyone by not using it, whereas if you use it wrongly, you could!), but it's important to be able to recognize it. Other forms of the plain style. -나 (-na), -니 (-ni), -자 (-ja) and -라 (-ra) are plain-style endings which look a little different from the standard endings - (느)ㄴ다 (- [nŭ]nda) and -다 (-da). The first two are question forms (use them to ask a question in the plain style); the third and fourth are the *let's* and the command forms of the plain style.

2 The informal style

Korean also has another very important system of addressing those younger than you or very close to you, in addition to the plain style. In fact, it is perhaps even more common and it is very easy.

All you have to do is take the polite style of the verb (present, past or future) and take off the −요(-yo) particle! That's all there is to it:

내 마음에 꼭 들어 (**nae maǔm-e kkok tǔrǒ**) *I like it very much*
그런데 이거 봐 (**kǔrǒnde igǒ pwa**) *But look at this*
질이 별로 안 좋아 (**chil-i pyǒllo an choa**) *The quality is not very good*

The one exception is the copula: instead of taking the −이에요 (-**ieyo**) form and taking off the −요, the informal style of the copula is −야(-**ya**) after a vowel, and −이야(-**iya**) after a consonant:

저 사람은 한국 사람이야 (**chǒ saram-ǔn hanguk saram-iya**)
That person is a Korean

김 선생님은 의사야 (**kim sǒnsaengnim-ǔn ǔysa-ya**)
Mr Kim is a medical doctor

Insight

The informal style (used between close friends or to those younger than you) is easier than the plain style. You create it simply by taking off the −요 (-**yo**) of the regular polite style. Easy!

3 Use of the particle −(으)로(-[ǔ]ro)

The particle −(으)로(-[**ǔ**]ro) has various functions, some of which you have learned already. Here is a list of its different uses.

- instruments: *by, by means of*

  기차로 와요 (**kich'a-ro wayo**)
  come by train

  손으로 만들어요 (**son-ŭro mandŭrŏyo**)
  make by hand

- cause, reason: *because of*

  교통사고로 죽었어요 (**kyot'ong sago-ro chugŏssŏyo**)
  (He) died (because of/in) a traffic accident

  개인적인 이유로 거절했어요 (**kaeinjŏgin iyu-ro kŏjŏl
  haessŏyo**)
  (I) refused for a private reason

- stuff, raw material: *from, of*

  이 집은 나무로 만들었어요 (**i chib-ŭn namu-ro
  madŭrŏssŏyo**)
  This house is made of wood

  와인은 포도로 만들어요 (**wain-ŭn p'odo-ro madŭrŏyo**)
  Wine is made from grapes

- unit, measure, degree: *by*

  영국에서는 파운드/킬로로 팔아요 (**yŏngug-esŏ-nŭn
  p'aundŭ/ k'iro-ro p'arayo**)
  They sell by the pound/kilo in Britain

- direction: *towards*

  런던으로 갔어요 (**london-ŭro kassŏyo**)
  (He) went to London

우리 집으로 오세요 (uri cib-ŭro oseyo)
Please come to my house

4 More on modifiers

In Unit 9 you learned how to make modifiers with ─는(-nŭn) for
processive verbs and ─(으)ㄴ(-[ŭ]n) for descriptive verbs. You
learned how they could be used with the noun 거(것)(kŏ [kŏt]) to
mean *the act of* (verb)*ing*.

In fact, you can use modifiers in front of any noun and, as
you would expect, their function is to modify the noun, to tell
you something about the noun they modify. Here is a good
example:

제가 먹는 사과 (che-ga mŏng-nŭn sagwa)

Here the noun is 사과(sagwa) (*apple*), and 제가 먹는(chega
mŏngnŭn) (from the verb 먹-) is modifying the noun 'apple'.
The meaning of the phrase *is the apple I am eating*. In English,
we put the noun first, and afterwards the modifying phrase
([which] I am eating), but in Korean it is the other way round.
The noun and its modifying phrase can then be used as part of a
sentence, as with any other noun. For example, you might want
to say *the apple I am eating has gone bad* or *where is the apple
I am eating?* You could do this in Korean like this (the modifying
phrases are in brackets and you can see that they are optional;
the sentences would make perfect sense without them, but the
modifying phrases show which particular apple you are talking
about):

(제가 먹는) 사과가 썩었어요 ([che-ga mŏng-nŭn] sagwa-ga
ssŏgŏssŏyo)

(제가 먹는) 사과가 어디 있어요 ([che-ga mŏng-nŭn] sagwa-
ga ŏdi issŏyo)?

Do you think it suits me?

🔊 CD 1, TR 11, 01:45

Minho tries the clothes on and they have another discussion.

점원	야, 아주 멋있는데요.
민호	(to Byongsoo) 나한테 어울리니?
병수	응, 잘 어울려. 그런데 좀 작은 것 같다.
점원	좀 큰 걸 입어보실래요?
민호	네.
점원	여기 있어요.

A little while later.

병수	그게 더 잘 맞는다.
점원	야, 아주 근사해요.
민호	그런데 얼마지요?
점원	삼만 이천원이에요.
민호	뭐라고요?
점원	왜요? 싼 거에요. 겨우 삼만 이천원인데요 뭐.
병수	제가 생각해도 좀 비싼 것 같은데요.
민호	남대문 시장에서는 비슷한 게 팔천원이에요.
점원	아, 네, 남대문하고는 비슷해 보여도 질이 달라요. 남대문 시장에서 옷을 사면 두세 달 만에 못 쓰게 돼서 새 옷을 사야 되거든요.
병수	그러면 이옷이 남대문 시장 옷보다 네 배나 더 오래 가요?

| 점원 | 적어도요. 그리고 훨씬 더 잘 맞아요. |
| 민호 | 음, 가서 생각 좀 다시 해봐야겠어요. |

Chŏmwon	Ya, aju mŏshin-nŭndeyo.
Minho (to Byongsoo)	Na-hant'e ŏulli-ni?
Byongsoo	Ŭng, chal ŏullyŏ. Kŭrŏnde chom chagŭn kŏt kat-ta.
Chŏmwon	Chom k'ŭn gŏ-l ibŏ-boshi-llaeyo?
Minho	Ne.
Chŏmwon	Yŏgi issŏyo.

A little while later.

Byongsoo	Kŭ-ge tŏ chal man-nŭnda.
Chŏmwon	Ya, aju kŭnsa haeyo.
Minho	Kŭrŏnde, ŏlma-jiyo?
Chŏmwon	Samman ich'ŏn won-ieyo.
Minho	Mworaguyo?
Chŏmwon	Waeyo? Ssan kŏ-eyo. Kyŏu samman-ich'ŏn won-indeyo mwo.
Byongsoo	Che-ga saenggak hae-do, chom pissan kŏt kat'ŭndeyo.
Minho	Namdaemun shijang-esŏ-nŭn pisut han ke p'alch'ŏn won-ieyo.
Chŏmwon	A, ne, Namdaemun-hago-nŭn pisŭt hae-poyŏ-do chir-i tallayo. Namdaemun shijang-esŏ os-ŭl sa-myŏn tu se tal man-e mot ssŭ-ge toe-sŏ sae os-ŭl sa-ya toe-gŏdŭnyo.
Byongsoo	Kurŏmyŏn i-osh-i Namdaemun shijang ot-poda ne-bae-na orae kayo?
Chŏmwon	Chŏgŏ-do-yo. Kŭrigo hwŏlsshin tŏ chal majayo.
Minho	Um, ka-sŏ saenggak chom tashi hae-bwa-yagessŏyo.

Phrases and expressions

che-ga saenggak hae-do	it seems to me
kyŏu samman-ich'ŏn won-indeyo mwo	it's only 32,000 won (it's not much)
chŏgŏ-do-yo	at least
ka-sŏ saenggak chom tashi hae-bwa-yagessŏyo	I'll have to go away and think about it

ŭng	응	yes (casual form)
maj-	맞-	to fit well (maj + nunda = man-nunda)
kŭnsa ha-	근사하-	look super, look good
kyŏu	겨우	only
pisŭt ha-	비슷하-	look similar
tarŭ-	다르-	be different (polite style: tallayo)
man-e	만에	within, in only (two or three months)
ssŭ-ge	쓰게	usable
toe-	되-	become
bae	배	double, (two) times
orae	오래	long
ka-	가-	here: last, endure
hwolsshin	훨씬	by far, far and away

Grammar 20

1 Ending sentences with 뭐(mwo)

Sometimes Koreans will add 뭐(**mwo**) to the end of certain sentences as a kind of afterthought. It has no real translation (despite literally meaning *what!*), and you don't need to use it yourself. It means something like *you know, isn't it* or *I think,* but you should not try to translate it or think that it has any great significance when you come across it.

2 Even if it looks the same

This dialogue has a rather complex verb in it which is a good example of how Korean uses particles and compound verbs in quite complicated ways to build up important meanings. The form is 비슷해 보여도(**pisŭt hae poyŏ-do**). We will work through it slowly to see how it is formed.

The basic verb is 비슷하-(**pisŭt ha-**) which means *is similar*. To this the verb 보이-(**poi-**) (*to look like, to appear*) has been added to give the meaning *to look similar, to appear similar*. You have seen verbs compounded before with the verbs 주-(**chu-**) and 보-(**po-**) and you will remember that these verbs are added onto the polite style of the main verb, with the -요 (**-yo**) particle taken off (for example, 먹어 보세요[**mŏgŏ-bo-seyo**], *please try eating it*). This example is just the same; the polite style of *is similar* is taken (비슷해요[**pisŭt haeyo**]), the 요 (**yo**) is removed (비슷해-[**pisŭt hae-**]) and the next verb 보이-(**poi-**) is added (비슷해 보이-[**pisut hae poi-**]).

You have also learned the form -(어)도(-[**ŏ]do**) before, which means *even though*, and once again this is added to the polite style of the verb, minus the 요(**yo**).

This means that the meaning of the entire verb set 비슷해 보여도 (**pisŭthae poyŏdo**) is *even though it looks similar, even though it appears similar*.

3 Use of the verb toe-

The verb 되-(**toe-**) means *is okay, (it) will do*, and it can be used after verbs with the particle -도(-**do**) (*even though*), to mean *it's okay if… .* Here are two examples:

나가도 돼요(naga-do toeyo) *it's okay to go out* (lit: *even if/even though you go out, it's okay/it will do*)

먹어도 돼요(mŏgŏ-do toeyo)? *is it okay to eat this?* (lit: *even if/though I eat this, is it okay?*)

This is a very useful pattern and is often used by Koreans to ask for and to give permission.

Another meaning of the verb 되-(toe-) is *becomes*. You saw it in the dialogue with the word 못 쓰게(mot ssŭ-ge) (*unusable*), meaning *it becomes unusable*. You can add the ending -게(-ge) onto other verb stems, and follow it with 되-(toe-) to say that something becomes or comes to a particular state. Here are some other examples:

못 먹게 됐어요(mon mŏk-ke toessŏyo)
It has become inedible (it's gone off!)

한국 여자하고 결혼하게 됐어요(Hanguk yŏja-hago
kyŏrhonha-ge toessŏyo)
I came to marry a Korean girl

> ## Insight
> Take off the -요 (-yo) of the regular polite style and add -도
> 돼요 (-do toeyo)? to ask for permission. 먹어도 돼요
> (mŏgŏ-do toeyo)? means *is it okay if I eat (it)?*

4 Speech styles and honorifics

We are taking this opportunity to remind you about the essential difference between speech styles and honorifics in Korean. It is absolutely essential that you are clear about the distinction, which is why we are going over it again and giving you a few more examples.

Remember, speech styles are decided according to the person you are talking to. Mostly you will use the polite style, but in formal situations you might use the formal style (which you will learn later), and with close friends and young people or children you might use the informal style or the plain style.

The person you are talking *about*, however, will govern whether or not you use an honorific. There is thus no incompatibility between honorifics and informal speech styles. Imagine you are talking to a child and asking the child where his grandad has gone. You would use the informal or plain style (because you are talking to a child) and you would use an honorific (because you are talking about grandad, who is an older, esteemed person).

When you are addressing someone as 'you' and talking about them, things will be much more straightforward. If you are asking a child what he is doing, you would use an informal style and, of course, no honorific since the person you are talking about (the child) is not an honorific person. In contrast, if you are talking to a professor and asking him what he is doing, you might use the polite or even the formal style and you would certainly use an honorific.

Here are a couple of examples of different combinations of speech styles and honorifics. Make sure you understand in each case the social level of the person being addressed and the social level of the person being spoken about:

민호, 할아버지 뭐 하시니(minho, haraběji mwo ha-shi-ni?)
Minho, what does your grandad do?

민호, 너 뭐 하니(minho, nŏ mwo ha-ni)?
Minho, what do you do?

선생님, 할아버지 뭐 하세요(sŏnsaengnim, haraběji mwo ha-se-yo?)
Professor, what does your grandad do?

선생님, 민호 뭐 해요(sŏnsaengnim, Minho mwo hae-yo?)
Professor, what does Minho do?

5 Do you want to?/do you feel like?

The pattern –(으)ㄹ래요(-[ŭ]llaeyo) can be added to the stems of processive verb bases (present tense) to ask in a casual way if someone wants to do or feels like doing something. You met it in the phrase 한번 입어 보실래요(han-bŏn ibŏ-boshi-llaeyo), where it is added to the honorific form of 입어보–(ibŏ-bo-) (*to try on*) to give the meaning *would you like to try it on?* Other examples would be:

커피 마실래요(k'ŏp'i mashi-llaeyo)?
Do you want to drink coffee, do you fancy some coffee?

노래방에 갈래요(noraebang-e ka-llaeyo)?
How about going to a noraebang?

Practice

1 Put the following sentences into the plain style.

a 이 옷이 정말 좋아요!
b 비가 와요.
c 뭘 하세요?
d 밥을 먹고 있어요.
e 걱정하고 있어요?

f 조금 더 기다리면 버스가 올 거에요.
g 밥 먹어요.
h 어제 밤 어디 갔어요?
i 조심했어요?

2 Translate the following phrases into Korean using the modifier forms you have learned in this lesson.

    a *clothes made of cotton*
    b *the beer we drank yesterday*
    c *the book Mr Kim is reading*
    d *the shirt he is wearing*
    e *the film we saw last year*
    f *the food I hate*

3 Join the following two sets of information with –어/아도 (**-ŏ/a-do**) to give the meaning 'even if A, then B' (or, 'even though A, B'). For example, the first will be: *Even if it looks good, it isn't.*

    a *It looks good*   *it isn't*
    b *It's expensive*   *it'll be tasty*
    c *It's raining*   *I want to go out*
    d *I don't like him*   *I'll have to meet him*
    e *It's a bright colour*   *it doesn't suit you*
    f *I've got a headache*   *thinking of going to a noraebang*

4 Make up a dialogue between two people arguing about which film to see on TV tonight. One of them wants to see a film which the other one says they saw last year. He wants to see a different film, but the other thinks it's on too late and that it's boring anyway. To help you, here are three phrases that you might like to use:

그것은 우리가 작년에 본 영화잖아요!
열 두시가 너무 늦었어요? 무슨 말이에요?!
정말 재미없는 것 같아요.

Now say the dialogue aloud using the informal style for all the verb endings and taking out any honorific suffixes you might have used.

5 Translate the following sentences into Korean.

a *That person who speaks Korean well is coming.*
b *I don't like those clothes you bought yesterday.*
c *He's a stylish man.*
d *Even though the quality is better, it's four times as expensive.*
e *Can I try on those clothes you are wearing?*
f *What did you say?*
g *Please take care when you are driving at night, even though you haven't been drinking.*
h *Do you have anything similar?*

6 You are looking for a new bag and come across the following pair. Compare one with the other (price, quality, size, colour) and say which one you would like to buy.

TEN THINGS TO REMEMBER

1 Buying clothes and asking *does it suit me?*

2 Asking if you can try something on

3 Exclamations like *wow!* and *hey!*

4 Descriptions of clothing: whether things look good/stylish, etc.

5 The plain style – what it is, and how it's used

6 The informal style

7 How to say *I'll have to (go away and) think about it*

8 Sentences with *toe-* (*it's okay to …* and *it has become*)

9 Asking if someone feels like doing something with -(**ŭ**)**llaeyo**

10 How to say *even though it looks similar …*

12

Do you have a spare room?/ The towel is dirty and the food is cold

In this unit you will learn
* *about booking hotels and inquiring about vacancies and facilities*
* *about making complaints when things don't go quite as they should*
* *more about the formal style of speech and the future tense*
* *quoted speech and reporting what other people said*

Do you have a spare room?

◀) **CD 1, TR 12**

Mr Lee is looking for a couple of rooms in a hotel.

손님	빈 방 있어요?
주인	네 있어요. 침대방을 드릴까요, 온돌방을 드릴까요?
손님	침대방 하나하고 온돌방 하나 주세요.
주인	네 알겠습니다.

침대방은 하루에 오만원이고 온돌방은
하루에 사만 원입니다.
얼마 동안 묵으시겠습니까?

손님 우선 삼일 동안요. 그리고 좀 더 묵을지도
몰라요.

주인 오일 이상 예약하시면 5% 할인해
드리는데요.

손님 아, 그럼 우리 집사람하고 좀 의논해
봐야겠어요.
아침식사도 포함되어 있지요?

주인 네, 물론 아침식사도 포함되어 있습니다.
7시부터 10시 사이에 지하 식당에 가시면
됩니다.
그리고 이천원만 더 내시면 손님 방까지
배달도 해드립니다.

손님 아니오, 직접 식당에 가서 먹겠어요.
이 호텔에 또 무슨 시설들이 있습니까?

주인 수영장, 사우나, 오락실, 노래방, 스텐드바,
그리고 한식당과 양식당이 있습니다.

손님 방에 텔레비젼과 전화도 있나요?

주인 물론입니다. 그리고 미니바도 있습니다.

손님 오, 아주 훌륭하군요. 오일 동안 예약하는
게 좋을 것 같아요.
아마 우리 집사람도 좋아할 거에요.

Sonnim	Pin pang issŏyo?
Chuin	Ne, issŏyo. Ch'imdaebang-ŭl tŭrilkkayo, ondolbang-ŭl tŭrilkkayo?
Sonnim	Ch'imdaebang hana-hago ondolbang hana chuseyo.
Chuin	Ne, algessŭmnida.
	Ch'imdaebang-ŭn haru-e oman won-i-go
	ondolbang-ŭn haru-e samman won-i-mnida.
	Ŏlma dongan mugŭshigessŭmnikka?

Sonnim	Usŏn sam-il dongan-yo. Kŭrigo chom tŏ mug-ŭljido mollayo.
Chuin	O-il isang yeyak ha-shimyŏn o-p'ŏsent'ŭ harin hae-tŭrinŭndeyo.
Sonnim	A, kŭrŏm uri chipsaram-hago chom ŭynon hae-bwayagessŏyo.
	Ach'im shiksa-do p'oham toeŏ itjiyo?
Chuin	Ne, mullon ach'im shiksa-do p'oham toeŏ issŭmnida. Ilgop-shi-but'ŏ yŏl-shi sai-e chiha shiktang-e ka-shimyŏn toemnida.
	Kŭrigo ich'ŏn won-man tŏ nae-shimyŏn sonnim pang-kkaji paedal-do hae-dŭrimnida.
Sonnim	Aniyo, chickchŏp shiktang-e ka-sŏ mŏkkessŏyo.
	I-hot'er-e tto musŭn shisŏl-dŭr-i issŭmnikka?
Chuin	Suyŏngjang, sauna, orakshil, noraebang, sŭt'endŭba, kŭrigo hanshiktang-gwa yangshiktang-i issŭmnida.
Sonnim	Pang-e t'ellebijyŏn-gwa chŏnhwa-do innayo?
Chuin	Mullon-imnida. Kŭrigo miniba-do issŭmnida.
Sonnim	O, aju hullyung ha-gunyo! O-il dongan yeyak hanŭn ke cho-ŭl kŏt kat'ayo. Ama uri chipsaram-do choa ha-lkŏeyo.

Phrases and expressions

ŏlma dongan mug-ŭshigessŏyo?	*how long will you be staying for?*
chom tŏ muk-ŭljido mollayo	*we may stay longer (I don't know if we might …)*
chipsaram-hago chom ŭynon hae-bwayagessŏyo	*I'll have to discuss it with my wife*
chikchŏp shiktang-e ka-sŏ mŏkkessŏyo	*we'll go to the restaurant to eat*
o-il dongan yeyak hanŭn ke cho-ŭl kŏt kat'ayo	*it seems like it would be a good idea to book for five nights*

pin	빈	empty, vacant, free (of seats and rooms)
pang	방	room
ch'imdaebang	침대방	room with bed
ch'imdae	침대	bed
ondolbang	온돌방	room with bed on floor
haru-e	하루에	per day
haru	하루	one day (duration)
ŏlma dongan	얼마 동안	how long
dongan	–동안	during
muk-	묵–	stay, lodge, spend the night
isang	이상	more than
yeyak ha-	예약하–	reserve, book
harin ha-	할인하–	give a discount
harin	할인	discount
ŭynon ha-	의논하–	discuss
ach'imshiksa	아침식사	breakfast
ach'im	아침	morning; breakfast (abbreviated form)
ach'im ha-	아침하–	have breakfast
p'oham doeŏ iss-	포함되어 있–	be included
sai-e	사이에	between
chiha shiktang	지하 식당	basement restaurant
chiha	지하	basement
paedal ha-	배달하–	deliver
chikchŏp	직접	direct(ly)
shisŏl	시설	facility
suyŏngjang	수영장	swimming pool
suyŏng ha-	수영하–	swim
sauna	사우나	sauna

orakshil	오락실	*amusements* (electronic games, etc.)
sŭt'endŭba	스텐드바	*bar* (standing bar)
hanshiktang	한식당	*Korean restaurant* (serving Korean food)
yangshiktang	양식당	*Western restaurant*
miniba	미니바	*mini-bar*
hullyung ha-	흘륭하–	*is excellent, great*

Grammar 21

1 *The formal style*

The formal style is the last important speech style for you to learn. It is used in formal situations, often by officials or representatives (such as the hotel worker in the dialogue), but it can be used by anybody when some formality is called for. It is perhaps slightly more common among men than women and, if you are a man, it is a good idea to say some sentences in the formal style occasionally, as if you always use the polite style it can sound to Koreans as though your Korean is a bit effeminate. It is quite common to mix formal and polite speech styles in this way, with some sentences in the formal style and some in the polite style.

To make statements in the formal style (that is, normal sentences which state facts, not questions, commands or suggestions), you add the ending –(스)ㅂ니다(-[**sŭ**]**mnida**) to the stem of the verb (either the present stem, past stem, or honorific present or past stem). Note that the ending is spelt -(**sŭ**)**pnida**, but pronounced -(**sŭ**)**mnida**. To consonant stems you add the form –습니다 (-**sŭmnida**), and to vowel stems –ㅂ니다(-**mnida**):

	wear	*buy*
stem	입–(ip-)	사–(sa-)
	입습니다(ipsǔmnida)	삽니다(samnida)
past	입었–(ibǒss-)	샀–(sass-)
	입었습니다	샀습니다
	(ibǒssǔmnida)	(sassǔmnida)
honorific	입으시–(ibǔshi-)	사시–(sashi-)
	입으십니다	사십니다
	(ibǔshimnida)	(sashimnida)
hon past	입으셨–(ibǔshyǒss-)	사셨–(sashyǒss-)
	입으셨습니다	사셨습니다
	(ibǔshyǒssǔmnida)	(sashyǒssǔmnida)

Note that the past formal forms have a treble -s, and so are spelt for example, 샀습니다(sass-sǔmnida). We just write two ss in romanization, however. You will recognize these formal statements from expressions like 미안합니다(mian hamnida), 죄송합니다(choesong hamnida) and 알겠습니다 (algessǔmnida). All those expressions are almost always used in the formal style.

To make questions in the formal style, you add the ending –(스) ㅂ니까?(-[sǔ]mnikka?) as follows:

	wear	*buy*
stem	입–(ip-)	사–(sa-)
	입습니까(ipsǔmnikka)?	삽니까(samnikka)?
past	입었–(ibǒss-)	샀–(sass-)
	입었습니까(ibǒssǔmnikka)?	샀습니까 (sassǔmnikka)?
honorific	입으시–(ibǔshi-)	사시–(sashi-)
	입으십니까(ibǔshimnikka)?	사십니까 (sashimnikka)?

hon past	입으셨–(ibŭshyŏss-)	사셨–(sashyŏss-)
	입으셨습니까	사셨습니까
	(ibŭshyŏssŭmnikka)?	(sashyŏssŭmnikka)?

Commands in the formal style always go on honorific present stems, and the ending is –ㅂ시오(-**pshio**) (pronounced rather as if it were –ㅂ시요[-**pshiyo**]):

stem	입–(ip-)	사–(sa-)
honorific stem	입으시–(ibŭshi-)	사시–(sashi-)
formal command	입으십시오	사십시오
	(ibŭshipshio)	(sashipshio)

You have already learned how to make suggestions in the formal style, way back in the early lessons of the course: –(으)ㅂ시다 (-[ŭ]**pshida**); 입읍시다(ibŭpshida) (let's wear it), 삽시다(sapshida) (let's buy it)

Note that this form can be added to an honorific stem, to express the feeling of formal style: 입으십시다 (ibushipshida), 사십시다 (sashipshida).

Insight

The formal style is used in formal situations to talk to people older or more important than you, or to show respect. You don't have to use it all the time; speakers will often mix their styles between the polite and the formal style in the same conversation. This is perfectly okay.

To make the formal style, add the form –습니다 (-**sŭmnida**); –습니까 (-**sŭmnikka**) for questions to verb stems ending in a consonant; and add –ㅂ니다 (-**mnida**); –ㅂ니까 (-**mnikka**) for questions to verb stems ending in vowels.

2 The future marker 겠(-kess)

The future marker 겠(-kess) can be added to any present stem (normal or honorific) to make a future stem. You can then add verb endings to this (such as the polite or formal styles, or a clause ending, such as 지만[-jiman]) in the normal way. You have two good examples in this unit:

얼마 동안 묵으시겠어요?
(Ŏlma dongan mugŭshi-gess-ŏyo)?
How long will you be staying for?

집사람하고 의논해봐야겠어요
(Chipsaram-hago ŭynon hae-bwaya-gess-ŏyo)
I will have to discuss with my wife ...

The 겠 future marker is used in the ending 야겠어요 (-yagessŏyo) (as in the second example) which you have already learned. It is also used in certain idiomatic phrases like 알겠습니다(algessŭmnida) and 모르겠습니다(morŭgessŭmnida) (*I understand and I don't understand*).

Although this form does express the future (it can also be used to express probability), the most common way to put a normal sentence into the future is with the -(으)ㄹ 거에요(-[ŭ]l kŏeyo) form which you have already learned. -(으)ㄹ 거에요 is a more useful form than -겠 for most situations, and the precise difference between them is something that you do not really need to worry about for this course. It is sufficient to be able to recognize the -겠 as the future marker, and to know that it can be used to make future stems which can then be used in other constructions.

Insight

The future marker 겠-(-kess-) can be added to verbs to specify a future sense; verb endings are then added in the normal way, in whatever style is appropriate for the conversation. However, the most common way of making a future form is to use the −(으)ㄹ 거에요 (-[ŭ]l kŏeyo) form that you learned much earlier in this course.

3 I don't know whether

You can say that you don't know whether you will do something or other by adding −(으)ㄹ지도 모르−(-[ŭ]lji-do morŭ-) to a verb stem. The example from the dialogue was 좀 더 묵을지도 몰라요 (**chom tŏ mug-ŭlji-do mollayo**) (*I don't know whether we will stay a bit longer, it might be that we stay a bit longer*). Here are a couple of other examples:

졸업할지도 몰라요
(**chorŏp ha-lji-do mollayo**)
I don't know whether I'll graduate (or not)

갈 수 있을지도 모릅니다
(**ka-l su iss-ŭlji-do morŭmnida**)
I don't even know if I'll be able to go or not

4 If you do, it will be okay

The sentence 가시면 됩니다(**ka-shimyŏn toemnida**) means *if you go, it will be okay*, and this pattern, one clause ending in −면 (-**myŏn**), plus a form of the verb 되−(**toe-**) is a common pattern. In the context of the dialogue, it is used to say that breakfast is available between certain times, so that if they go to the restaurant between those times, *it will be okay*. It can be used to ask for permission to do something: 지금 가면 돼요(**chigŭm ka-myŏn toeyo**)? (*is it okay to go now?*).

A very similar pattern is used in the next dialogue, where there is a similar sentence to this: 저한테 말하면 안 돼요(**chŏ-hant'e mal ha-myŏn an toeyo**)? (*can't you tell me? if you tell me, won't it be okay?*). A similar use would be 밖에 나가면 안 됩니까(**pakk-e**

naga-myŏn an toemnikka)? (*can't I go outside? won't it be okay if I go outside?*).

The next dialogue is quite advanced in parts and you should be satisfied if you understand the gist of what is going on. If you can understand the details of the dialogue then you can be sure that your Korean is coming on very well indeed.

Insight

Giving permission. Use the form – (으)면 돼요 (-[ŭ]myon toeyo) to give permission.

The towel is dirty and the food is cold

🔊 **CD 1, TR 12, 02:22**

Unfortunately, the hotel didn't turn out to be as good as it looked ...

손님	지배인 좀 바꿔주세요.
종업원	실례지만, 무슨 일이세요?
손님	이 호텔 서비스에 대해서 할 말이 있어요.
종업원	죄송하지만 저한테 말씀하시면 안될까요?
손님	지배인한테 직접 말하고 싶은데요.
종업원	좋습니다. 잠깐 기다리세요.

A little while later.

지배인	네, 지배인입니다. 말씀하시지요.
손님	이 호텔 서비스에 문제가 많은 것 같아요. 직원들이 불친절하고 무뚝뚝해요. 그리고 오늘 아침에 식당에 갔는데 음식이 다 식어 있었어요. 어제도 마찬가지였고요.

지배인	그래요? 정말 죄송합니다.
	웨이터한테 말씀하셨습니까?
손님	물론 종업원 아가씨한테 얘기했지요.
	그런데 아가씨가 불친절한데다가 제
	한국말을 못 알아듣겠다고 하면서
	음식에 아무 문제가 없다고 했어요.
	음식이 다 식었고 맛이 없는데도
	말이에요.
지배인	아, 정말 죄송합니다.
	항상 최선의 봉사를 하려고 노력하는데도
	가끔 실수가 발생합니다.
	제가 즉시 식당 종업원들에게
	얘기하겠습니다.
손님	그리고 또 있어요.
	오늘 아침 수건을 갈아달라고 했는데
	수건이 너무 더러웠어요.
	그리고 내 아들 방은 아직까지 청소도 안
	했어요.
지배인	그것 참 이상하군요.
	손님처럼 불평하는 경우가 지금까지
	없었는데요.
손님	그것뿐이 아니에요. 내 방의 텔레비젼은
	고장이 났고, 냉장고 문은 열리지도
	않아요.
	솔직히 말해서 이 호텔 서비스하고
	시설은 엉망이네요.
지배인	죄송합니다. 그렇지만 저희도 손님처럼
	불평많은 사람은 필요없으니까 오늘
	당장 나가 주세요.
	요금은 다시 환불해드리겠습니다.

Sonnim	Chibaein chom pakkwo-juseyo.
Chongŏbwon	Shillye-jiman, musŭn ir-iseyo?
Sonnim	I-hot'el sŏbisŭ-e taehaesŏ ha-l mar-i issŏyo.
Chongŏbwon	Choesong ha-jiman chŏ-hant'e malssŭm ha-shimyŏn an toe-lkkayo?
Sonnim	Chibaein-hant'e chikchŏp mal ha-go ship'ŭndeyo.
Chongŏbwon	Chosŭmnida. Chamkkan kidariseyo.

A little while later.

Chibaein	Ne, chibaein-imnida. Malssŭm hashijiyo.
Sonnim	I-hot'el sŏbisŭ-e munje-ga man-ŭn kŏt kat'ayo. Chigwon-dŭr-i pulch'injŏl ha-go muttukttuk haeyo. Kŭrigo onŭl ach'im-e shiktang-e kannŭnde ŭmshig-i ta shigŏ issŏssŏyo. Ŏje-do mach'angaji-yŏt-goyo.
Chibaein	Kŭraeyo? Chŏngmal choesong hamnida. Weit'ŏ-hant'e malssŭm hashyŏssŭmnikka?
Sonnim	Mullon chongŏbwon agasshi-hant'e yaegi haetjiyo. Kŭrŏnde agasshi-ga pulch'inchŏlha-ndedaga che hangung mar-ŭl mot aradŭt-ket-tago ha-myŏnsŏ ŭmshig-e amu munje-ga ŏp-tago haessŏyo. Ŭmshig-i ta shig-ŏt-ko mash-i ŏmnŭnde-do mar-ieyo.
Chibaein	A, chŏngmal choesong hamnida. Hangsang ch'oesŏn-ŭy pongsa-rŭl ha-ryŏgo noryŏk hanŭnde-do kakkŭm shilsu-ga palsaeng hamnida. Chega chŭkshi shiktang chongŏbwon-dŭr-ege yaegi ha-gessŭmnida.
Sonnim	Kŭrigo tto issŏyo. Onŭl ach'im sugŏn-ŭl kara-dallago haennŭnde sugŏn-i nŏmu tŏrŏwossŏyo. Kŭrigo nae adŭl pang-ŭn ajik-kkaji ch'ŏngso-do an haessŏyo.

Chibaein	Kŭ-gŏt ch'am isang ha-gunyo. Sonnim ch'ŏrŏm pulp'yŏng hanŭn kyŏngu-ga chigŭm-kkaji ŏpsŏnnŭndeyo.
Sonnim	Kŭ-gŏt-ppun-i anieyo. Nae pang-ŭy t'ellebijyŏn-ŭn kojang nat-ko naengjanggo mun-ŭn yŏlli-ji-do anayo. Soljikhi mal hae-sŏ i-hot'el sŏbisŭ-hago shisŏr-ŭn ŏngmang-i-neyo.
Chibaein	Choesong hamnida. Kŭrŏch'iman chŏhŭy-do sonnim-ch'ŏrŏm pulp'yŏng manŭn saram-ŭn p'iryo ŏps-ŭnikka onŭl tangjang naga-juseyo. Yogŭm-ŭn tashi hwanpul hae-dŭrigessŭmnida.

Phrases and expressions

... -e taehaesŏ ha-l mar-i issŏyo	*I have something to say about ...*
	there's something I want to say about ...
chŏ-hant'e malssŭm ha-shimyŏn an toelkkayo?	*wouldn't it be all right to tell me?*
	can't you just tell me?
ŏje-do mach'angaji-yŏtgoyo	*it was exactly the same yesterday as well*
mot ara-dŭt-ket-tago ha-	*say that (one) couldn't understand*
amu munje ŏp-tago haessŏyo	*(she) said that there wasn't any problem*
mashi-ŏmnŭnde-do mar-ieyo	*I'm saying (emphasis!) that the food even tasted bad*
sugŏn-ŭl kara-tallago haessŏyo	*I asked (her) to change the towel*
solchikhi mal hae-sŏ	*honestly speaking; to tell the truth; in fact ...*

chibaein	지배인	*manager* (of hotel or facility)
sŏbisŭ	서비스	*service*
(*noun*)-e taehaesŏ	–에 대해서	*concerning* (noun), *about* (noun)

ha-l mal	할 말	*something to say*
malssŭm ha-	말씀하-	*speak, say* (of someone honorific, often in phrase **malssŭm haseyo!**)
malssŭm haseyo	말씀하세요	*please tell me, please say it* (honorific)
-e	-에	*about, concerning*
munje	문제	*problem*
chigwon	직원	*employee*
pulch'inchŏl ha-	불친절하-	*be unhelpful, be unkind, be impolite*
muttukttuk ha-	무뚝뚝하-	*be stubborn, be blunt*
shigŏ iss-	식어 있-	*be bad, have gone off, cold, be stale etc.*
mach'angaji-eyo	마찬가지에요	*be the same, be identical*
weit'ŏ	웨이터	*waiter*
yaegi ha-	애기하-	*talk, tell*
-nŭndedaga	-는데다가	*on top of* (clause ending, onto verbs, like the **-nŭnde** pattern)
ara-dŭl-	알아듣-	*understand* (**l/t** verb like **tul-**, *listen*; **ara-dŭrŏyo**, **ara-dŭt-ko** etc.)
... tago ha-	-다고 하-	*saying* (this pattern shows quoted speech; see note 4)
-myŏnsŏ	-면서	*while* (see note 5)
shik-	식-	*get cold*
mash-i ŏps-	맛이 없-	*be tasteless, be unpleasant (to eat)*
noryŏk ha-	노력하-	*make effort, strive*
shilsu	실수	*mistake*
shilsu ha-	실수하-	*make a mistake*
palsaeng ha-	발생하-	*occur, happen*

QUICK VOCAB

chŭkshi	즉시	*immediately*
sugŏn	수건	*towel*
kal-	갈-	*change (a towel, a platform, clothes etc.)*
kara-ip-	갈아입-	*change clothes*
kara-t'a-	갈아타-	*change (platform, trains etc.)*
tŏrŏp-	더럽-	*be dirty (polite: **tŏrŏwoyo**, p-verb like **kakkap-** etc.)*
ajik	아직	*yet, still*
ch'ŏngso ha-	청소하-	*clean, clean up*
ch'am	참	*very*
-ch'ŏrŏm	-처럼	*like*
pulp'yŏng ha-	불평하-	*complain*
kyŏngu	경우	*circumstance, situation (here: occurrence*
-ppun	-뿐	*only*
kojang na-	고장나-	*break down*
kojang nassŏyo	고장났어요	*be broken down*
naengjanggo	냉장고	*refrigerator*
mun	문	*door*
yolli-ji an(h)-	열리지 않-	*does not open*
ŏngmang	엉망	*rubbish, awful, appalling*
tangjang	당장	*immediately*
yogŭm	요금	*fee*
hwanpul ha-	환불하-	*reimburse*

Grammar 22

1 Concerning

You can say what you are talking, discussing, writing or reading about in Korean with the construction –에 대해서 (-e taehaesŏ) which is added to the noun which describes what it is you are talking about. Here are some examples:

정치에 대해서 이야기했어요
(chŏngch'i-e taehaesŏ iyagi haessŏyo)
(we) talked about politics

서비스에 대해서 불평했어요
(sŏbisŭ-e taehaesŏ pulp'yŏng haessŏyo)
(he) complained about the service

날씨에 대해서 물어봤어요
(nalssi-e taehaesŏ murŏ-bwassŏyo)
(he) asked about the weather

2 The future modifier

We have already taught you a bit about the future modifier
-(으)ㄹ(-[ŭ]l) and here is the opportunity to give you a few more examples, the first one taken from the dialogue. You will remember that modifiers are added to verbs which then modify or describe the noun which they precede. We've put the modifier phrase in brackets to help you spot the pattern, and likewise its literal meaning in English:

서비스에 대해서 (할 말이) 있어요
(sŏbisŭ-e taehaesŏ (ha-l mar-i) issŏyo)
(words to say) I've got some things to say about the service

(갈 시간이) 됐어요
([ka-l shigan-i] twaessŏyo)?
(time to go) is it time to go? (lit. *has it become time to go?*)

집에 (먹을 것이) 있어요
(chib-e (mŏg-ŭl kŏsh-i) issŏyo)?
(thing to eat) is there anything to eat at home?

3 On top of that

You have learned the word 게다가(**kedaga**) which means *on top of that* and you can use a similar form to add to verbs. You use the −(으)ㄴ데(**-[ŭ]nde**) or −는데(**-nŭnde**) imminent elaboration form plus −다가(**-daga**), so that the completed forms look like 좋은데다가(**cho-ŭndedaga**) (*on top of being good*); 가는데다가 (**ka-nŭndedaga**) (*on top of going*) and so on. Here are two examples in sentences:

이 옷이 질이 좋은데다가 싸요
(**I-osh-i chir-i cho-ŭndedaga ssayo**)
These clothes are good quality and, on top of that, they're cheap

비가 오는데다가 추워요
(**Pi-ga o-nŭndedaga ch'uwoyo**)
It's raining and, on top of that, it's cold

4 Quotations and reported speech

This unit introduces you to the rather complicated matter of reported speech in Korean. Reported speech is when you say what someone else said to you. For example, 'He said *he was going* to the shops.' What the person said literally, of course, was 'I'm going to the shops', but when we report what someone said we change it to something like, 'He said he was going to the shops.' This section is designed so that you will be able to recognize reported speech in Korean and use some of the forms yourself. It is not designed to teach reported speech comprehensively. If you wish to know more, you should consult an advanced grammar book. What we tell you here is more than you need to get by.

To report speech in Korean you use the plain style of the verb: 먹는다(**mŏng-nunda**), 산다(**sanda**), 간다(**kanda**), 좋다(**chot'a**) etc., plus −고 하−(**-ko ha-**). Remember that the plain style can be formed on any verb stem – past present or future, and honorifics. Here are three examples: the first sentence gives you what the person actually said, the second one gives the reported speech form, 'he said' or 'he says':

나는 집에 가요
(na-nŭn chib-e kayo)
I'm going home

집에 간다고 해요
(chib-e kanda-go haeyo) (plain style of
가– = 간다)
he says he's going home

사람들이 많습니다
(saram-dŭr-i mansŭmnida)
there are a lot of people

사람들이 많다고 했어요
(saram-dŭr-i mant'a-go haessŏyo) (plain style of 많– = 많다)
he said there were a lot of people

날씨가 좋았어요
(nalsshi-ga choassŏyo)
the weather was good
(Mr Kim speaking)

김 선생님이 날씨가 좋았다고 했어요
(Kim sŏnsaengnim-i nalssi-ga choat-tago haessŏyo) (plain style past of 좋– = 좋았다)
Mr Kim said that the weather had been good

Note that suggestions and commands can be quoted in the same way:

집에 갑시다
(chib-e kapshida)
let's go home

집에 가자고 했어요
(chib-e kaja-go haessŏyo)
(가자 = plain style suggestion of 가–)
he suggested we go home

밥 먹어라
(pap mŏgŏra)
eat your food!

밥 먹으라고 했어요
(pap mŏg-ŭrago haessdyo)
he told (him/me) to eat his/my food

Questions are a little more complicated and you only need to be able to recognize them as having –냐–(-nya-) or –느냐–(-nunya-) in them: you will then know what they are when someone uses the form.

Insight

To report what someone said, put the verb in the plain style, and add –고 했어요 (-ko haessŏyo) to the end.

5 While

You can say that you are doing something while you are doing something else by adding –(으)면서(-[ŭ]myŏnsŏ) to the 'while' clause. For example, to say that you were talking (while you watched TV), you would say: 텔레비젼을 보면서 이야기했어요(t'ellebijyŏn-ŭl po-myŏnsŏ iyagi haessŏyo). Here are a couple of other examples.

한국말 배우면서 음악을 들어요
(Hangung mal paeu-myŏnsŏ ŭmag-ul turŏyo)
I listen to music while I study Korean

먹으면서 말해 보세요
(Mŏg-ŭmyŏnsŏ mal hae-boseyo)
Please tell me while you're eating

6 Even though: –는데도(-nŭnde-do)

You have learned the imminent elaboration form –는데(-nŭnde) which indicates that you have not finished what you are saying yet and that there is more to come. You have also learned –도(-do), added to the polite style minus –요(-yo) to mean *even though*. The combined 도 form –는데도(-nŭndedo) also means *even though* (*so and so*), but has a stronger emphasis than simply –도. Thus, 노력하는데도 가끔 실수가 발생합니다(noryŏk ha-nŭnde-do kakkŭm shilsu-ga palsaeng hamnida) (from the dialogue) means *even though we (really) are trying, occasionally mistakes happen.*

The other –는데도 form from the dialogue is a way of putting special emphasis on what you have just said. You saw it in the phrase 음식이 다 식었고 맛이 없는데도 말이에요(ŭmshig-i ta

shig-ŏt-go mash-i ŏmnŭnde-do marieyo). The waiter had just told Mr Lee that there was no problem with the food, and then Mr Lee adds: *even though (despite the fact that) the food was off and was tasteless.* The 말이에요(**mar-ieyo**) bit on the end means something like *that's what I'm saying* and adds strong emphasis to what has just been said.

7 Quoted requests

Back to reported speech again. When you ask something to be done for your benefit (by using a compound verb with 주-(**chu-**), as in 해주세요(**hae-juseyo**) (*please do it for me*) and then report what you have just said, as in *I asked him to (do it for me)*, there is a special rule to remember. Instead of saying something like (해주라고 [**hae-ju-rago**]) 했어요(**haessŏyo**), you swop the verb 주-(**chu-**) and the -라-(**-ra-**) which follows it with the verb 달라 (**talla**), to give 해 달라고 했어요(**hae-dallago haessŏyo**) (*I asked him to do it for me*).

You saw this in the phrase 수건을 갈아달라고 했는데도… (**sugŏn-ŭl karadallago haennŭndedo …**) (*I asked her to change the towels for me …*). Do not worry about this pattern; this note is merely to explain what is going on in the dialogue and to enable you to recognize the form.

Practice

1 You are thinking of sending your children to a new school in Korea and you have a meeting with one of the teachers to chat about the school. Before you go, you jot down some questions you want to ask about the school. Can you put them into Korean in full sentences?

  a *How many students?* (학생: *student*)
  b *What facilities?*

c *Is it possible to study Korean and Chinese?*
d *How many students studying Korean?* (*how many*: 몇 명)
e *What time is lunch?*
f *Is it okay to go home to eat at lunchtime?*

2 You go to make a booking at a hotel with the following requirements. The receptionist asks you the following questions, for which you must prepare answers in Korean.

a 뭘 도와드릴까요?
b 침대방 드릴까요?
c 아이들이 몇 살이에요? (아이: *child*)
d 얼마 동안 묵으시겠어요?
e 아침 식사 배달해드릴까요?

3 Put the following sentences into the formal style.

a 무엇을 하셨어요?
b 침대방 하나 주세요.
c 저 사람은 김 선생님이세요?
d 나는 백화점에 간다.
e 라디오를 들으면서 책을 읽어요.

4 Translate the following sentences into English.

a 일주일 이상 예약하시면 10% 할인해드립니다.
b 솔직히 말해서 그런 사람을 싫어해요.
c 아침 벌써 먹었다고 했어요.
d 온돌방은 하루에 이만원이에요.
e 일곱시에 일어나시면 됩니다.
f 요금은 다시 환불해드릴 수 없습니다.
g 침대방 두 개 주세요.
h 이 호텔에 대해서 할 말이 있으시면 지배인한테 말해주세요.

5 Ask if there are the following facilities at the hotel at which you are staying.

6 Translate the following into Korean.

a *How long are you booking for?*
b *I told the bank clerk immediately.*
c *What facilities are there at the hotel?*
d *There seem to be a lot of problems with my car.*
e *My son still hasn't got up.*
f *We'll go straight to the bar and have a drink.*

g *Mr Kim is an impolite person.*

h *It would be a good idea to stay for three nights.*

7 Your hotel room has a few problems, as you can see in the picture. Write out a series of complaints, making your language as strong as you can.

TEN THINGS TO REMEMBER

1 Asking for a room/checking availability of accommodations

2 Checking if breakfast is included

3 Responding when someone asks how long you will be staying for

4 Asking what facilities a hotel has

5 The formal style – what it is and how to recognize it

6 The future particle and modifier

7 How to ask for the manager

8 How to complain

9 How to say *the food was cold and the service was bad!*

10 The expression to say that something does or doesn't work/is broken

13

Two to Taegu/I don't want to go there!

In this unit you will learn

- *how to buy train tickets*
- *how to ask for information about catching the train you want*
- *how to discuss going out for meals and drinks together*

Two to Taegu

◆) CD 1, TR 13

매표원	뭘 도와드릴까요?
박선생	오늘 저녁 대구 가는 기차가 있나요?
매표원	네, 두 가지가 있는데요, 완행은 5 시 30 분이고 직행은 7 시 45 분이에요.
박선생	시간은 얼마나 걸려요?
매표원	직행은 3 시간 걸리고, 완행은 4 시간 30 분 걸립니다.
박선생	가격은요?
매표원	완행은 만 팔천원이고, 직행은 사만 오천원입니다.
	직행은 좌석이 얼마 남지 않았습니다.
박선생	네 자리를 함께 예약할 수 있을까요?

매표원	잠깐만 기다려보세요. 확인 좀
	해보겠습니다.
	아, 네. 네 자리가 있군요!
	흡연석을 원하세요, 금연석을
	원하세요?
박선생	금연석으로 부탁합니다.
매표원	편도를 드릴까요, 왕복을 드릴까요?
박선생	왕복으로 주세요.
매표원	언제 돌아오시겠어요?
박선생	일요일 저녁에요.
매표원	6 시 30 분 기차가 있는데, 완행이에요.
	일요일 저녁에는 직행 기차는
	없는데요.
박선생	그러면 일요일 오후에는요?
매표원	2 시 30 분에 직행 기차가 있어요.
박선생	그거 좋군요. 그걸로 주세요.
매표원	모두 삼십육만원입니다.
박선생	몇 번 홈에서 기차가 떠나지요?
매표원	아직 모릅니다. 출발 시간 전에
	전광판을 봐주세요.
박선생	네, 알겠어요. 고맙습니다.

Maep'yowon	Mwol towa-dŭrilkkayo?
Mr Pak	Onŭl chŏnyŏk Taegu kanŭn kich'a-ga innayo?
Maep'yowon	Ne. Tu kaji-ga innŭndeyo. Wanhaeng-ŭn
	tasŏt-shi samship-pun-igo chikhaeng-ŭn
	ilgop-shi sashibo-bun-ieyo.
Mr Pak	Shigan-ŭn ŏlma-na kŏllyŏyo?
Maep'yowon	Chikhaeng-ŭn se shigan kŏlli-go,
	wanhaeng-ŭn ne shigan samship-pun
	kŏllimnida.
Mr Pak	Kagyŏg-ŭn-yo?

Maep'yowon	Wanhaeng-ŭn man p'alch'ŏn won-igo, chikhaeng-ŭn samman och'ŏn won-imnida. Chikhaeng-ŭn chwasŏg-i ŏlma nam-ji anassŭmnida.
Mr Pak	Ne chari-rŭl hamkke yeyak ha-l su iss-ŭlkkayo?
Maep'yowon	Chamkkan-man kidaryŏ-boseyo. Hwagin chom hae-bogessŭmnida. A, ne. Ne chari-ga it-kunyo. Hŭbyŏnsŏg-ŭl wonhaseyo, kŭmyŏnsŏg-ŭl wonhaseyo?
Mr Pak	Kŭmyŏnsŏg-ŭro put'ak hamnida.
Maep'yowon	P'yŏndo-rŭl tŭrilkkayo? Wangbog-ŭl tŭrilkkayo?
Mr Pak	Aniyo. Wangbog-ŭro chuseyo.
Maep'yowon	Ŏnje tora-oshigessŏyo?
Mr Pak	Iryoil chŏnyŏg-eyo.
Maep'yowon	Yŏsŏt-shi samship-pun kich'a-ga innŭnde, wanhaeng-ieyo. Iryoil chŏnyŏg-enŭn chikhaeng kich'a-nŭn ŏmnŭndeyo.
Mr Pak	Kŭrŏmyŏn iryoil ohu-nŭn-yo?
Maep'yowon	Tu-shi samship-pun-e chikhaeng kich'a-ga issŏyo.
Mr Pak	Kŭ-gŏ cho-k'unyo. Kŭ-gŏllo chuseyo.
Maep'yowon	Modu samshimyuk man won-imnida.
Mr Pak	Myŏt pŏn hom-esŏ kich'a-ga ttŏna-jiyo?
Maep'yowon	Ajik morŭmnida. Ch'ulbal shigan jŏn-e chŏnkwangp'an-ŭl pwa-juseyo.
Mr Pak	Ne, algessŏyo. Komapsumnida.

Phrases and expressions

mwol towa-dŭrilkkayo?   *how can I help you?*
olma nam-ji anassŭmnida   *there are only a few left*

QUICK VOCAB

Taegu	대구	*a Korean city*
wanhaeng	완행	*slow train (also called* **mugunghwa**)
chikhaeng	직행	*fast train, express train (also called* **saemaŭl[ho]**)

kagyŏk	가격	*price*
chwasŏk	좌석	*seating, places*
nam-	남-	*be left* (over), *remain*
chari	자리	*seat*
hamkke	함께	*together*
hwagin ha-	확인하-	*check, confirm*
hŭbyŏnsŏk	흡연석	*smoker* (compartment)
kŭmyŏnsŏk	금연석	*no smoking compartment*
wonha-	원하-	*want, require*
put'ak ha-	부탁하-	*make a request*
p'yŏndo	편도	*single*
wangbok	왕복	*return*
hom	홈	*platform*
ch'ulbal	출발	*departure*
ch'ulbal ha-	출발하-	*depart*
chŏngwangp'an	전광판	*electronic notice board*
pwa-juseyo	봐주세요	*please look at*

Grammar 23

1 –을까요 (-ŭlkkayo) *To ask questions*

In some of the earlier units of this course you learned –을까요 (-ŭlkkayo) as a pattern meaning *shall we?* As you will have seen in this unit, it is also sometimes used to ask a question: 네 자리를 함께 예약할 수 있을까요(ne chari-rŭl hamkke yeyak ha-l su issŭlkkayo)? (*is it possible to book four seats together?*). There are several patterns like this in Korean where certain verb endings do not always have their basic meaning. The context will always make clear to you which is the correct meaning and in most cases –(으)ㄹ까요 does mean *shall we?* and is used to make suggestions.

2 Making requests

Koreans have a word for *favour* (as in *do a favour for someone*), 부탁(**put'ak**) and you saw it used in the sentence 금연석으로 부탁합니다(**kŭmyŏnsŏg-ŭro put'ak hamnida**). To say *I have a favour to ask*, you say either 제가) 부탁 있어요([**che-ga**] **put'ak issŏyo**) and then say what the request is or else say the request, and then add 부탁합니다(**put'ak hamnida**) or 부탁해요(**put'ak haeyo**) (*please, I ask you to do it as a favour*).

3 Before and after

You have already learned the nouns 전(**chŏn**) and 후(**hu**) which mean *before* and *after*, respectively. They can be used with nouns, as in 출발 시간 전에(**ch'ulbal shigan jŏn-e**) (*before the time of departure*), or 식사 후에(**shiksa hu-e**) (*after the meal*). They can also be used with verbs, although in a slightly different way.

To say *before* (verb) you add –기 전에(**-ki jŏn-e**) to the stem, as in the following examples: 시작하기 전에(**shijak ha-gi jŏn-e**) (*before we begin ...*) or 학교에 가기 전에(**hakkyo-e ka-gi jŏn-e**) (*before (I/you) go to school*).

To say *after* (verb) you add ‑(으)ㄴ 후에(**-[ŭ]n hu-e**) (or ‑(으)ㄴ 다음에(**-[ŭ]n taum-e**), which has the same meaning) to the verb stem of a processive verb. This ‑(으)ㄴ is the past modifier which you have already learned (the present modifier, you will recall, is ‑는, as in 가는), e.g. 먹은 후에(**mŏg-ŭn hu-e**) (*after eating*); 학교에 간 다음에(**hakkyo-e ka-n taum-e**) (*after going to school*).

In the next dialogue there is more new grammar, but the most important thing is the colloquial language that is used. There are several examples of constructions being used in ways similar to, but not quite the same as, what you have seen before and your aim should be to get the drift of what is going on, and not to be put off by the colloquialisms and (at times) seeming lack of grammar rules! This is what it will be like when you first go to Korea and listen to Koreans talking to each other. With a little practice at concentrating on the drift of what is being said, you will find that the Korean you have learned in this course will stand you in good stead.

I don't want to go there!

◀) **CD 1, TR 13, 02:15**

Some colleagues are discussing what they will do after work.

윤선생	오늘 저녁 일 끝나고 뭐 할 거에요?
백선생	일 끝나고요? 모르겠어요. 아직 계획 없어요.
윤선생	저녁이나 같이 먹으러 갈까요?
백선생	좋은 생각이네요. 그런데 우리 둘만 가요?
윤선생	다른 사람도 부르지요. 김 선생하고 이 선생한테 얘기해볼까요?

백선생	좋지요. 어이, 김 선생, 이 선생! 오늘 저녁 밥 먹으면서 소주 한 잔 어때요?
김선생	좋아요. 그런데 어디로 갈 거에요?
윤선생	글쎄요, 그냥 불고기하고 소주 한잔 하려고요. 그리고 나서 노래방에도 가고요.
김선생	술 마시는 건 좋은데, 저는 불고기는 별로에요. 그리고 노래하는 건 딱 질색이에요.
백선생	아, 그럼 불고기 말고 다른 거 먹으면 되잖아요. 그리고 노래하지 말고 그냥 듣기만 하세요.
김선생	그거 괜찮은 생각이네요. 그런데 오늘 돈이 별로 없는데....
윤선생	걱정 마세요. 오늘 저녁은 내가 한턱 낼게요.
김선생	아 그럼, 좋습니다.
백선생	이 선생은 어때요? 같이 가시겠어요?
이선생	글쎄요, 저도 가고 싶은데, 저는 인천에 가서 싱싱한 생선회를 먹고 싶은데요.
백선생	에이, 인천은 너무 멀어요. 그리고 생선회는 요즘 너무 비싸고요.
윤선생	게다가 저는 생선회를 못 먹어요.
이선생	좋아요, 좋아. 그냥 해본 소리에요. 오늘은 저도 따라가서 불고기에 소주나 먹을 수밖에 없겠네요.

Mr Yun	Onŭl chŏnyŏk il kkŭnna-go mwo ha-l kŏeyo?
Mr Paek	Il kkŭnna-go-yo? Morŭgessŏyo. Ajik kyehoek ŏpsŏyo.
Mr Yun	Chŏnyŏk-ina kach'i mŏg-ŭrŏ ka-lkkayo?
Mr Paek	Cho-ŭn saenggag-ineyo. Kŭrŏnde uri tŭl-man kayo?
Mr Yun	Tarŭn saram-do purŭ-jiyo. Kim sŏnsaeng-hago I sŏnsaeng-hant'e yaegi hae-bolkkayo?
Mr Paek	Cho-ch'iyo. Ŏi, Kim sŏnsaeng, I sŏnsaeng! Onŭl chŏnyŏk pap mŏg-ŭmyŏnsŏ soju han jan ŏttaeyo?
Mrs Kim	Choayo. Kŭrŏnde ŏdi ka-l kŏeyo?
Mr Yun	Kŭlsseyo. Kŭnyang pulgogi-hago soju han jan ha-ryŏgoyo. Kŭrigo nasŏ noraebang-e-do ka-go-yo.
Mrs Kim	Sul mashinŭn kŏn cho-ŭnde chŏ-nŭn pulgogi-nŭn pyŏllo-eyo. Kŭrigo norae hanŭn kŏn ttak chilsaeg-ieyo.
Mr Paek	A, kŭrŏm pulgogi malgo tarŭn kŏ mŏg-ŭmyŏn toe-janayo. Kŭrigo norae ha-ji malgo kŭnyang tŭt-kiman haseyo.
Mrs Kim	Kŭ-gŏ koench'anŭn saenggag-ineyo. Kŭrŏnde onŭl ton-i pyŏllo ŏmnŭnde …
Mr Yun	Kŏkchŏng maseyo. Onŭl chŏnyŏg-ŭn nae-ga han t'ŏk nae-lgeyo.
Mrs Kim	A, kŭrŏm. Chosŭmnida.
Mr Paek	I sŏnsaeng-ŭn ŏttaeyo? Kach'i kashigessŏyo?
Mrs Lee	Kŭlsseyo. Chŏ-do ka-go ship'ŭnde, chŏ-nŭn Inch'ŏn-e ka-sŏ shingshing han saengsŏn hoe-rŭl mŏk-ko ship'ŭndeyo.
Mr Paek	Ei, Inch'ŏn-ŭn nŏmu mŏrŏyo. Kŭrigo saengsŏn hoe-nŭn yojŭm nŏmu pissa-goyo.
Mr Yun	Kedaga chŏ-nŭn saengsŏn hoe-rŭl mon mŏgŏyo.
Mrs Lee	Choayo. Choa. Kŭnyang hae-bon sori-eyo. Onŭr-ŭn chŏ-do ttara-ga-sŏ pulgogi-e soju-na mŏg-ŭl su pakk-e ŏpkenneyo.

Phrases and expressions

il kkŭnnago

after finishing work

ajik kyehoek ŏpsŏyo

I don't have any plans yet

cho-ŭn saenggag-ineyo		*that's a good idea*
uri tŭl-man kayo?		*is it just the two of us going?*
kŭnyang soju han jan haryŏgoyo		*we were just thinking of having a soju*
chŏ-nŭn pulgogi-nŭn pyŏllo-eyo		*I don't really like pulgogi*
norae hanŭn kŏn ttak chilsaeg-ieyo		*I really hate singing*
norae ha-ji malgo tŭt-kiman haseyo		*don't sing, just listen instead*
kŭnyang hae-bon sori-eyo		*I was just saying it (don't take it too seriously)*
soju-na mŏg-ŭl su pakk-e ŏp-kenneyo		*there's nothing for it (no alternative) but to eat soju*
han t'ŏk naelgeyo		*I'll pay (for everyone); it's on me*

QUICK VOCAB

kyehoek	계획	plan(s)
purŭ-	부르–	call
ŏi	어이!	hey! (used to call close friends and colleagues)
pap mŏk-	밥 먹–	have a meal
kŭnyang	그냥	simply, just
kŭrigo nasŏ	그리고 나서	after that
-ko nasŏ	–고 나서	after (added to verb stems)
pyŏllo	별로	not particularly, not really (fond of)
ttak chilsaeg-ieyo	딱 질색이에요	hate, is awful (to me)
(noun) malgo	말고	not (noun), instead of (noun) (when suggesting an alternative)
-kiman haseyo	–기만 하세요	just do (verb)
pyŏllo ŏps-	별로 없–	have almost none, scarcely have any
inch'ŏn	인천	Korean port near Seoul
sshingshing ha-	싱싱하–	be fresh
saengsŏn	생선	fish

hoe	회	*raw meat*	
ei	에이	*hey, come off it!*	
kedaga	게다가	*on top of that*	
ttarŭ-	따르–	*follow*	
-(ŭ)l su pakk-e ŏps-	–(으)ㄹ 수 밖에 없–	*there is nothing for it but to* (verb)	

Grammar 24

1 *More ways of saying 'afterwards'*

You can add the ending –고 나서(-**ko na-sŏ**) to any present tense processive verb base to mean *after* (verb):

일하고 나서 술 한 잔 합시다(**Il ha-go na-sŏ sul hanjan hapshida**)
After finishing work let's have a drink

–고 나서 can be abbreviated to –고서(-**kosŏ**), and sometimes even to just –고.

2 *Informal sentences*

This dialogue shows the way in which Koreans can add particles to the end of verbs in colloquial speech to give extra nuances to what they are saying. They can also make incomplete sentences which they complete simply by adding the polite particle –요(-**yo**). You do not need to worry about learning rules for this kind of thing, since in most circumstances you will want to use a more formal and grammatical style of speaking when you begin to speak Korean in Korea. It is very useful to recognize what is going on in colloquial speech, however, and as you spend more time speaking with Koreans you will quickly learn to do this kind of thing for yourself.

You can miss out the rest of this section if you wish, as
the explanation may seem a bit complicated. Your main
task should be to completely familiarize yourself with the
dialogue, almost to the extent of being able to say it by
heart. For the adventurous, however, here are two sentences
from the dialogue with an explanation of how they have
been constructed.

소주 한 잔 하려고요 (Soju han jan haryŏgoyo)

You have previously met the -(으)려고(-[ŭ]ryŏgo) pattern,
with the meaning *with the intention of*. Normally it is used in
the pattern (clause A)-**ŭryŏgo** (clause B), as in 한국말 배우려고
책 샀어요(hangung mal paeu-ryŏgo ch'aek sassŏyo), but here
the pattern is simply (clause A)-**uryŏgo-yo**. Clause B has been
omitted in casual speech and the polite particle added to round the
construction off. The full form would have been something like
소주 한잔 하려고 어느 술집이나 갈까 해요(soju han jan haryŏgo
ŏnŭ sulchib-ina kalkka haeyo) (*we were thinking of going to some
pub or other to have a drink*), but this is cut down to what would
translate as *to have a drink* – or, in better English, *we were just
thinking of going for a drink* and is made into a sentence simply be
adding -요 to the -(으)려고 pattern.

그리고 나서 노래방에도 가고요 **(Kŭrigo na-sŏ norae-bang-e-do ka-go-yo)**

This means *after that (we were thinking of) going to a* noraebang *too*. The −고 at the end is the clause ending −고 that normally means *and* when you are going to add another clause. However, in this case, the meaning is *as well, in addition*. This sentence is being added to the one that has been said previously to indicate that this is also part of the plan as well. Then the particle -요 is added to round it all off.

3 Negatives with 별로 **(pyŏllo)**

Sentences with negative verbs in them (with 안 and 못) can be modified by inserting the word 별로 **(pyŏllo)** in them, to mean *not particularly*. This will be clearer with examples:

고기를 별로 안 좋아해요 **(kogi-rŭl pyŏllo an choa haeyo)**
I don't particularly like meat

별로 가고 싶지 않아요 **(pyŏllo ka-go ship'chi anayo)**
I don't particularly want to go

별로 재미 없어요 **(pyŏllo chaemi ŏpsŏyo)**
it's not particularly interesting

The dialogue also has a 별로 sentence in it, which is slightly different. 저는 불고기는 별로에요 **(chŏ-nŭn pulgogi-nŭn pyŏllo-eyo)**. This is a more colloquial form, putting the copula onto the end of the word 별로. But you can see that it is in a sense an abbreviated form of 저는 불고기는 별로 좋아하지 않아요 **(chŏ-nŭn pulgogi-nŭn pyŏllo choa ha-ji anayo)**, so the pattern is essentially the same. You should stick to the full form with a negative verb most of the time and leave the colloquial, abbreviated form to native speakers.

Insight

The term 별로 (**pyŏllo**), with a negative verb, is a very useful
term which has the meaning of *(not) particularly*.

4 Not one thing, but another instead

You can stay *instead of* (noun), or *not* (noun) by putting the
word 말고(**malgo**) after the noun, as you can see in these
examples:

사과 말고 고기 삽시다(**sagwa malgo kogi sa-pshida**)
*Let's not buy apples, let's buy meat; instead of apples, let's
buy meat*

잡지 말고 신문을 읽는 거 좋아해요(**chapji malgo shinmun-
ŭl ing-nŭn kŏ choa haeyo**)
It's not magazines, it's newspapers I enjoy reading

불국사 말고 산에 가는 게 어때요(**pulguksa malgo san-e
ka-nŭn ke ŏttaeyo**)?
How about going to the mountain instead of Pulguksa?

You can use a similar pattern to say *instead of* (verb). Simply add
−지 말고(**-ji malgo**) (this is the same −지[**-ji**] that you use in the
long negative, or in −지 마세요(**-ji maseyo**)). Look at the following
examples, the first is from the dialogue:

노래하지 말고 듣기만 하세요(**norae ha-ji malgo tut-kiman
haseyo**)
Don't sing (do a song), just listen (instead)

커피 마시지 말고 차나 드세요(**k'ŏp'i mashi-ji malgo ch'a-na
tuseyo**)
Don't drink coffee, have some tea or something instead

왜 공부하지 말고 이야기만 하라고 해요(wae kongbu ha-ji malgo iyagi-man hara-go haeyo)?
Why are you staying just talking and not studying (instead)?

5 Just doing something

The sentence 듣기만 하세요(tŭt-kiman haseyo) means *just listen!* The form -기만 하-(-kiman ha-) added to processive verbs means *just* (verb) or *only* (verb). Here are examples:

말하지 않고 먹기만 했어요(mal ha-ji an-k'o mŏk-kiman haessŏyo)
We didn't say anything, we just ate

듣기만 해요(tŭt-kiman haeyo)?
Are you only listening (rather than participating)?

6 There's nothing for it, but to...

When you feel you have no option but to do something or other, or that you are obliged to do something, you can use the pattern -(으)ㄹ 수밖에 없-(-[ŭ]l su pakk-e ŏps-). Here are examples:

갈 수밖에 없어요(Ka-l su pakk-e ŏpsŏyo)
There's nothing for it but to go; I'll have to go

비싸지만 살 수밖에 없어요(Pissa-jiman sa-l su pakk-e ŏpsŏyo)
Although it's expensive, there's nothing for it but to buy it

Insight

The form -(으)ㄹ 수밖에 없어요 (-[ŭ]l su pakk-e ŏpsŏyo) is used to mean *there's nothing for it but to...* or *I'm going to have to ...* It's a relatively common form, and worth remembering.

Practice

1 Translate the following sentences into English.

a 좌석이 얼마 남지 않았어요.
b 다른 거 먹으면 안돼요.
c 왕복을 드릴까요?
d 등산하는 건 딱 질색이에요.
e 제가 갈 수밖에 없겠네요.
f 그냥 야구하려고요.
g 오늘 오후 목포에 가는 기차 있어요?
h 그거 괜찮은 생각이네요.

2 For each of the following, say that you will go out *before* doing them and then that you will go out *after* doing them.

a *(Eating) lunch.*
b *Telephoning your mother.*
c *Having fun* (놀-[**nol-**]).
d *Reading the newspaper.*

3 Look at the following information about train availability and then answer the questions.

열차(기차) 시간표			
목적지	출발	도착	
서울	8:00	11:00	직행
대구	20:00	23:30	직행
부산	7:00	12:00	완행
광주	13:00	18:00	완행
서울	10:00	15:00	완행
대전	14:00	16:00	직행

a 밤 늦게 대구에 가고 싶어요. 기차가 몇 시에
출발해요?
b 서울에 가는 직행은 몇 시에 떠나요?
c 언제 도착해요?
d 대전에 가는 완행 있어요?
e 부산에 가는 완행 기차 있어요?

4 Make up three sentences saying that there is nothing for it but
to …

  a *go home*
  b *pay the money*
  c *get up at six in the morning*

5 Make up a set of sentences, each one using the following sets
of information and using (noun)-말고 or (verb)-지 말고. For
example, for the first one you could make up a sentence which
said *I want to eat fruit, not meat.*

6 Translate the following sentences into Korean.

    a *Buy something to eat before the departure time.*
    b *Shall we have a talk to your parents?*
    c *I'd like to go, too, but it's a long way.*
    d *Can I book three seats together?*
    e *Let's go to Inchŏn, not to Seoul.*
    f *What shall we do after finishing work?*
    g *When are you going to come back?*
    h *Do you like eating raw fish?*

TEN THINGS TO REMEMBER

1 The terms for *before* and *after*

2 How to say you don't *particularly* want to go, or that you don't find something *particularly* interesting

3 The construction for *there's nothing for it but to ...*

4 Saying *instead of* (e.g. *let's buy apples instead of bananas*)

5 How to ask if there is a train to Pusan this evening

6 How to book four non-smoking seats together

7 How to ask what platform a train leaves from

8 How to ask how long a journey takes

9 Asking what someone is doing after work this evening

10 How to say you'll pay (for drinks or a meal)

14

....

Review

....

Introduction

So, you have virtually reached the end of this course. This
unit contains more exercises which practise the situations and
grammar you have been learning in the last six units. Most
of these exercises are Korean to English or English to Korean
translations, since that is the best way to check that you have
really mastered the material in the units. Make sure you are
comfortable with the topics in the list that follows and be sure
to revise the grammar notes for any of the major patterns you
are not quite happy with. It would be a good idea also to read
through all the dialogues in the units once again. You will find
there are things that you felt a bit uneasy about at the time that
are now clearer to you and you are sure to understand more fully
what is going on grammatically in the dialogues. Even though
you have reached the end of the course, you will find that simply
reading through the dialogues every so often will help you to
retain the things you have learned.

....

Topic revision

The following list shows the main topics that have been covered in
the last six units. You should feel capable of handling these topics at
a simple level should you need to when you are in Korea. If you feel

unsure about a particular topic, you should go over the dialogue again more thoroughly, and revise the expressions and vocabulary that go with it. Of course there will still be many things that you are not able to say in Korean, but with the tools we have given you you should be able to succeed in carrying out many language tasks, some at quite a high level, and should have a more fascinating and enjoyable experience as a result whenever you visit Korea or communicate with Korean people.

1 advanced phone conversations
2 cancelling appointments
3 dating and talking about other people
4 describing what you did
5 buying presents
6 retorting
7 police officers and traffic offences
8 lost property
9 describing objects
10 feeling ill
11 getting medicine
12 buying and comparing clothes
13 trying on clothes
14 booking into a hotel and asking about facilities
15 complaining
16 train journeys
17 arranging to go out

Practice

1 Translate the following into English.

a 어머니가 영화를 좋아하시니까 아버지 대신 극장에 가면 돼요.

b 스트레스가 원인인 것 같아요.

c 사실 아주 중요한 서류가 들어 있어요.

d 청바지가 못 쓰게 됐어요.

e 우리 집사람이 아마 알고 있을 거에요.

f 내일 저녁 일 끝내고 산에 갈 계획 있어요?

g 당신은 내 의견을 항상 좋아하지 않아요.

h 우리 방문은 열리지도 않아요.

i 도서관이 어디인지 좀 가르쳐 주시겠어요?
  (도서관 = *library*)

j 그렇게 술을 많이 마셨어요?

k 요즘 아주 유행하는 스타일이에요.

l 면허증 좀 보여주세요.

2 For each of the following pictures make up a question which asks if someone has ever tried doing them. Then make up an answer which says *yes, I have* and another which says *you did it yesterday, as a matter of fact*. (*dance*: 춤 추-)

3 Make up an appropriate response to the following questions or requests.

  a 김 선생님 좀 바꿔주세요.

  b 영화구경을 좋아하세요?

c 데이트할 때 보통 어디 가세요?
d 이 청바지 질이 어때요?
e 약속을 자주 취소하는 사람이세요?

4 Translate the following into Korean.

  a *I really didn't see the sign.*
  b *You can wear it with jeans.*
  c *I'm ringing to cancel my appointment.*
  d *Is there a telephone and TV in the room?*
  e *The service is rubbish!*
  f *We bought him socks last year.*
  g *It looks a bit small.*
  h *I thought so.*
  i *I'd like to go to Inchŏn and eat raw fish.*
  j *What does your car look like?*
  k *Would you write a letter for me?*
  l *My head hurts so much I can't sleep.*

5 Your friend has a new girlfriend and you quiz him about her. Make up questions to fill in the following fact file:

Name _____
Age _____
Occupation _____
Father's name _____
How met? _____
What do together? _____
Likes/Dislikes _____

6 Translate the following into English.

  a 잘못하면 아주 위험해요.
  b 복동씨한데 전할 말이 있어요?
  c 손님방까지 배달해드립니다.
  d 어제 여기 왔었는데요. 잠바를 놓고 갔어요.
  e 아가씨가 질이 좋다고 했어요.

f 여자 친구 생겨서 매일 나가는 것 같아요.

g 이야기하지 말고 듣기만 하세요.

h 식후에 한 알씩 하루 두 번 드세요.

i 이거 봐. 질이 별로 안 좋아.

j 혹시 어디 갔는지 아세요?

k 새 텔레비젼은 어떨까요?

l 남대문에서는 비슷한 게 두 배나 더 싸요.

7 Complete the following dialogue.

A 내일 저녁에 시간 있어요?

You *(No, an urgent matter has come up. Why?)*

A 그냥 나가고 싶었는데요.

You *(How about Monday?)*

A 월요일날은 아버지 생신이에요.

You *(Really? Will there be a party?)*

A 아니요. 그냥 식당에 가서 같이 저녁 하는 거에요.

You *(What are you going to buy for him?)*

A 양말요. 항상 양말 사요.

You *(How about Tuesday? Do you have time then?)*

A 네, 좋아요. 나이트 클럽 갈까요? (나이트 클럽: night club)

You *(That's a good idea.)*

8 Rewrite the dialogue in question 7 using the informal and plain styles of speech.

9 Put the following sentences into the formal style.

a 지금 어디 가세요?

b 주문했어요?

c 일곱시에 일어나요.

d 빨리 해주세요.

e 저 사람은 불친절한 사람이에요.

10 The following pictures tell what you did last Saturday. Write an account of what you did, putting in as many details as you can according to what the pictures suggest.

11 Translate the following into Korean.

a *I started meeting her often from that time.*
b *Don't be surprised even if you have no energy (strength).*
c *You help this time.*
d *Although it might look similar, it isn't.*
e *Be (more) careful from now on.*
f *We'll go straight to the restaurant and eat.*
g *It's turned out well then. Goodbye!*
h *This evening I'll pay.*
i *What time did you leave our department store?*
j *Mistakes do happen.*
k *Shall I introduce you?*
l *Would you like to try it on?*

Translation of dialogues

Unit 1

Where are you off to?

Sangmin	Jaemin! Hello/How are you!
Jaemin	Hello! How have you been getting along?
Sangmin	Fine, fine. Where are you going?
Jaemin	Right now I'm off to the city centre.
Sangmin	What are you going to do in the city centre?
Jaemin	I'm going to buy some bread.
Sangmin	I'm also going to buy bread in the city centre.
Jaemin	Let's go together!
Sangmin	Yes, let's.

Cheers!

Sangmin	Excuse me/Waiter! Do you have any soju?
Ajŏssi	Yes, yes. We have. Soju, beer, western spirits – all of them.
Sangmin	Well then, give us a beer and one soju, please.
Ajŏssi	Yes. I understand.
Sangmin	And we also need some snacks/side dishes. What do you have?
Ajŏssi	Fruit, squid, dry snacks, p'ajŏn – we've got all of those.
Sangmin	Then give me some fruit and some squid, please.
Ajŏssi	Here you are.
Sangmin	Thank you. Enjoy it! (Good appetite!)
Sangmin	Cheers!

Unit 2

Long time, no see!

Mr Pak	Mr Kim! How are you?
Mr Kim	Ah, Mr Pak! Hello there!
Mr Pak	Long time, no see!

Mr Kim	Yes, that's right. It's really been a long time.
Mr Pak	How have you been getting along?
Mr Kim	Yes, fine. How's business these days?
Mr Pak	It's so-so.
	This is my wife.

Mr Kim	Oh, really? Pleased to meet you. I've heard a lot about you.
Mr Pak's wife	Pleased to meet you. I'm Yunhuy Jang.
Mr Kim	I'm Jinyang Kim. I'm pleased that I've met you.

It's not me!

Mr O	Excuse me!
Mr Lee	Yes?
Mr O	Are you the Korean language teacher?
Mr Lee	No. I'm not a Korean language teacher. I'm a Japanese language teacher.
Mr O	Ah, I'm sorry. Isn't this the Korean department's office?
Mr Lee	No, this isn't the Korean department. This is the Japanese department.
Mr O	Right. Where is the Korean department office, please?
Mr Lee	It's over there.

Mr O	Excuse me, is this the Korean department's office?
Mr Kim	Yes. What brings you here? (Can I help you?)
Mr O	I've come to meet the Korean language teacher.

Unit 3

Sorry, wrong number!

Tony	Hello? I'm sorry, but can I speak to Mr Kim, please?
Mr Pak	There is no such person here.
Tony	Isn't that 389 2506?
Mr Pak	No. You've dialled the wrong number.
Tony	I'm sorry.

Tony	Hello? I'm sorry, but can I speak to Mr Kim, please?
Mr Kim's wife	Wait a moment, please.
Mr Kim	Yes? Speaking.
Tony	Ah, hello. I'm Tony from the British embassy.
Mr Kim	Ah, hello! Long time, no see!
Tony	Do you have any free time this lunchtime?
Mr Kim	Yes, I do.
Tony	Then I'd like to buy you lunch.
Mr Kim	Yes, fine. Let's meet at 12 in front of Lotte Hotel.
Tony	Great. So, I'll see you in a little while.

Are you ready to order yet?

Waiter	Welcome! Please take a seat over here.
Mr Kim	Thank you.
Waiter	Would you like anything to drink?
Mr Kim	We'll have some beer first, please.
Mr Kim	Do you like Korean food?
Tony	Yes, I like it a lot, but I can't eat spicy food so well.
Mr Kim	Then let's eat pulgogi or kalbi.
Tony	Yes, fine. And I'd like to eat some naengmyon as well.
Waiter	Would you like to order?
Tony	Pulgogi for two people and two dishes of naengmyon, please.
Waiter	Would you like water naengmyon or pibim naengmyon?
Tony	Water naengmyon, please.
Waiter	Enjoy your meal!
Tony	Waiter! More water and more kimchi, please.

Unit 4

How much is it altogether?

Assistant	What are you looking for?
Chris	Do you have dictionaries?

Assistant	Yes. A Korean dictionary?
Chris	Yes, I'd like both a Korean–English dictionary and an English–Korean dictionary.
Assistant	Here you are.
Chris	How much is it?
Assistant	Each volume is 10,000 won; 20,000 won all together.
Chris	Do you have Chinese character dictionaries also?
Assistant	We have three kinds of Chinese character dictionary.
Chris	The cheapest one, please.
Assistant	Just a moment ... here it is.
Chris	Thank you. How much is it altogether?
Assistant	The Chinese character dictionary is 30,000 won ... therefore altogether it's 50,000 won.
Chris	The cheapest one is 30,000 won? How much is the most expensive one, then?! 100,000 won?!
Assistant	Oh, I'm sorry; I've made a mistake. It's 30,000 won altogether. Would you like a receipt?
Chris	Yes please.
Assistant	Okay. Here it is. Goodbye!
Chris	Goodbye.

Finding the way

Mr Pak	Excuse me, can you tell me where the bank is around here?
Bank Clerk A	If you go left at that post office over there, there is the Sangŏp bank.
Mr Pak	Thank you.
Mr Pak	I'd like to change some English money into Korean money.
Bank Clerk B	We don't deal with foreign currency at this bank. Please go to the Korea Exchange Bank.
Mr Pak	Where is there a Korea Exchange Bank?

Bank Clerk B	Cross over the road and go towards Chongno. At the crossroads in Chongno, if you go right there is a Korea Exchange Bank.
Mr Pak	Is it far from here?
Bank Clerk B	No. It's about five minutes on foot.

Unit 5

Is this the bus for Tongdaemun market?

Mr Kim	Excuse me, is there a bus for Tongdaemun market here?
Mr Lee	I don't have a clue, I'm not from Seoul.
Mr Kim	Excuse me, is there a bus to Tongdaemun market from here?
Mrs O	No. You can't get a bus to Tongdaemun market from here. But if you get bus number 20 it will take you to Namdaemun market.
Mr Kim	Namdaemun market? What is there at Namdaemun market?
Mrs O	What is there? There's nothing they don't sell at Namdaemun market.
Mr Kim	Are there more goods than at Tongdaemun market?
Mrs O	In my opinion Namdaemun market has more goods than Tongdaemun, and is more interesting. However, they don't sell monkeys at Namdaemun market. They do sell them at Tongdaemun.
Mr Kim	Is that true?! Although ... I don't need a monkey.
Mrs O	Then take the number 20 bus.
Mr Kim	Where do I get it?
Mrs O	Take it at the stop straight across the road.
Mr Kim	How much is the fare?
Mrs O	My, you must be a real stranger here (country bumpkin)! It's 900 won.
Mr Kim	Thank you.
Mrs O	Hurry up. The bus is coming!

This fruit doesn't look too good!

| **Minja** | How much are the apples here? |
| **Chŏmwon A** | One box is 30,000 won. |

Minja	That's too expensive. Will you cut the price a bit?
Chŏmwon A	Okay, you can take a box for 28,000 won.
Minja	It's still expensive.
Chŏmwon A	Then go and try somewhere else! Bad luck all morning (today, since the morning)!
Minja	These apples don't look too good (fresh). Some of them have gone bad.
Chŏmwon B	Really? Then I'll cut the price a bit for you.
Minja	How much will you give me them for?
Chŏmwon B	Just give me 31,000 won.
Minja	What?! That's even more expensive than the stall next door!
Chŏmwon B	All right. Then just give me 27,000 won.
Minja	Please cut me a bit more off the price.
Chŏmwon B	All right, then! Just pay 25,000 a box.
Minja	Thank you. Three boxes please.

Unit 6

Off to the mountains

Mr Kim	The weather's really good today.
Tony	Yes. The weather's better in Korea than in England.
Mr Kim	What are you going to do tomorrow? If you don't have anything on, shall we go to the mountains?
Tony	I do want to go, but tomorrow I decided to go shopping at Tongdaemun market with my wife.
Mr Kim	How about next Sunday, then?
Tony	Next Sunday I'm thinking of going to Pulguksa with some friends from university.
Mr Kim	Next Sunday won't do either, then. When would be okay?
Tony	The Sunday after that would probably be fine.
Mr Kim	All right. Then let's go that following Sunday.
Tony	I like mountain climbing too. But there aren't many mountains in Britain so I haven't been able to do much. By the way, which mountain shall we go to?
Mr Kim	Tobongsan mountain would be convenient.

Tony	Then shall we meet at the entrance to Tobongsan mountain?

I've got a nasty headache!

Jaehoon	I'm going into town. Shall we go together?
Yongtae	I don't know ... I don't feel too good.
Jaehoon	You don't feel well *again*? You're always pretending to be ill!
Yongtae	No I'm not. That's not true. Today I really am ill.
Jaehoon	What is it this time?
Yongtae	I've got a nasty headache. My head hurts.
Jaehoon	Is that all? Don't worry – it's perhaps because the weather is hot.
Yongtae	I don't think so. I have stomach ache as well.
Jaehoon	Is it bad?
Yongtae	Yes. It hurts a lot.
Jaehoon	Then let's go to the chemist to buy some medicine.
Yongtae	I can't. I have no energy (strength). Besides, my legs hurt.
Jaehoon	Your legs, too? It seems like your whole body hurts! Is there anywhere that doesn't hurt?
Yongtae	Shut up! Don't make fun of me. I need some medicine.
Jaehoon	I've got a cure-all medicine here – it's alcohol! It's better than medicine, you know!
Yongtae	Don't make jokes. I can't drink alcohol. I really need to go to the hospital.

Unit 8

She's just gone out

Mr Yun	Hello?
Jaemok	Hello. Can I speak to Chongmin, please?
Mr Yun	Yes, hold on, please.
	I'm sorry, she was here until a little while ago, but she has just gone out.
Jaemok	Oh dear. Have you any idea where she might have gone?
Mr Yun	I don't have a clue. Just a moment. Maybe my wife will know.

Mrs Yun	Tonight Chongmin has gone out to see a movie with her boyfriend.
Jaemok	Really? That's strange, she was supposed (lit: *decided*) to meet me this evening …
Mrs Yun	Oh dear. Well, she's gone out on a date with a different guy and she won't be back until late.
Jaemok	Oh well, it's turned out well then – I was just ringing up to cancel. Something came up today.
Mrs Yun	Oh really? It has turned out well. Do you have a message for Chongmin?
Jaemok	No, I don't. Goodbye.

What did you do last night?

Yongtae	Taegyu, how are you doing?!
Taegyu	Hi there! How are things?
Yongtae	Nowadays I'm a bit busy. I've (just) got a girlfriend, so I'm even more busy!
Taegyu	I thought so. What's her name?
Yongtae	She's called Kim Chongmin. She graduated last year from Seoul National University. Now she's working for Hyundai cars.
Taegyu	How did you meet?
Yongtae	My friend did an introduction for me. At first I didn't like her that much, but a month later we met by chance at a party. We started meeting regularly from then on.
Taegyu	And now you're meeting her and dating nearly every day, are you?
Yongtae	More or less!
Taegyu	I tried to ring you last night, but you'd gone out then too. Where did you go last night?
Yongtae	Last night? I don't remember. I expect we went somewhere or other.
Taegyu	You don't remember?! Had you drunk so much?!
Yongtae	You mean *me* drinking? (lit: *who was drinking?*) You're the one who drinks every day (on the contrary).

Taegyu	Anyhow, where did you go?
Yongtae	We went to a noraebang, my girlfriend really likes noraebangs.
Taegyu	Where did you go after coming out of the noraebang?
Yongtae	We played a bit of table tennis.
Taegyu	Is that all? Tell me honestly!
Yongtae	It's true! Nothing happened!

Unit 9

We bought him that last year!

Wife	It's Grandad's birthday tomorrow.
Husband	What, already?
Wife	Yes. We're going to have to decide what to buy him.
Husband	Can't you decide? I'm busy.
Wife	I always decide. Please help this time.
Husband	All right. Why don't we buy him a jumper?
Wife	He's got ten already. He doesn't need another one.
Husband	What about a shirt then?
Wife	He doesn't need a shirt either.
Husband	A book?
Wife	You know he doesn't like reading.
Husband	Since Grandma likes reading it would be okay if she read it instead!
Wife	Don't joke. Try making a better suggestion.
Husband	What about an umbrella?
Wife	He doesn't go out when it rains.
Husband	Some socks, then?
Wife	We bought him that last year.
Husband	How about a new electric razor?
Wife	We bought him that the year before. Besides, he doesn't shave himself properly (*frequently*).
Husband	You see?! You don't like my suggestions. You'd better decide, like I said at first!

I'm sorry, I really didn't know!

Policeman	Excuse me. Please show me your driving licence.
Driver	Why? What's the matter?

Policeman	You really don't know?
Driver	What are you talking about?
Policeman	Just look at the cars parked here. The cars have all been parked in the same direction.
Driver	So what?
Policeman	Okay then, didn't you see that red one-way signpost over there?
Driver	Ah, it's a one-way street! I'm sorry. I really didn't know.
Policeman	You've committed a serious offence. It's very dangerous and there is a large fine if you go into a one-way street the wrong way.
Driver	I really didn't see the sign. Please let me off this once.
Policeman	Be careful from now on. The fine is 50,000 won.
Driver	Thank you very much and keep up the good work.

Unit 10

What did you do with it?

Sonnim	Excuse me, I was here yesterday with some friends and I left my bag behind.
Chongŏbwon	Just let me go and have a look. Can you describe your bag?
Sonnim	Yes . . . it's very big, black and made of leather.
Chongŏbwon	There's a briefcase. Is that it?
Sonnim	No, it's not a briefcase.
Chongŏbwon	No, we don't seem to have anything. Was there anything important inside?
Sonnim	Yes, actually. There were some important documents, some books and my bank cards.
Chongŏbwon	Please wait a moment. I will ask the manager.
Sajang	Hello, how can I help you?
Sonnim	I've lost my bag – yesterday I ate here and left it behind (*put it down and left*).
Sajang	What time did you leave the restaurant?
Sonnim	About 11 p.m., I think.

Sajang	Around closing time … Ah yes, I remember now. There was a bag when we were cleaning this morning.
Sonnim	What did you do with it?
Sajang	I sent it to the police station. They are keeping it there.
Sonnim	Can you tell me where the police station is?
Sajang	Yes, go out of the restaurant and turn left and it's on the third (*small*) street on your right.
Sonnim	Thank you very much. Goodbye.

Nasty headaches

Yaksa	Hello, can I help you?
Mr Pak	Yes, I've got a very bad headache; I wonder if you could give me some medicine.
Yaksa	Yes, certainly. When did you get it?
Mr Pak	It came yesterday. I've been working very hard and have had a lot of stress – probably overwork and stress is the reason.
Yaksa	It could be. Do your eyes hurt at all?
Mr Pak	Yes, they do a bit.
Yaksa	Have you been able to sleep?
Mr Pak	No, my head hurts too much, and so I can't sleep.
Yaksa	I see. It's probably linked to stress, then. I recommend these tablets.
Mr Pak	How often should I take them?
Yaksa	You can take one every four hours while it's very bad. When it gets a bit easier, then just take one tablet after meals three times a day.
Mr Pak	Are there any side-effects?
Yaksa	When you take the medicine you will feel drowsy so take care. Don't be surprised if you feel tired easily.
Mr Pak	Okay. Thank you very much.

Unit 11

Would you like to try it on?

Minho	Look at that shirt; it's really nice.
Byongsoo	Well, I think the design is a bit old-fashioned.
Minho	No, I like them. Agassi, how much are those shirts?
Chŏmwon A	8,000 won.

Minho	Wow, that's really cheap.
Byongsoo	Yeah, but look at it, the quality's not very good.
Minho	Oh, I don't know. Shall we go and look somewhere else then?
Chŏmwon B	Welcome! What are you looking for?
Minho	Yes, I'm looking for casual shirts. (*Something in*) a bright colour. Something stylish and good quality which I can wear with jeans.
Chŏmwon B	What about these? This style is very popular at the moment.
Minho	What is it made of?
Chŏmwon B	100% cotton. Would you like to try one on?
Minho	Yes, please . . . Does it suit me?

Do you think it suits me?

Chŏmwon	Ah, that looks very nice.
Minho	Do you think it suits me?
Byongsoo	Yes. But it seems/looks a bit small.
Chŏmwon	Would you like to try a bigger one?
Minho	Yes, please.
Chŏmwon	Here you are.
Byongsoo	That looks a bit better.
Chŏmwon	Ah, that looks super.
Minho	By the way, how much is it?
Chŏmwon	32,000 won.
Minho	What?
Chŏmwon	Why? That's a very good price. Only 32,000 won.
Byongsoo	It sounds a bit expensive to me!
Minho	At Namdaemun they had a similar one for only 8,000 won.
Chŏmwon	Ah yes, at Namdaemun. It looks the same, but the quality is very different. If you buy clothes at Namdaemun, they become unusable in just two or three months, so you have to buy new ones.
Byongsoo	Well, I don't know. Do you reckon this shirt will last four times as long, then?
Chŏmwon	Oh, at least. And it will be a much better fit.
Minho	Mmm. I'll go and think about it, I think.

Unit 12

Do you have a spare room?

Sonnim	Do you have any free rooms, please?
Chuin	Yes, we do. Would you like beds or sleeping on the floor?
Sonnim	One with bed and one with floor sleeping.
Chuin	Certainly. It will be 50,000 won for the room with a bed, and 40,000 for the room with floor sleeping. How many nights are you staying?
Sonnim	Three nights, please. We may stay a little longer than that (I don't know).
Chuin	If you book for five nights or more, we offer a 5% discount.
Sonnim	Oh, I'll talk about that with my wife. Is breakfast included in the price?
Chuin	Yes, breakfast is included. Between 7 and 10 a.m. please go to the basement restaurant. Or you can have breakfast brought to your room for 2,000 won extra per person.
Sonnim	No, we'll go to the restaurant, thank you. What other facilities does the hotel have?
Chuin	We have a swimming pool, a sauna, a games room, a noraebang, a bar, a Korean restaurant and a western one.
Sonnim	Is there a TV and a phone in the rooms?
Chuin	Of course, and there is also a mini-bar.
Sonnim	Oh, that's excellent. It would be better to book for five nights, then. My wife will probably like that.

The towel is dirty and the food is cold

Sonnim	Excuse me, I'd like to speak to the manager, please.
Chongŏbwon	Excuse me, but is there a problem?
Sonnim	Yes, I have something to say about the hotel service.
Chongŏbwon	Is there any chance you can tell me what the problem is?
Sonnim	I'd like to speak to the manager direct about it.
Chongŏbwon	Very well, sir. Hold on a moment please.

Chibaein	Hello, I'm the manager. What is the problem?
Sonnim	It seems that there are many problems with the service at this hotel. The staff are unfriendly and unhelpful; this morning we went in for breakfast and the food was cold. Yesterday it was the same.
Chibaein	Really? I'm very sorry to hear that. Did you speak to the waitress about it?
Sonnim	Of course I spoke to the waitress! She was impolite, and while saying that she couldn't understand my Korean, she said that the food was fine. It wasn't; it was cold and the taste was awful.
Chibaein	I'm extremely sorry, sir. We always try to do our best, but sometimes mistakes happen. I'll make sure that I speak to the kitchen staff right away.
Sonnim	And that's not all. This morning I asked for my towel to be changed and the new towel was very dirty and they still haven't cleaned my son's room.
Chibaein	This is strange. We don't usually get any complaints like this.
Sonnim	Even that is not all. The television in our room has broken down and the fridge door won't even open. I have to say that quite frankly the service and facilities are rubbish.
Chibaein	I'm sorry but we also don't need guests like you who complain so much in our hotel. Please leave right away. We will refund your money.

Unit 13
Two to Taegu

Maep'yowon	Can I help you?
Mr Pak	Are there any trains to Taegu this evening, please?
Maep'yowon	Yes, there are two trains, a slow one at 5.30, and a fast one at 7.45.
Mr Pak	How long do they take?

Maep'yowon	The fast one takes three hours, the slow one four hours 30 minutes.
Mr Pak	What about the price?
Maep'yowon	Yes, the slow one is 18,000 won, the fast 45,000 won, and we only have a few seats left for the fast one.
Mr Pak	Can we book four seats together?
Maep'yowon	Please wait a minute. Just let me check ... yes, that's fine. There are four seats available. Non-smoking or smoking?
Mr Pak	Non-smoking, please.
Maep'yowon	Would you like single tickets or return?
Mr Pak	No, return please.
Maep'yowon	When are you coming back?
Mr Pak	Sunday evening.
Maep'yowon	There's a train at 6.30; but it's a slow one. There is no fast train on Sunday evening.
Mr Pak	What about Sunday afternoon?
Maep'yowon	Yes, there's one at 2.30.
Mr Pak	That'll be okay. We'll take the fast one, please.
Maep'yowon	That will be 360,000 won altogether, please.
Mr Pak	What platform does the train go from?
Maep'yowon	I don't know yet. Before the time of departure look at the electronic notice board.
Mr Pak	Okay, thank you very much.

I don't want to go there!

Mr Yun	What are you doing after work this evening?
Mr Paek	After work? Don't know. I haven't got anything planned.
Mr Yun	What about going out for a meal?
Mr Paek	Sounds a good idea. Just the two of us?
Mr Yun	We could invite some others. What about Mrs Kim and Mrs Lee?
Mr Paek	Yeah, sure! Hey, Mrs Kim, Mrs Lee! Do you fancy going out for a meal tonight?
Mrs Kim	Okay, but where are we going to?

Mr Yun	We could go and eat pulgogi, and of course we could drink soju and then go out to a noraebang or something.
Mrs Kim	I like drinking, but I don't particularly like pulgogi, and I hate singing.
Mr Paek	Well *you* don't have to eat pulgogi, you can have something else. And you can just listen instead of singing.
Mrs Kim	Yeah, that's fair enough. But I don't have much spare cash right now.
Mr Yun	Don't worry. I'll buy.
Mrs Kim	Yes, okay then. That's nice of you.
Mr Paek	What about you, Mr Lee, would you like to come?
Mrs Lee	I would like to go, but I'd prefer to go out to Inchŏn and eat raw fish, though.
Mr Paek	No, it's too far and it's too expensive.
Mr Yun	Besides, I can't eat raw fish.
Mrs Lee	Okay, okay, it was only an idea. I guess I'll just have to come and eat pulgogi and soju!

Key to exercises

Exercises on Korean alphabet
Exercise 3: **1** Pakistan **2** Mexico **3** New Zealand
4 The Netherlands **5** Sweden **6** Denmark **7** Indonesia
8 Poland **9** Canada **10** America

Exercise 4: **1** hotel **2** piano **3** computer **4** television
5 radio **6** taxi **7** lemon **8** ice cream **9** hamburger
10 sandwich **11** orange juice **12** tennis **13** camera **14** tomato

Exercises on romanization
Exercise 1: **1** 재민 **2** 가요 **3** 지금 **4** 양주
5 마른 안주 **6** 중국 **7** 마시다 **8** 밥 **9** 진짜
10 우리

Exercise 2: **1** Ŏttaeyo? **2** Saram **3** Sŏnsaengnim **4** Aniyo
5 Samushil **6** Mannada **7** Miguk **8** Hakkyo **9** Taesagwan
10 Chŏmshim

Unit 1
Exercise 1: **a** Chigŭm ilbon-e kayo. 지금 일본에 가요.
b Ajŏssi, maekchu issŏyo? 아저씨, 맥주 있어요? **c** Mwo sa-
rŏ kage-e kayo? 뭐 사러 가게에 가요? **d** Yangju-hago ojingŏ
chuseyo. 양주하고 오징어 주세요. **e** Kŭrigo anju-do chuseyo.
그리고 안주도 주세요. **f** Na-do kage-e kayo. 나도 가게에
가요. **g** Maekchu-hago marŭn anju-hago pap ta issŏyo. 맥주하고
마른 안주하고 밥 다 있어요.
Or, Marŭn anju-hago maekchu-hago pap ta issŏyo. 마른 안주하고
맥주하고 밥 다 있어요.

Exercise 2: **a** ppang issŏyo. 빵 있어요. **b** maekchu issŏyo.
맥주 있어요. **c** sulchip issŏyo. 술집 있어요. **d** kwail issŏyo.
과일 있어요.

Exercise 3: **1** Hakkyo-e kayo. 학교에 가요. **2** Kamsa hamnida. 감사합니다. **3** Annyŏng haseyo! 안녕하세요. **4** Ne, chal chinaessŏyo. 네, 잘 지냈어요. **5** Maekchu mashi-rŏ sulchib-e kayo. 맥주 마시러 술집에 가요. **6** Kŭrŏm, maekchu-hago soju chuseyo. 그럼 맥주하고 소주 주세요.

Exercise 4: **a** kayo 가요 Chigŭm hakkyo-e kayo. 지금 학교에 가요. **b** issŏyo 있어요 Soju issŏyo? 소주 있 어요? **c** sayo 사요 Mwo sayo? 뭐 사요? **d** mŏgŏyo 먹어요 Kim sŏnsaengnim ppang mŏgŏyo. 김 선생님 빵 먹어요. **e** ŏpsŏyo 없어요 Ojingŏ ŏpsŏyo. 오징어 없 어요. **f** haeyo 해요 wo ha-rŏ sulchib-e kayo? 뭐 하러 술 집에 가요? **g** anjayo 앉아요 Anjayo! 앉아요!

Exercise 5: **a** Kage-esŏ mwo sayo? 가게에서 뭐 사요? Or Mwo sa-rŏ kage-e kayo? 뭐 사러 가게에 가요? **b** Kim sŏnsaengnim, annyŏng haseyo! 김 선생님, 안녕하세요! **c** Kŭ-daum-e mwo haeyo? 그 다음에 뭐 해요? **d** Chigŭm shinae-e kayo? 지금 시내에 가요? **e** Ŏdi kayo? 어디 가요? **f** Maekchu-hago kwail-hago ppang – ta issŏyo! 맥주하고 과일하 고 빵 – 다 있어요! **g** Pap-do chuseyo. 밥도 주세요 **h** Ojingŏ yŏgi issŏyo. Mashikke tŭseyo! 오징어 여기 있어요. 맛있게 드세요! **i** Yangju ŏpsŏyo. Kŭrŏm maekchu hana chuseyo. 양주 없어요. 그럼 맥주 하나 주세요. **j** P'ajŏn-hago soju hana chuseyo. 파전하고 소주 하나 주세요.

Exercise 6: **a** Ajŏssi, ojingŏ chuseyo. 아저씨, 오징어 주세요. **b** Ajŏssi, wisk'i chuseyo. 아저씨, 위스키 주세요. **c** Ajŏssi, mul chuseyo. 아저씨, 물 주세요.

Exercise 7: **a** One soju, one beer and some dry snacks. **b** Squid, fruit, western spirits and one beer.

Exercise 8
a A: Annyŏnghaseyo? Ŏdi kayo? 안녕하세요? 어디 가요?
　B: Ne. Annyŏnghaseyo? Kage-e kayo. 네, 안녕하세요. 가게에 가요.
　A: Na-do kage-e kayo. Kach'i kayo. 나도 가게에 가요. 같이 가요.

B: Ne. Kach'i kayo. Kŭrigo sul mashi-rŏ sulchip-e kayo.
네. 같이 가요. 그리고 술 마시러 술집에 가요.

b A: Chal chinaessŏyo? 잘 지냈어요?

B: Ne. Chal chinaessŏyo. 네. 잘 지냈어요.

A: (to the waiter) Ajŏssi, maekchu hana-hago soju hana chuseyo. 아저씨, 맥주 하나하고 소주 하나 주세요.

Waiter: Ne. Algessŏyo. 네. 알겠어요.

A: Kŭrigo anju-do chuseyo. Mwo issŏyo? 그리고 안주도 주세요. 뭐 있어요?

Waiter: Kwail-hago ojingŏ-hago marŭn anju issŏyo.
과일하고 오징어하고 마른 안주 있어요.

A: Kŭrŏm kwail chuseyo. 그럼 과일 주세요.

Unit 2

Exercise 1:   **a** ssi, do, e   **d** ga   **b** rŏ, e, yo   **e** nŭn, i   **c** ŭn

Exercise 2:   **a** O sŏnsaengnim annyŏng haseyo! Hoesa-nŭn ŏttaeyo? 오 선생님 안녕하세요! 회사는 어때요?   **b** Misesŭ Cho annyŏng haseyo! Saŏb-ŭn ŏttaeyo? 미세스 조, 안녕하세요! 사업은 어때요?   **c** Pak sŏnsaengnim annyŏng haseyo! Kajog-ŭn ŏttaeyo? 박 선생님 안녕하세요! 가족은 어때요?   **d** Taegyu-ssi annyŏng haseyo! Hakkyo-nŭn ŏttaeyo? 태규씨 안녕하세요! 학교는 어때요?   **e** Misŭ Pak, annyŏng haseyo? Kŏngang-ŭn ŏttaeyo? 미스 박, 안녕하세요! 건강은 어때요?

Exercise 3:   Ne, oraeganman-ieyo. Chal chinaessŏyo?
네, 오래간만이에요. 잘 지냈어요? Yojŭm choayo [= it's good at the moment]. 요즘 좋아요. Samushir-e kayo. 무실에 가요. Chŏgi-eyo. 저기에요. Kim sŏnsaengnim manna-rŏ kayo. 김 선생님 만나러 가요.

Exercise 4:   **a** I-gŏsh-i ojingŏ-eyo. 이것이 오징어에요.
b I-gŏsh-i chaeg-ieyo. 이것이 책이에요.   **c** I-gŏsh-i sagwa-eyo. 이것이 사과에요.   **d** I-gŏsh-i shinmun-ieyo. 이것이 신문이에요.
e I-gŏsh-i chapchi-eyo. 이것이 잡지에요.   **a** I-gŏsh-i ojingŏ-ga anieyo. 이것이 오징어가 아니에요.   **b** I-gŏsh-i chaeg-i anieyo. 이 것이 책이 아니에요.   **c** I-gŏsh-i sagwa-ga anieyo. 이것이

사과가 아니에요. **d** I-gŏsh-i shinmun-i anieyo. 이것이 신문이 아니에요. **e** I-gŏsh-i chapchi-ga anieyo. 이것이 잡지가 아니에요.

Exercise 5: **a** Excuse me, are you Mr Pak? **b** No, I'm not Mr Pak. Mr Pak is the Chinese teacher. This is the Chinese department office. **a** Ah, I'm sorry. Excuse me, but could you tell me where the Korean department is? **b** It's over there. I'm going to see (meet) a teacher (someone) at the Korean department also. **a** Let's go together then.

Exercise 6: **a** Miguk saram-iseyo? 미국 사람이세요? Ne, miguk saram-ieyo. 네, 미국 사람이에요. Aniyo, miguk saram-i anieyo. 아니요, 미국 사람이 아니에요. **b** I sŏnsaengnim-iseyo? 이 선생님이세요? Ne, I sŏnsaengnim-ieyo. 네, 이 선생님이에요. Aniyo, I sŏnsaengnim-i anieyo. 아니요, 이 선생님이 아니에요. **c** Chungguk sŏnsaengnim-i aniseyo? 중국 선생님이 아니세요? Ne, chungguk sŏnsaengnim-ieyo. 네, 중국 선생님이에요. Aniyo, chungguk sonsaengnim-i anieyo. 아니요, 중국 선생님이 아니 에요. **d** Paek sŏnsaengnim adŭr-i anieyo? (or, aniseyo) 백 선생 님 아들이 아니에요? Ne, Paek sŏnsaengnim adŭr-ieyo. 네, 백 선 생님 아들이에요. Aniyo, Paek sŏnsaengnim adŭr-i anieyo. 아니요, 백 선생님 아들이 아니에요. **e** Hakkyo sŏnsaengnim aniseyo? 학교 선생님 아니세요? Ne, hakkyo sŏnsaengnim-ieyo. 네, 학교 선 생님이에요. Aniyo, hakkyo sŏnsaengnim-i anieyo. 아니요, 학교 선생님이 아니에요.

Exercise 7: **a** Pak Sangmin-ieyo. 박상민이에요. A, kŭraeyo? Mannasŏ pangapsŭmnida. 아, 그래요? 만나서 반갑습니다. **b** Yojŭm hakkyo-nŭn ŏttaeyo? 요즘 학교는 어때요? **c** Sillye hamnida. Ilbonmal sŏnsaengnim-iseyo? 실례합니다. 일본말 선 생님이세요? **d** Ajŏssi, ojingŏ issŏyo? Ojingŏ ŏttaeyo? Choayo. 아저씨, 오징어 있어요? 오징어 어때요? 좋아요. **e** Hankuk hakkwa samushir-i anieyo? Ne. Aniyo. 한국학과 사무실이 아니 에요? 네. 아니에요. **f** Chŏ-nŭn Woo sŏnsaengnim-i anieyo. A, kŭraeyo? Choesong-hamnida. 저는 우 선생님이 아니에요. 아, 그래요? 죄송합니다. **g** Uri chungguk mal sŏnsaengnim-iseyo. Kŭraeyo? Malssŭm mani tŭrŏssŏyo. 우리 중국말 선생님이세요.

그래요? 말씀 많이 들었어요. **h** Ilbon kage-eyo? 일본 가게에요?
i Na-do hanguk sǒnsaengnim manna-rǒ kayo. 나도 한국 선생님
만나러 가요. **j** Pak sǒnsaengnim puin manna-rǒ wassǒyo. 박 선
생님 부인 만나러 왔어요. **k** Hanguk hakkwa-ga ǒdi-eyo? 한국
학과가 어디에요? **l** Hakkyo samushir-i ǒdi-eyo? 학교 사무실이
어디에요?

Exercise 8
A Annyǒng haseyo? 안녕하세요?
B A! Annyǒng haseyo? 아! 안녕하세요?
A Oraeganman-ieyo. 오래간만이에요.
B Ne. Kǔraeyo. Chinccha oraeganman-ieyo. 네, 그래요. 진짜
오래간만이에요.
A Chal chinaessǒyo? 잘 지냈어요?
B Ne. Chal chinaessǒyo. Yojǔm saǒb-ǔn ǒttaeyo? 네. 잘
지냈어요. 요즘 사업은 어때요?
A Kǔjǒ kǔraeyo. 그저 그래요.
(signalling to his son) Uri adǔr-ieyo. 우리 아들이에요.
B A! Kǔraeyo. Pangapsǔmnida. 아! 그래요. 반갑습니다.

Exercise 9:
Yǒgi-nǔn chunguk hakkwa samushir-i anieyo.
여기는 중국학과 사무실이 아니에요. Chunguk mal sǒnsaengnim-i
ǒpsǒyo. 중국말 선생님이 없어요.

Unit 3
Exercise 1: **a** Pak sǒnsaengnim-hago Misesu Kim manna-go
ship'ǒyo. 박 선생님하고 미세스 김 만나고 싶어요.
b Ppang-hago kwail sa-go ship'ǒyo. 빵하고 과일 사고 싶어요.
c Pulgogi-hago kalbi mǒk-ko ship'ǒyo. 불고기하고 갈비 먹
고 싶어요. **d** Yǒngo sǒnsaengnim-hago ilbonmal sǒnsaengnim
kidari-go ship'ǒyo. 영어 선생님하고 일본말 선생님 기다리고 싶
어요. **e** Maekchu-hago wisk'i mashi-go ship'ǒyo. 맥주하고 위
스키 마시고 싶어요. **f** Ojingǒ-hago naengmyǒn chumun ha-go
ship'ǒyo. 오징어하고 냉면 주문하고 싶어요. Second part: Pak
sǒnsaengnim-ina Misesu Kim manna-go ship'ǒyo; ppang-ina kwail
sa-go ship'ǒyo, etc. 박 선생님이나 미세스 김 만나고 싶어요; 빵이
나 과일 사고 싶어요, etc.

Exercise 2: 김 선생님: 오팔이–오구이공 (Kim sŏnsaengnim: o-p'al-i-o-gu-i-gong.) 재민: 이구일–육사팔이 (Chaemin: i-gu-il-yuk-sa-p'al-i.) 의사: 육육육–공이삼일 (ŭysa: yuk-yuk-yuk-gong-i-sam-il.) 피터: 공일육이삼–이구육공 (P'it'ŏ: kong-il-yuk-i-sam-i-gu-yuk-kong.) 박 선생님: 공일오일육팔칠구일공이 (Pak sŏnsaengnim: kong-il-o-il-yuk-p'al-ch'il-gu-il-gong-i.)

Exercise 3: **a** Hanguk ŭmshik choa haseyo? 한국 음식 좋아하세요? **b** Chŏ-nŭn Hilton Hotel-ŭy Sangmin-ieyo. 저는 힐튼 호텔의 상민이에요. **c** Yŏlshi-e hakkyo ap'esŏ mannapshida. 열시에 학교 앞에서 만납시다. **d** Onŭl chŏmshim-e shigan-i issŏyo? 오늘 점심에 시간이 있어요? **e** Usŏn mul chom chuseyo. 우선 물 좀 주세요. **f** Maeun kŏ chal mot (pron: mon) mŏgŏyo. 매운 거 잘 못 먹어요. **g** Kalbi saminbun-hago naengmyŏn tu-kŭrŭt chuseyo. 갈비 삼 인분하고 냉면 두 그릇 주세요.

Exercise 4: **a** Na-nŭn Ilbon taesagwan-e mot kayo. 나는 일본 대사관에 못 가요. **b** Chigŭm chŏmshim mŏg-ŭro shiktang-e mot kayo. 지금 점심 먹으러 식당에 못 가요. **c** Jaemin-ssi-nŭn Sangmin-ssi mot kidaryŏyo (or, kidariseyo). 재민씨는 상민씨 못 기다려요 (or 기다리세요). **d** Sangmin-ssi maeun kŏ mon mŏgŏyo. 상민씨 매운 거 못 먹어요. **e** (Chungguk taesagwan ap'esŏ) Misesu Jang mon mannayo. (중국 대사관 앞에서) 미세스 장 못 만나요. **f** Paekhwajŏm-e mot kayo. 백화점에 못 가요.

Exercise 5: **a** kaseyo 가세요 kapshida 갑시다 **b** chumun haseyo 주문하세요 chumun hapshida 주문합시다 **c** poseyo 보세요 popshida 봅시다 **d** anjŭseyo 앉으세요 anjŭpshida 앉읍시다 **e** kidariseyo 기다리세요 kidaripshida 기다립시다 **f** saseyo 사세요 sapshida 삽시다 **g** mannaseyo 만나세요 mannapshida 만납시다

E.g. Kim sŏnsaengnim chamkkan kidariseyo. 김 선생님 잠깐 기다리세요. Yŏlshi-e hakkyo-e kapshida. 열시에 학교에 갑시다.

Exercise 6: The first sentence says something is good (irrespective of whether or not you personally like it) and the second says that you like it (irrespective of its quality).

Exercise 7: **a** Chunguk mal-lo malhapshida. 중국말로 말합시다.
b Paekhwachŏm-e kapshida. 백화점에 갑시다. **c** Maekchu-na
wain mashipshida. 맥주나 와인 마십시다 **d** Migug-e kago ship-
jiman mot kayo. 미국에 가고 싶지만 못 가요. **e** Wisk'i cho-
ch'iman mon mashyŏyo. 위스키 좋지만 못 마셔요.
f Kim sŏnsaengnim-hant'e chŏnhwa hago ship-jiman, chalmot
kŏrŏssŏyo. 김 선생님한테 전화하고 싶지만, 잘못 걸었어요.

Exercise 8: **a** 97 **b** 53 **c** 207 **d** 867 **e** 34495

Exercise 9: **a** I like spicy food, but I can't eat Korean (well).
Or, Although I like spicy food, I can't eat Korean. **b** Excuse me,
where is the British embassy? **c** Please sit down over here (at this
side). Would you like anything to drink? **d** Do you have
(some/free) time? Let's meet later, then. **e** Mr Kim? Just a
moment ... I'm sorry, but there is no such person here. You've
misdialled. **f** Is that 863-0542?

Exercise 10: Yŏl-tu-shi-e hakkyo ap'-esŏ mannapshida. 열두시
에 학교 앞에서 만납시다.

Unit 4
Exercise 1: **a** kŭrŏn 그런 tarŭn 다른 kaseyo 가세요
b kamyŏn 가면 **c** -jiman –지만 sajŏn 사전 **d** yŏgisŏ 여기서
oshippun 오십분 **e** chŏ-nŭn 저는 ŭy 의 **f** uch'eguk 우체국
orŭn 오른 ŭnhaeng 은행 **g** chongnyu-ga 종류가 **h** modu 모두
tŭrilkkayo 드릴까요 **i** ieyo 이에요 saŏp 사업 **j** pissan 비싼
ship'ŏyo 싶어요

Exercise 2: **a** movie **b** what (him) **c** none **d** word
e bread

Exercise 3: **a** Yŏboseyo. Kim sŏnsaengnim chom pakkwo
chuseyo. 여보세요. 김 선생님 좀 바꿔주세요. **b** Naeil shigan
issŭseyo? 내일 시간 있으세요? **c** Kŏgi Hankuk taesakwan
anieyo? 거기 한국 대사관 아니에요? **d** Uri chip saram-ieyo.
우리 집사람이에요. **e** Yŏngo sajŏn issŏyo? 영어 사전 있어요?

f Hanguk umshik choahaseyo? 한국 음식 좋아하세요?
g Maekchu mashi-go ship'ŏyo? 맥주 마시고 싶어요?

Exercise 4: **a** Han gwon-e paek won-ssig-ieyo. 한 권에 백원씩
이에요. Kŭrŏnikka modu sa-baek won-ieyo. 그러니까 모두 사백
원이에요. **b** Han jan-e ch'il-paek won-ssig-ieyo. 한 잔에 칠백원
씩이에요. Kŭrŏnikka modu ch'ŏn-sa-baek won-ieyo. 그러니까 모
두 천 사백원이에요. **c** Han kae-e i-ch'ŏn won-ssig-ieyo. 한 개
에 이천원씩이에요. Kŭrŏnikka modu man-i-ch'ŏn won-ieyo. 그러
니까 모두 만이천원이에요. **d** Han byŏng-e ch'ŏn-o-baek won-
ssig-ieyo. 한 병에 천 오백원씩이에요. Kŭrŏnikka modu sa-ch'ŏn-
o-baek won-ieyo. 그러니까 모두 사천 오백원이에요. **e** Han
sangja-e yuk-ch'ŏn won-ssig-ieyo. 한 상자에 육천원씩이에요.
Kŭrŏnikka modu man-p'al-ch'ŏn won-ieyo. 그러니까 모두 만 팔천
원이에요.

Exercise 5: **a** sŏ   ŭro   i   **b** i   e   esŏ   **c** ŭl   ŭro
d ŭn/i   rŭl   **e** nŭn   ŭl   na   **f** nŭn   i   **g** ŭl   ina   **h** ga
i e   ieyo

Exercise 6: **a** chaek se kwon 책 세 권, chaek yŏdŏl kwon 책 여
덟 권, chaek sŭmul-du kwon 책 스물두 권. **b** ir-il 일일, sam-il 삼
일, yukship-ch'ir-il 육십칠일. **c** han saram 한 사람, ilgop saram
일곱 사람, sŏrŭn-ne saram 서른네 사람. **d** ojingŏ se mari 오징
어 세 마리, ojingŏ ahop mari 오징어 아홉 마리, ojingŏ yŏl-ne mari
오징어 열 네 마리. **e** tu pyŏng 두 병, yŏl pyŏng 열 병. **f** kae
ahop mari 개 아홉 마리, kae han mari 개 한 마리. **g** chŏn won
천 원, man won 만 원.

Exercise 7: **a** Marŭn anju an chumun haeyo. 마른 안주 안 주
문해요. **b** O-bun an kŏllyŏyo. 오분 안 걸려요. **c** Maekchu an
tŭseyo. 맥주 안 드세요. **d** Sŏnsaengnim an kidariseyo. 선생님 안
기다리세요. **e** Chaek an ilgŏyo. 책 안 읽어요.

Exercise 8: **a** Sillye-jiman, yŏgi shiktang issŏyo? 실례지만, 여
기 식당 있어요? **b** Naengmyŏn mon mŏgŏyo. Kalbi-do mon
mŏgŏyo. 냉면 못 먹어요. 갈비도 못 먹어요. **c** Ŏlma-eyo? Han
chŏpshi-e i-ch'ŏn won ..., kŭrŏnikka modu yuk-ch'ŏn won-ieyo.
얼마에요? 한 접시에 이천원···, 그러니까 모두 육천원이에요.

d Yŏgisŏ oencchog-ŭro kaseyo. 여기서 왼쪽으로 가세요. O-bun kamyŏn, Chongno sagŏri-ga issŏyo. 오분 가면, 종로사거리 가 있어요. Oencchog-ŭro kaseyo. 왼쪽으로 가세요. Ŭnhaeng-i orŭncchog-e issŏyo. 은행이 오른쪽에 있어요. **e** Cheil ssan kŏ ŏlma-eyo? 제일 싼 거 얼마에요? **f** Kŏrŏsŏ ship-pun cchŭm kŏllyŏyo. 걸어서 십분쯤 걸려요. **g** Yŏgi Hanguk oehwan ŭnhaeng chijŏm-i ŏpsŏyo. 여기 한국 외환은행 지점이 없어요. **h** Ton-ŭl chom pakku-go ship'ŏyo. O-man won cchŭm issŏyo. 돈을 좀 바꾸고 싶어요. 오만원쯤 있어요. **i** Hanguk-e yŏl kaji chongnyu-ŭy kimch'i-ga issŏyo. 한국에 열 가지 종류의 김치가 있어요. **j** Hanguk mal sajŏn-ŭl tŭrilkkayo? 한국말 사전을 드 릴까요? **k** Ŏttŏn chongnyu-rŭl tŭrilkkayo? 어떤 종류를 드릴 까요? **l** Cheil ssan kŏ chuseyo. 제일 싼 거 주세요. **m** Kim sŏnsaengnim-i nappŭn saram-ieyo? 김 선생님이 나쁜 사람이에요? **n** Uch'egug-e kaseyo? Choayo. Annyŏnghi kaseyo. 우체국에 가세요? 좋아요. 안녕히 가세요.

Exercise 9:

Clerk	Mwol ch'ajŭseyo? 뭘 찾으세요?
Child	Uyu issŏyo? 우유 있어요?
Clerk	Ne, issŏyo. 네, 있어요.
Child	Uyu tu pyong-hago ppang chom chuseyo. 우유 두 병하고 빵 좀 주세요.
Clerk	Yŏgi issŏyo. 여기 있어요.
Child	Ŏlmaeyo? 얼마에요?
Clerk	Sam ch'ŏn won-ieyo. 삼천원이에요.
Child	Maekchu-hago kogi-hago sagwa-hago kimch'i-do issŏyo? 맥주하고 고기하고 사과하고 김치도 있어요?
Clerk	Ne, issŏyo. 네, 있어요.
Child	Ŏlmaeyo? 얼마에요?
	etc., etc., etc.

Unit 5

Exercise 1: a 아니요. 남대문 시장이 동대문 시장보다 더 재미 있어요. **b** 동대문 시장에서 원숭이는 안 팔아요. **c** 이십번 버 스를 타면 남대문 시장에 가요. **d** 네. 남대문 시장에는 안 파는 게 없어요. **e** 바로 길 건너편 정류장에서 타요.

Exercise 2: **a** Aniyo. Na-nŭn mot kayo. 아니요. 나는 못 가요. **b** Namdaemun shijang ap'esŏ Kim sŏnsaengnim mannayo. 남대문 시장 앞에서 김 선생님 만나요. **c** Kŭrŏm tarŭn te-e ka-boseyo. 그럼 다른 데에 가보세요. **d** Sambaek oship won-ieyo. 삼백 오십원이에요. **e** Hanguk choa ha-jiman hangungmal chaemi ŏpsŏyo. 한국 좋아하지만 한국말 재미없어요.

Exercise 3: **a** Kim sonsaengnim(ŭy) kae-gunyo! 김 선생님(의) 개군요! **b** O sŏnsaengnim puin-ishigunyo! 오 선생님 부인이시군요! **c** Ilbon ch'aeg-igunyo! 일본 책이군요! **d** Hanguk oehwan ŭnhaeng-igunyo! 한국 외환 은행이군요! **e** Hyŏngjun-igunyo! 형준이군요! **f** Chunggungmal sŏnsaengnim-ishigunyo! 중국말 선생님이시군요!

Exercise 4: **a** Hanguk ŭmshig-i ilbon ŭmshik-poda tŏ mashi issŏyo. 한국 음식이 일본 음식보다 더 맛이 있어요. **b** Yŏgi-nŭn kŏgi-poda tŏ man(h)ayo. 여기는 거기보다 더 많아요. **c** Kich'a-nŭn bŏsŭ-poda tŏ pallayo. 기차는 버스보다 더 빨라요. **d** Kim sŏnsaengnim-i Pak sŏnsaengnim-poda chaesu tŏ cho(h)ayo. 김 선생님이 박 선생님보다 재수 더 좋아요. **e** Namdaemun shijang-i Tongdaemun shijang-poda tŏ pissayo. 남대문 시장이 동대문 시장 보다 더 비싸요.

Exercise 6: **a** Wow, it's expensive here! Let's go and try next door (at the next door shop). **b** They do sell them here, but if you go somewhere else (to a different place) it's cheaper. **c** Where do you catch a bus for (going to) Seoul city centre? **d** I haven't had any luck all morning! **e** Japan is more expensive than Korea. Mind you (however ...), Korea is expensive too. **f** There are more English people in Korea than I thought. **g** I'll cut the price for you. You can take a box for 13,000 won. **h** Would you like to order? **i** Since this isn't Korea (since we're not in Korea) there are few places selling kimchi. **j** You want to know if we've got monkeys? Go and try at Tongdaemun market!

Exercise 7: The acceptable sequences are: a, c, d, h.

Exercise 8: **a** I sajŏn-i pissa-neyo. 이 사전이 비싸네요. **b** Taegyu-ga o-neyo. 태규가 오네요. **c** Mwol ha-neyo?

뭘 하네요? **d** I shinmun-i chŏngmal chaemi in-neyo. 이 신문이 정말 재미있네요.

Exercise 9: **a** 이 사람이 박 선생님이고 저 사람 강 선생님이에요. **b** 어머니는 책 읽고 아버지는 텔레비를 봐요. **c** 고기 못 먹고 사과도 못 먹어요. **d** 십일번 버스가 남대문 시장에 가고, 이십번 버스는 동대문 시장에 가요. **e** 상준(도) 버스 타고 명택도 버스 타요.

Exercise 10: O-ship-ch'il-pŏn bŏsŭ-ga hakkyo-e kanŭn bŏsŭ-eyo. 오십칠번 버스가 학교에 가는 버스에요. Ship-p'al-pŏn bŏsŭ-nŭn shinae-e kayo. 십팔번 버스는 시내에 가요.

Unit 6

Exercise 1: **a** ap'ŭl kŏeyo 아플 거에요 **b** mŏgŭl kŏeyo 먹을 거에요 **c** ŏpsŭl kŏeyo 없을 거에요 **d** ka-giro haessŏyo 가기로 했어요 **e** sa-giro haessŏyo 사기로 했어요 **f** mŏk-kiro haessŏyo 먹기로 했어요 **g** polkka haeyo 볼까 해요 **h** halkka haeyo 할까 해요 **i** kalkka haeyo 갈까 해요 **j** kalkkayo? 갈까요? **k** mannalkkayo? 만날까요? **l** t'alkkayo? 탈까요?

Exercise 2: Naeil-ŭn shyop'ing halkka haeyo. 내일은 쇼핑할까 해요. Hal ir-i manasŏ nŏmu pappayo. 할 일이 많아서 너무 바빠요. Taehak tongch'ang-hago golf hagiro haessŏyo. 대학 동창하고 골프 하기로 했어요. Tŭngsan-ŭl an choa haeyo. 등산을 안 좋아해요.

Exercise 3

A Mŏri-ga ap'ayo. 머리가 아파요.
B Mani ap'ayo? 많이 아파요?
A Kŭraeyo. Mani ap'ayo. 그래요. 많이 아파요.
B Kŭrŏm yag-ŭl sarŏ yakkug-e kapshida. 그럼 약을 사러 약국에 갑시다.
A Na-nŭn mot kayo. Tari-do ap'ayo. 나는 못 가요. 다리도 아파요.
B A! Yŏgi tut'ong yag-i issŏyo. 아! 여기 두통약이 있어요.
A Kŭraeyo? Komawoyo. 그래요? 고마워요.

Exercise 4:   **a** nolliji maseyo (or, shikkŭrŏwoyo) 놀리지 마세요 (or 시끄러워요)   **b** an toegennneyo (or, chaesu ŏmneyo!) 안 되겠네요 (or 재수 없네요!)   **c** chŏnshin-i ta ap'ŭgunyo 전신이 다 아프군요   **d** mworaguyo? (or, shikkŭrŏwoyo) 뭐라구요? (or 시끄러워요)   **e** shikkŭrŏwoyo 시끄러워요.   **f** ch'akkak haessŏyo 착각했어요.   **g** kŭrŏch'i anayo 그렇지 않아요.   **h** anin kŏt kat'ayo 아닌 것 같아요.   **i** kŏkjŏng haji maseyo 걱정하지 마세요.   **j** mworaguyo? 뭐라구요?

Exercise 5:   **a** ppalli t'apshida 빨리 탑시다.   **b** Shigan-ŭn in- 시간은 있-   **c** an choayo 안 좋아요.   **d** kach'i kalkkayo? 같이 갈까요?   **e** kŭ saram puin-i an choayo 그 사람 부인이 안 좋아요.

Exercise 6:   **a** kedaga 게다가   **b** kŭlsseyo 글쎄요   **c** kŭrŏch'iman (kŭraedo would be even better) 그렇지만 (그래도)   **d** kŭrŏch'iman 그렇지만   **e** kŭrigo 그리고

Exercise 7:   **a** Kogi-rŭl choa haji anayo. 고기를 좋아하지 않아요.   **b** Chigŭm kaji mot haeyo. 지금 가지 못 해요.   **c** Chumun haji anayo. 주문하지 않아요.   **d** I sagwa-ga shingshing haji anayo. 이 사과가 싱싱하지 않아요.   **e** Bŏsŭ t'aji mot haeyo. 버스 타지 못 해요.

Exercise 8:   Mŏri-ga ap'-ayo. Tari-do ap'-ayo. Ŭmshig-ŭl mot mŏg-ŏyo. 머리가 아파요. 다리도 아파요. 음식을 못 먹어요.

Unit 7

Exercise 1:   **a** Then let's go together.   **b** Do you have (free) time today at lunchtime?   **c** It's really been a long time (since we've seen each other).   **d** I'm not the Japanese language teacher.   **e** I'm sorry. I made a mistake.   **f** Next Monday will perhaps be okay.   **g** Since I'm not from Seoul either, I really don't know.   **h** So your whole body hurts, then?! Is there anywhere that doesn't hurt?   **i** I'd like to change English currency into Chinese.   **j** And I'd like to eat some naengmyon as well.   **k** Give us some dried snacks and some Korean pancake, please. I You can take them for 20,000 won a box.

Exercise 2: **a** Se-shi-eyo. 세시에요 **b** Yŏdŏl-shi pan-ieyo. 여덟 시 반이에요. Or, Yŏdŏl-shi sam-ship-pun-ieyo. 여덟시 삼십 분이에요. **c** Yŏl-shi sa-ship-o-pun-ieyo. 열 시 사십오분이에요. **d** Ilgop-shi i-ship-pun-ieyo. 일곱시 이십분이에요. **e** Yŏsŏt-shi ship-pun-ieyo. 여섯시 십분이에요. **f** Yŏdŏl-shi ship-o pun-ieyo. 여덟 시 십오분이에요.

Exercise 3: **a** haeyo 해요, ha-go 하고, ha-pshida 합시다. **b** tadayo 닫아요, tat-ko 닫고, tat-ŭpshida 닫읍시다. **c** p'arayo 팔아요, p'al-go 팔고 p'a-pshida 팝시다. **d** pappayo 바빠요, pappŭ-go 바쁘고, pappŭ-pshida 바쁩시다. **e** umjigyŏyo 움직여요, umjigi-go 움직이고, umjigi-pshida 움직입시다.

Exercise 4: **a** San-e kapshida. 산에 갑시다. **b** Undongha-rŏ san-e kayo. 운동하러 산에 가요. **c** Yu-wol ship-i-ir-e kapshida. 유월 십이일에 갑시다. **d** Yŏdŏl-shi-e mannapshida. 여덟 시에 만납시다. **e** Kyohoe ap'-esŏ mannapshida. 교회 앞에서 만납시다.

Exercise 6: E.g. Ŏdi kayo? 어디 가요? Kage-e kayo. 가게에 가요. Mwo sa-rŏ kage-e kayo? 뭐 사러 가게에 가요? Ojingŏ sa-rŏ kayo. 오징어 사러 가요.

Exercise 7: **a** 박 선생님은 7 시 30 분에 일어나요. **b** 힐튼 호텔에서 이 선생님의 부인을 만나요. **c** 중국 음식을 먹어요. **d** 영화 보러 극장에 가요. **e** 11시에 자요.

Exercise 8: **a** Chukku-rŭl choa ha-ji anayo. T'enisŭ choa haeyo. 축구를 좋아하지 않아요. 테니스 좋아해요. **b** Aniyo, maeun kŏ chal mon mŏgŏyo. Kalbi mŏg-ŭl su issŏyo. 아니요, 매운 거 잘 못 먹어요. 갈비 먹을 수 있어요. **c** Aniyo, mani an payo. Kŭrŏch'iman radio-rŭl mani tŭrŏyo. 아니요, 많이 안 봐요. 그렇지만 라디오를 많이 들어요. **d** Chal mot pullŏyo. Ŭmag-ŭl (music) chal tŭrŏyo. 잘 못 불러요. 음악을 잘 들어요. **e** Aniyo, chunggungmal paeu-ji anayo. Yŏngŏ paewoyo. 아니요, 중국말 배우지 않아요. 영어 배워요.

Exercise 9: **a** Kyohoe-esŏ yŏngguk taesagwan-ŭn mŏl-ji anayo.
교회에서 영국 대사관은 멀지 않아요. **b** I kunch'ŏ-e hanguk
oehwan unhaeng-i ŏpsŏyo. Sangŏp unhaeng-ŭn issŏyo. 이 근처에
한국외환은행이 없어요. 상업은행은 있어요. **c** Hakkyo-ga
ŭnhaeng yŏp'-ieyo. 학교가 은행 옆이에요. **d** Chegwajŏm-i
mŏrŏyo. 제과점이 멀어요. **e** Ne. Uch'egug-ŭn taesagwan-poda
tŏ mŏrŏyo. 네. 우체국은 대사관보다 더 멀어요. **f** Hakkyo-e
karyŏmyŏn, kŏrŏsŏ saship-o-pun cchŭm kŏllyŏyo. 학교에 가려면
걸어서 사십오 분쯤 걸려요. **g** Uch'egug-ŭn chegwajŏm yŏp'-
ieyo. 우체국은 제과점 옆이에요.

Exercise 11: **a** 나도 영어를 공부하러 학교에 가요. **b** 가게 밖
에서 만납시다. 나중에 봐요. **c** 맛있게 드세요. (많이 드세요)
d 정말 병원에 가야겠어요. **e** 그럼 만오천원만 내세요.
f 십오분쯤 걸려요. **g** 요즘 사업은 어때요? **h** 제일 싼 거 주
세요. **i** 요즘 날씨가 좋아요. **j** 한국 대사관에서 박 선생님을
만나러 왔어요. **k** 매운 거 못 먹어요. **l** 우체국 가는 버스가 여
기 서요?

Unit 8
Exercise 1: **a** 학교에 갔어요. **b** 맥주 많이 마셨어요.
c 약속을 못 지켰어요. **d** 친구를 만났어요. **e** 영화를 보고 싶
었어요. **f** 도봉산에 갈까 했어요.

Exercise 2: **a** Hae-juseyo. 해주세요. **b** Shyop'ing hae-juseyo.
쇼핑해주세요. **c** Chŏmshim sa-juseyo. 점심 사주세요. **d** Kim
sŏnsaengnim-hant'e chŏnhwa hae-juseyo (or better, hae-jushigessŏyo).
김 선생님한테 전화해주세요 (or 해 주시겠어요?) **e** Yag-ŭl
sa-juseyo. 약을 사주세요. **f** Shijak hae-juseyo. 시작해주세요.

Exercise 3: ach'im-e 아침에..., -kiro haessŏyo –기로 했어요...,
kŭrŏch'iman 그렇지만..., saengyŏso 생겨서..., kŭrŏnikka
그러니까..., ha-ryŏgo 하려고..., haessŏyo 했어요..., chik'yŏssŏyo
지켰어요

Exercise 4: **a** 오늘 학교에 못 가요. 머리가 아프거든요. **b** 일
요길 날에 시내에 못 가요. 다른 약속이 있거든요. **c** 오늘 밤 탁

구 못 쳐요. 팔이 아프기 시작했거든요. **d** 노래방에 가요? 나는
안 가요. 노래방을 싫어하거든요. **e** 재민씨 못 가요? 그럼 잘 됐
네요. 나도 못 가거든요.

Exercise 5: **a** Taehak tongch'anghoe-ga issŏyo. 대학 동창회
가 있어요. **b** Friday, 10th, June. **c** Chipsaram-hago shyop'ing
haryŏgo haeyo. 집사람하고 쇼핑하려고 해요. **d** Tobongsan-e
karyŏgo haeyo. 도봉산에 가려고 해요 **e** From Friday, 17th June.
f Tony-hago chŏmshim-ŭl mŏgŏssŏyo. 토니하고 점심을
먹었어요.

Exercise 6: **a** Please try the soup! (Have a taste of …)
b Pulguksa han bŏn ka-boseyo. 불국사 한번 가보세요.
c Even though you're busy, go and see. **d** Have you never
tried playing table tennis? Then have a go! **e** Jaemin-ssi ajik
an wassŏyo? Kŭrŏm chogŭm tŏ kidaryŏ-boseyo. 재민씨 아직 안
왔어요? 그럼 조금 더 기다려 보세요.

Exercise 7: **a** Pappŭn ir-i saengyŏ-sŏ, mot kayo. (Or, kal su
ŏpsŏyo). 바쁜 일이 생겨서 못 가요. (or 갈 수 없어요) **b** Chib-e
ŭmshig-i ŏpsŏ-sŏ, shiktang-e kayo. 집에 음식이 없어서, 식당에
가요. **c** Saŏb-i an choa-sŏ, ton-i ŏpsŏyo. 사업이 안 좋아서, 돈
이 없어요. **d** Pakk-e naga-sŏ kidari-pshida. 밖에 나가서 기다립
시다. **e** Sangmin-ssi chib-e ka-sŏ mwol halkkayo? 상민씨 집에
가서 뭘 할까요? **f** Sinae-e ka-sŏ kwail chom sa-o-seyo. 시내에
가서 과일 좀 사 오세요.

Exercise 8: **a** Yaksog-ŭl ch'wisoha-ryŏgo chŏnhwa haess-ŏyo.
Ir-i saenggyŏt-kŏdŭnyo. 약속을 취소하려고 전화했어요. 일이
생겼거든요. **b** Sangmin-ssi-nŭn t'akku ch'i-rŏ panggum nagass-
ŏyo. 상민씨는 탁구 치러 방금 나갔어요. **c** Chŏŭm-enŭn
Kimch'i-ga kŭrŏk'e maŭm-e tŭl-ji anan-nŭnde (Or, Kimch'i-rŭl
pyŏllo choaha-ji anan-nŭnde), iksuk haejyŏss-ŏyo. 처음에는 김치
가 그렇게 마음에 들지 않았는데 (or 김치를 별로 좋아하지 않았
는데), 익숙해졌어요. **d** Ŏnje chorŏphaess-ŏyo? 언제 졸업했어
요? **e** Sulchip-esŏ uyŏnhi manass-ŏyo. 술집에서 우연히
만났어요. **f** Isangha-neyo! K'ŭrisŭ-nŭn pŏlssŏ torawass-ŏyo.
이상하네요! 크리스는 벌써 돌아왔어요. **g** Ŏje pam-e mwo

haess-ŏyo? Solchikhi mal hae-boseyo. 어제밤에 뭐 했어요? 솔직히
말해보세요.

Exercise 9: T'enisŭ hae bwass-ŏyo? 테니스 해봤어요? Nonggu
hae bwass-ŏyo? 농구 해봤어요? Sinmun ilg-ŏ bwass-ŏyo? 신문 읽
어 봤어요? Yŏngguk ŭmshik mŏg-ŏ bwass-ŏyo? 영국 음식 먹어 봤
어요?

Unit 9
Exercise 1: **a** P'at'i-e sŏnsaengnim-i oshilkka(-bwa)
kŏkchŏng-ieyo. 파티에 선생님이 오실까(봐) 걱정이에요.
b Ŭmshig-i mojaralkka(-bwa) kŏkchŏng-ieyo. 음식이
모자랄까(봐) 걱정이에요. **c** Kim sŏnsaengnim-i an
oshilkka(-bwa) kŏkchŏng-ieyo. 김 선생님이 안 오실까(봐) 걱정
이에요. **d** Yŏja ch'ingu-ga tangshin-ŭl an choahalkka(-bwa)
kŏkchŏng-ieyo. 여자 친구가 당신을 안 좋아할까(봐) 걱정이
에요. **e** Pi-ga olkka(-bwa) kŏkjŏng-ieyo. 비가 올까봐
걱정이에요.

Exercise 2: 김 선생님 대학교 선생님이세요. 런던 대학교에서
한국말을 가르치시고 일본말도 가르치세요. 매일 아침 공원에 가
셔ㅓ산책하세요. 개하고 같이 가세요. 공원은 아주 좋아요. 김선
생님의 개는 고기를 잘 먹어요. 작년부터 부인도 가끔 산책하기
시작하셨어요. 부인도 가시면 둘이 식당에 가서서 커피 한잔 마
시세요.

Exercise 3: **a** Yag-ŭl sa-yagessŏyo. 약을 사야겠어요.
b Chwiso ha-ryŏgo chŏnhwa hae-yagessŏyo. 취소하려고 전화해야
겠어요. **c** Sajŏn-ŭl sa-yagessŏyo. 사전을 사야겠어요. **d** Tora-
ga-yagessŏyo. 돌아가야겠어요. **e** Shinmun-ŭl pwa-yagessŏyo.
신문을 봐야겠어요.

Exercise 4: **a** Muŏs-ŭl salkka kyŏlchŏng hae-yagessŏyo.
무엇을 살까 결정해야겠어요. **b** Muŏs-ŭl ibulkka kyŏlchŏng
hae-yagessŏyo. 무엇을 입을까 결정해야겠어요. **c** Ŏdi anjŭlkka
kyŏlchŏng hae-yagessŏyo. 어디 앉을까 결정해야겠어요.
d Muŏs-ŭl chumun halkka kyŏlchŏng hae-yagessŏyo. 무엇을 주문

할까 결정해야겠어요. **e** Chumar-e ŏdi kalkka kyŏlchŏng
hae-yagessŏyo. 주말에 어디 갈까 결정해야겠어요.

Exercise 5: **a** Na-do o-l su issŏyo? 나도 올 수 있어요? **b** Igŏ
mŏg-ŭl su issŏyo? 이거 먹을 수 있어요? **c** Na-rŭl naeil manna-l
su issŏyo? 나를 내일 만날 수 있어요? **d** Ilbonmar-ŭl mal ha-l
su ŏpsŏyo. 일본말을 말할 수 없어요. **e** Ton-i ŏps-ŏsŏ sa-l su
ŏpsŏyo. 돈이 없어서 살 수 없어요. **f** Yŏgi chuch'a ha'l su
ŏpsŏyo. 여기 주차할 수 없어요.

Exercise 6: **a** Ŏje sat-janayo. 어제 샀잖아요! **b** Aniyo, pŏlssŏ
kyŏrhon haet-janayo! 아니요, 벌써 결혼했잖아요! **c** Pŏlssŏ haet-
janayo. 벌써 했잖아요! **d** Ilkki shirŏ ha-janayo. 읽기 싫어하잖아
요! **e** Uri chipsaram-ieyo. Ŏje mannat-janayo. 우리 집사람이에
요. 어제 만났잖아요!

Exercise 7

A Naeir-i oppa saengir-ieyo. 내일이 오빠 생일이에요.

Mwol sa-dŭrilkka chŏng haeyagessŏyo. 뭘 사드릴까
정해야겠어요.

B Ch'ŏngbaji-rŭl sa-dŭrilkkayo? 청바지를 사드릴까요?

A Ch'ŏngbaji-nŭn pŏlssŏ yŏl pŏl-ina kat-ko issŏyo. 청바지는 벌써
열 벌이나 갖고 있어요.

B Kŭrŏmyŏn chaeg-ŭn ŏttŏlkkayo? 그러면 책은 어떨까요?

A Oppa-nŭn chaeg-ŭl sirŏhaeyo. 오빠는 책을 싫어해요.

B Kŭrŏm mannyŏnp'ir-ŭnyo? 그럼 만년필은요?

A Mannyŏnp'il-do tŏ isang p'iryo ŏpsŏyo. 만년필도 더 이상 필요
없어요.

B Kŭrŏm CD-nŭn? 그럼 씨디는?

A Changnyŏn-e sa dryŭŏt-janayo. 작년에 사드렸잖아요.

Unit 10

Exercise 1: **a** Naeil shigan issŏyo? 내일 시간 있어요?
b Yŏnggug-esŏ wan-nŭndeyo. 영국에서 왔는데요. **c** Ŏje
chŏnhwa haen-nŭndeyo. 어제 전화했는데요. **d** Kabang-ŭl nok'o

kassŏyo. 가방을 놓고 갔어요. **e** Sajŏn-ŭl sa-go ship'-ŭndeyo.
사전을 사고 싶은데요. **f** Kim sŏnsaengnim ŏdi kasyŏssŏyo?
김 선생님 어디 가셨어요?

Exercise 2: **a** 비가 오는 것 같아요. **b** 그 사람은 박 선생님인
것 같아요. **c** 독서를 싫어하는 것 같아요. **d** 동대문 시장에 간
것 같아요. **e** 김 선생님 오시는 것 같아요. **f** 가방을 여기 놓은
것 같아요.

Exercise 3: Aju k'ŭgo kŏmjŏng saeg-igo kajug-ŭro mandŭrŏssyo.
아주 크고 검정색이고 가죽으로 만들었어요.

Exercise 4: **a** Ŭmshig-ŭl mŏg-ŭl ttae iyagi (mal) ha-ji maseyo.
음식을 먹을 때 이야기(말)하지 마세요. **b** Chuch'a ha-l ttae
choshim haseyo. 주차할 때 조심하세요. **c** Shinae-e ka-l ttae
na-hant'e chŏnhwa hae-juseyo. 시내에 갈 때 나한테 전화해주
세요. **d** Yŏnghwa-ga kkŭnna-l ttae shiktang-e kapshida. 영화
가 끝날 때 식당에 갑시다. **e** Toch'ak haess-ŭl ttae maekchu
hana mashyŏssŏyo. 도착했을 때 맥주 하나 마셨어요. **f** Naga-l
ttae kach'i kapshida. 나갈 때 같이 갑시다.

Exercise 5: **a** Anyhow, what have you decided to do now?
b Didn't you see my girlfriend? If you see her (please) give me a call.
c If you get a bit better don't take the medicine any more.
d When will you graduate? What plans have you got after that?
e Are these papers important? Of course they're important! It's my
driving licence, stupid! **f** When we have a date, we often go to
see a movie.

Exercise 6: **a** K'ŭn shilsu-rŭl hasyŏssŏyo. 큰 실수를 하셨어요.
b Pam nŭtke toshi-e kamyŏn wihŏmhaeyo. 밤 늦게 도시에 가면
위험해요. **c** Kŭ sajŏn chom poyŏ jushigessŏyo? 그 사전 좀 보여
주시겠어요? Igŏ ŏdi-sŏ sashyŏssŏyo? 이거 어디서 사셨어요?
d Musŭn munje-ga innayo? 무슨 문제가 있나요? Ne. Nae yag-ŭl
irŏbŏri-n kŏt kat'ayo. 네. 내 약을 잃어버린 것 같아요. **e** Yojŭm
st'ŭresu-rŭl nŏmu mani pada-sŏ, pam-e cham-ŭl chal su ŏpsŏyo. 요
즘 스트레스를 너무 많이 받아서 밤에 잠을 잘 수 없어요.
f Kabang-ŭl irŏbŏri-syŏssŏyo? Mwo-ga tŭrŏ innayo? 가방을 잃어

버리셨어요? 뭐가 들어 있나요? **g** Nae saenggag-ŭl choaha-ji anch'anayo. 내 생각을 좋아하지 않잖아요. **h** Kŭraesŏ mwol hashyŏssŏyo? 그래서 뭘 하셨어요?

Exercise 7: Take two tablets every three hours while it's very bad. When it gets a bit better, then take one tablet before meal only at lunchtime.

Unit 11

Exercise 1: **a** 이 옷이 정말 좋다. **b** 비가 온다. **c** 뭘 하나? **d** 밥을 먹고 있다. **e** 걱정하고 있나? **f** 조금더 기다리면 버스가 올 거다. **g** 밥 먹는다. **h** 어제 밤 어디 갔니? **i** 조심했니?

Exercise 2: **a** Myŏn-ŭro mandŭn ot. 면으로 만든 옷. **b** Ŏje uri-ga mashin maekchu. 어제 우리가 마신 맥주. **c** Kim sŏnsaengnim-i il-ko innŭn chaek. 김 선생님이 읽고 있는 책. **d** Kŭ saram-i ip-ko innŭn shyŏch'ŭ. 그 사람이 입고 있는 셔츠. **e** Changnyŏn-e uri-ga pon yŏnghwa. 작년에 우리가 본 영화. **f** Nae-ga shirŏha-nŭn ŭmshik. 내가 싫어하는 음식.

Exercise 3: **a** Choa poyŏ-do, an choayo. 좋아 보여도, 안 좋아요. **b** Pissa-do, mash-i issŏyo. 비싸도, 맛이 있어요. **c** Pi-ga wa-do, naga-go ship'ŏyo. 비가 와도, 나가고 싶어요. **d** Kŭ saram-ŭl choaha-ji ana-do, manna-yagessŏyo. 그 사람을 좋아하지 않아도, 만나야겠어요. **e** Palgŭn saeg-ira-do, ŏulli-ji anayo. 밝은 색이라도, 어울리지 않아요. **f** Mŏri-ga ap'a-do, noraebang-e kalkka haeyo. 머리가 아파도, 노래방에 갈까 해요.

Exercise 4

A Musŭn yŏnghwa-rŭl polkkayo? 무슨 영화를 볼까요?

B _____rŭl popshida. ____를 봅시다.

A Kŭ-gŏn uri-ga changnyŏn-e pon yŏnghwa-janayo. 그건 우리가 작년에 본 영화잖아요.

_____rŭl popshida. ___를 봅시다.

B Kŭ-gŏn shigan-i nŏmu nŭjŏyo. 그건 시간이 너무 늦어요.

A Yŏldu-shi-ga nŏmu nŭjŏyo? Musŭn mar-ieyo?! 열두 시가 너무 늦어요? 무슨 말이에요?!

B Kŭraedo kŭ yŏnghwa-nŭn chŏngmal chaemi ŏmnŭn kŏt kat'ayo. 그래도 그 영화는 정말 재미 없는 것 같아요.

A Musŭn yŏnghwa-rŭl polkka? 무슨 영화를 볼까?

B _____rŭl poja. ___ 를 보자.

A Kŭ-gŏn uri-ga changnyŏn-e pon yŏnghwa-jana. 그건 우리가 작년에 본 영화잖아.

  _____rul poja. ___ 를 보자.

B Kŭ-gŏn shigan-i nŏmu nŭjo. 그건 시간이 너무 늦어.

A Yŏldu-shi-ga nŏmu nŭjo? Musŭn mar-iya?! 열두시가 너무 늦어? 무슨 말이야?!

B Kŭraedo kŭ yŏnghwa-nŭn chŏngmal chaemi ŏmnŭn kŏt kat'a. 그래도 그 영화는 정말 재미없는 것 같아.

Exercise 5: **a** Hangugmar-ŭl chal hanŭn saram-i wayo. 한국말을 잘 하는 사람이 와요. **b** Ŏje san os-ul choaha-ji anayo. 어제 산 옷을 좋아하지 않아요. **c** Kŭ saram-ŭn mŏshinŭn saram-ieyo. 그 사람은 멋있는 사람이에요. **d** Chir-i tŏ choa-do ne bae-na pissayo. 질이 더 좋아도 네 배나 비싸요. **e** Tangshin-i ip-go innŭn os-ŭl ibŏ pol su issŏyo? 당신이 입고 있는 옷을 입어볼 수 있어요? **f** Mworaguyo? 뭐라구요? **g** Sul mashi-ji anass-ŏdo, pam-e unjŏnhal ttae choshimhaseyo. 술 마시지 않았어도 밤에 운전할 때 조심하세요. **h** Pisŭt han kŏ issŏyo? 비슷한 거 있어요?

Unit 12

Exercise 1: **a** Haksaeng-i myŏnmyŏng-imnikka? 학생이 몇 명입니까? **b** Mŭsŭn shisŏl-dŭr-i issŭmnikka? 무슨 시설들이 있습니까? **c** Hangungmal-hago chunggungmar-ŭl kongbu hal su issŭmnikka? 한국말하고 중국말을 공부할 수 있습니까? **d** Myŏnmyŏng-i hangungmar-ŭl kongbu hamnikka? 몇 명이 한국말을 공부합니까? **e** Chŏmshim shigan-ŭn myŏt-shi-imnikka? 점심 시간은 몇 시입니까? **f** Chŏmshim shigan-e pap mŏg-ŭrŏ chip-e ka-do toemnikka? 점심 시간에 밥 먹으러 집에 가도 됩니까?

Exercise 2: **a** Pin pang issŏyo? 빈 방 있어요? **b** Ne. Ch'imdae-bang chuseyo. 네. 침대방 주세요. **c** Ilgop-sal-hago tasŏt-sar-ieyo. 일곱 살하고 다섯 살이에요. **d** Sam-il tongan-iyo. 삼일 동안이요. **e** Aniyo. Chikchŏp shiktang-e kasŏ mŏkkessŏyo. 아니요. 직접 식당에 가서 먹겠어요.

Exercise 3: **a** Muŏs-ŭl hashyŏsssŭmnikka? 무엇을 하셨습니까? **b** Chimdaebang hana chushipshio. 침대방 하나 주십시오. **c** Chŏ saram-ŭn Kim sŏnsaengnim-ishimnikka? 저 사람은 김 선생님이십니까? **d** Na-nŭn paekhwajŏm-e kamnida. 나는 백화점에 갑니다. **e** Radio-rŭl tŭr-ŭmyŏnsŏ ch'aeg-ŭl ilksŭmnida. 라디오를 들으면서 책을 읽습니다.

Exercise 4: **a** If you book for more than a week, we'll give you a 10% discount. **b** To be (perfectly) honest, I hate people like that. **c** He said that he had (or, he has) already eaten breakfast. **d** A room with a floor mattress is 20,000 won per day. **e** It will be okay if you get up at 7 o'clock. **f** We can't give you a refund (of the fare). **g** Two rooms with (Western) beds, please. **h** If you've got something to say (comments to make) about this hotel, please speak to the manager.

Exercise 5: **a** I hot'er-e sauna shisŏr-i issŭmnikka? 이 호텔에 사우나 시설이 있습니까? **b** Ach'im shiksa-rŭl paedal hae-jumnikka? 아침 식사를 배달해 줍니까? **c** I hot'er-e suyŏngjang-i issŭmnikka? 이 호텔에 수영장이 있습니까?

Exercise 6: **a** Myŏch'il tongan yeyak hasyŏsssŭmnikka? 며칠 동안 예약하셨습니까? **b** Chŭkshi unhaengwon-hant'e yaegi haessŭmnida. 즉시 은행원한테 얘기했습니다. **c** I hot'er-e musŭn shisŏl-dŭr-i issŭmnikka? 이 호텔에 무슨 시설들이 있습니까? **d** Nae ch'a-e munje-ga manŭn kŏt kat'-ayo. 내 차에 문제가 많은 것 같아요. **e** Nae adŭr-ŭn aji-kkaji irŏna-ji anassŏyo. 내 아들은 아직까지 일어나지 않았어요. **f** Uri-nŭn chŭkshi ba-e kasŏ sul mashil kŏeyo. 우리는 즉시 바에 가서 술 마실 거에요. **g** Kim sŏnsaengnim-ŭn pulch'injŏl han saram-ieyo. 김 선생님은 불친절한 사람이에요. **h** Sam-il tongan mungnŭn ke chok'essŏyo. 삼일 동안 묵는 게 좋겠어요.

Unit 13

Exercise 1: a There are not many seats left. **b** You can't eat something different. **c** Would you like a return ticket? **d** Mountain climbing is really awful. (*I really hate it …*) **e** It looks as if I'll have to go, then. **f** We were just going to have (*intending to have*) a game of baseball. **g** Is there a train going to Mokp'o this afternoon? **h** That's a decent idea (surprise!).

Exercise 2: a Chŏmshim mŏk-ki chŏn-e 점심 먹기 전에. Chŏmshim mŏg-ŭn taŭm-e 점심 먹은 다음에. **b** Ŏmŏni-hant'e chŏnhwa ha-gi chŏn-e 어머니한테 전화하기 전에. Ŏmŏni-hant'e chŏnhwa ha-n taŭm-e 어머니한테 전화한 다음에. **c** Nol-gi chŏn-e 놀기 전에. No-n taŭm-e 논 다음에. **d** Shinmum-ŭl ilk-ki chŏn-e 신문을 읽기 전에. Shinmun-ŭl ilk-ŭn taŭm-e 신문을 읽은 다음에.

Exercise 3: a 20.00 (10 p.m.) **b** 8.00 **c** 11.00 **d** No, there isn't. **e** Yes, there is.

Exercise 4: a Chib-e toraga-l su pakk-e ŏpsŏyo. 집에 돌아갈 수 밖에 없어요. **b** Ton-ŭl nae-l su pakk-e ŏpsŏyo. 돈을 낼 수 밖에 없어요. **c** Ach'im yŏsŏt-shi-e irŏna-l su pakk-e ŏpsŏyo. 아침 여섯 시에 일어날 수밖에 없어요.

Exercise 5: a Na-nŭn kogi malgo kwail mŏk-ko ship'-ŏyo. 나는 고기 말고 과일 먹고 싶어요. **b** Na-nŭn suyŏng malgo non-ggu ha-go ship'-ŏyo. 나는 수영 말고 농구하고 싶어요. **c** Na-nŭn shinmun malgo sosŏl chaek ilk-ko ship'-ŏyo. 나는 신문 말고 소설 책 읽고 싶어요. **d** Na-nŭn norae ha-ji malgo ŭmak tŭt-ko ship'-ŏyo. 나는 노래하지 말고 음악 듣고 싶어요.

Exercise 6: a Ch'ulbal shigan chŏn-e (or, Ch'ulbal ha-gi chŏn-e), mŏg-ŭl kŏ-rŭl saseyo. 출발 시간 전에 (or 출발하기 전에), 먹을 거를 사세요. **b** Pumonim-hant'e yaegi halkkayo? 부모님한테 얘기 할까요? **c** Na-do ka-go ship-chiman, nŏmu mŏrŏyo. 나도 가고 싶지만, 너무 멀어요. **d** Se chari-rŭl hamkke yeyak hal su issŏyo? 세 자리를 함께 예약할 수 있어요? **e** Sŏul malgo Inch'ŏn-e kapshida. 서울 말고 인천에 갑시다. **f** Il kkŭnna-n daŭm-e mwol

halkkayo? 일 끝난 다음에 뭘 할까요? **g** Ŏnje tora-o-shigessŏyo?
언제 돌아오시겠어요? **h** Saengsŏnhoe choaha-seyo? 생선회 좋
아하세요?

Unit 14
Exercise 1: **a** Since Mum likes watching movies, she can go
to the cinema instead of Dad. **b** It's probably due to stress.
c In fact (actually) there were some very important papers inside.
d (My) jeans have worn out (become unusable). **e** My wife will
perhaps know. **f** Tomorrow evening after work I'm planning to
go to the mountains. **g** You never like my ideas (**or**, opinions).
h The door to our room doesn't even open. **i** Could you tell
me where the library is, please (*lit:* could you teach me ...)?
j Did you drink so much alcohol (as that)? **k** It's a very popular
style nowadays. **l** Show me your driver's licence, please.

Exercise 2: **a** Yagu hae boshyŏssŏyo? 야구 해보셨어요?
Ne. Hae bwassŏyo. Sashir-ŭn ŏje hae bwassŏyo. 네. 해봤어요. 사
실은 어제 해봤어요. **b** Suyŏng hae boshyŏssŏyo? 수영 해보셨어
요? Ne. Hae bwassŏyo. Sashir-ŭn ŏje hae bwassŏyo. 네. 해봤어요.
사실은 어제 해봤어요. **c** T'aku hae boshyŏssŏyo? 탁구 해보셨어
요? Ne. Hae bwassŏyo. Sashir-ŭn ŏje hae bwassŏyo. 네. 해봤어요.
사실은 어제 해봤어요. **d** Ch'um ch'wo boshyŏssŏyo? 춤 춰보셨
어요? Ne. Hae bwassŏyo. Sashir-ŭn ŏje hae bwassŏyo. 네. 해봤어
요. 사실은 어제 해봤어요.

Exercise 3: **a** 죄송하지만 여기 그런 사람 없어요. **b** 아니요,
싫어합니다. **c** 데이트할 때는 보통 극장이나 공원에 가요.
d 별로 좋지 않은 것 같아요. **e** 아니요, 약속을 잘 지켜요.

Exercise 4: **a** Chŏngmallo p'yojip'an-ŭl mot pwassŏyo.
정말로 표지판을 못 봤어요. **b** Ch'ongbaji hago kach'i ibŭl su
issŏyo. 청바지하고 같이 입을 수 있어요. **c** Yaksog-ŭl ch'wiso
ha-ryŏgo chŏnhwa haessŏyo. 약속을 취소하려고 전화했어요.
d Pang-e chŏnhwa-hago t'erebi-ga issŏyo? 방에 전화하고 테레비
가 있어요? **e** Sŏbisu-ga ŏnmang-ieyo. 서비스가 엉망이에요.
f Changnyŏn-e kŭ saram-hant'e yangmar-ŭl sa juŏssŏyo. 작년에

그 사람한테 양말을 사주었어요. **g** Chom chag-ŭn kŏt kat'-ayo. 좀 작은 것 같아요. **h** Kŭrŏn chul arassŏyo. 그런 줄 알았어요. **i** Inch'ŏn-e kasŏ saengsŏnhoe-rŭl mŏk-ko ship'-ŏyo. 인천에 가서 생선회를 먹고 싶어요. **j** Cha-ga ŏttŏk'e saenggyŏssŏyo? 차가 어떻게 생겼어요? **k** P'yŏnji han jang ssŏ jushigessŏyo? 편지 한 장 써 주시겠어요? **l** Mŏri-ga nŏmu ap'asŏ cham-ŭl mot chayo. 머리가 너무 아파서 잠을 못 자요.

Exercise 5

Name:	Irŭm-i mwo-eyo? 이름이 뭐에요?
Age:	Myŏt-sar-ieyo? 몇 살이에요?
Occupation:	Chigŏb-i mwo-eyo? 직업이 뭐에요?
Father's name:	Abŏji irŭm-i mwo-eyo? 아버지 이름이 뭐에요?
How met:	Ŏttŏk'e mannass-ŏyo? 어떻게 만났어요?
What do together:	Hamkke (Kach'i) mwol haeyo? 함께 (같이) 뭘 해요?
Likes/dislikes:	Mwol choahaeyo? 뭘 좋아해요?
	Mwol sirŏhaeyo? 뭘 싫어해요?

Exercise 6: **a** If you do it wrong (*if you don't do it properly*), it's very dangerous. **b** Do you have a message for Poktong? **c** We deliver it to your room (*lit:* the guest's room). **d** I was here yesterday. I left my jumper. **e** The girl said that it was good quality. **f** I've got a new girlfriend and it seems as if we're out every day. **g** Don't talk; just listen. **h** Take one tablet twice a day after meals. **i** Look at this! The quality's pretty bad. **j** You wouldn't know where he/she has gone, would you? **k** How would a new television be? **l** A similar thing is about twice as cheap at Namdaemun.

Exercise 7: Anio, pappŭn ir-i issŏyo. Waeyo? 아니요, 바쁜 일이 있어요. 왜요? Woryoir-ŭn ŏttaeyo? 월요일은 어때요? Kŭraeyo?

P'at'i-ga issŏyo? 그래요? 파티가 있어요? Abŏji-hant'e mwol sa-dŭrilkkŏeyo? 아버지한테 뭘 사 드릴까요? Hwayoir-ŭn ŏttaeyo? Kŭ-ttae-nŭn shigan issŏyo? 화요일은 어때요? 그때는 시간 있어요? Cho-ŭn saenggag-ieyo. 좋은 생각이에요.

Exercise 8

Informal style:

A Naeil chŏnyŏg-e shigan-i issŏ? 내일 저녁에 시간이 있어?

You Ani, pappŭn ir-i issŏ. Wae? 아니. 바쁜 일이 있어. 왜?

A Kŭnyang naga-go ship'ŏnnŭnde. 그냥 나가고 싶었는데.

You Woryoir-ŭn ŏttae? 월요일은 어때?

A Woryoil-lar-ŭn abŏji saengshin-iya. 월요일 날은 아버지 생신이야.

You Kŭrae? P'at'i-ga issŏ? 그래? 파티가 있어?

A Ani. Kŭnyang shiktang-e kasŏ kach'i chŏnyŏk hanŭn kŏ-ya. 아니. 그냥 식당에 가서 같이 저녁 하는 거야.

You Abŏji-hant'e mwol sa-dŭrilkŏya? 아버지한테 뭘 사 드릴 거야?

A Yangmal. Hangsang yangmal sa. 양말. 항상 양말 사.

You Hwayoir-ŭn ŏttae? Kŭ ttae-nŭn shigan issŏ? 화요일은 어때? 그때는 시간 있어?

A Ŭng, choa. Naitŭ kalkka? 응. 좋아. 나이트 갈까?

You Cho-ŭn saenggag-iya. 좋은 생각이야.

Plain style:

A Naeil chŏnyŏg-e shigan-i iss-ni? 내일 저녁에 시간이 있니?

You Anida, pappŭn ir-i iss-ta. Wae? 아니다. 바쁜 일이 있다. 왜?

A Kŭnyang naga-go ship'ŏnnunde. 그냥 나가고 싶었는데.

You Woryoir-ŭn ŏttŏ-ni? 월요일은 어떠니?

A Woryoil-lar-ŭn abŏji saengshin-ida. 월요일 날은 아버지 생신이다.

You Kŭrae? P'at'i-ga iss-ni? 그래? 파티가 있니?

A Anida. Kŭnyang shiktang-e kasŏ kach'i chŏnyŏk hanŭn kŏ-da. 아니다. 그냥 식당에 가서 같이 저녁 하는 거다.

You Aboji-hant'e mwol sa-dŭrilkŏ-ni? 아버지한테 뭘 사 드릴 거니?

A Yangmal. Hangsang yangmal sa-nda. 양말. 항상 양말 산다.

You Hwayoir-ŭn ŏttŏ-ni? Kŭ ttae-nŭn shigan iss-ni? 화요일은 어떠니? 그때는 시간 있니?

A Ŭng, cho-t'a. Naitŭ kalkka? 응, 좋다. 나이트 갈까?

You Cho-ŭn saenggag-ida. 좋은 생각이다.

Exercise 9: **a** Chigŭm ŏdi kashimnikka? 지금 어디 가십니까? **b** Chumun haesssŭmnikka? 주문했습니까? **c** Ilgop shi-e irŏnamnida. 일곱시에 일어납니다. **d** Ppalli hae-jushipshio. 빨리 해주십시오. **e** Chŏ saram-ŭn pulch'inchŏl han saram-imnida. 저 사람은 불친절한 사람입니다.

Exercise 10: Ach'im ilgop-shi-e irŏnassŏyo. 아침 일곱시에 일어났어요. Ach'im-ŭl mŏg-ŭn daŭm-e ahop-shi-e kyohoe-e kassŏyo. 아침을 먹은 다음에 아홉 시에 교회에 갔어요. Yŏl-du-shi-e yŏja ch'ingu hago kach'i chŏmshim-ŭl mŏgŏssŏyo. 열두 시에 여자 친구하고 같이 점심을 먹었어요. Se-shi-e kich'a-rŭl t'ago Pusan-e kassŏyo. 세시에 기차를 타고 부산에 갔어요. Ilgop-shi-e yŏnghwa-rŭl pwassŏyo. 일곱시에 영화를 봤어요

Exercise 11: **a** 그때부터 그 여자를 자주 만나기 시작했어요. **b** 힘이 없어도 놀라지 마세요. **c** 이번에는 당신이 도와주세요. **d** 비슷해 보여도 비슷하지 않아요. **e** 지금부터 더 조심하세요. **f** 지금 (즉시) 식당에 가서 밥 먹을 거에요. **g** 그럼 잘 됐네요. 안녕히 계세요. **h** 오늘 저녁은 내가 낼게요 (or 살게요). **i** 우리 백화점을 몇 시에 떠나셨어요? **j** 실수가 발생합니다. **k** 당신을 소개할까요? **l** 입어보시겠어요?

Korean–English vocabulary

아 (a)! — *ah!*

아침 (ach'im) — *morning; breakfast* (abbreviated form)

아침하- (ach'im ha-) — *have breakfast*

아침식사 (ach'imshiksa) — *breakfast*

아들 (adŭl) — *son*

아가씨 (agassi) — *waitress!*, lit: = *girl, unmarried woman*

아직 (ajik) — *yet, still*

아저씨 (ajŏssi) — *waiter!*

아주 (aju) — *very*

알 (al) — *tablet*

알겠습니다 (algesssŭmnida) — *I understand; okay, right, fine* (formally)

아마 (ama) — *perhaps, probably*

안 (an) — *not* (used to make verbs negative)

아니에요 (anieyo) — *is not* (opposite of *-(i)eyo,* negative copula)

아니요 (aniyo) — *no*

앉- (anj-) — *sit* (stem)

안주 (anju) — *snacks or side dishes for drinks*

안녕히 가세요 (annyŏnghi kaseyo) — *goodbye (to someone who is leaving)*

안녕히계세요 (annyŏnghi kyeseyo) — *goodbye (to someone who is staying)*

안 파는 거 (an p'anŭn kŏ) — *something which is not sold, not available*

앞에서 (ap'esŏ) — *in front of*

아파요 (ap'ayo)	*hurts* (polite style)
아프- (ap'ǔ-)	*hurts* (stem)
아픈 (ap'ǔn)	*hurting, painful* (adjective)
알아들- (ara-dǔl-)	*understand* (l/t verb like tul-, listen; *ara-dǔroyo, ara-dǔt-ko* etc.)
째 (cchae)	*number* (time)
쪽 (cchok)	*side*
차 (ch'a)	*car* (short form)
찾- (ch'aj-)	*look for*
찾아보- (ch'aja-bo-)	*to have a look, to look for*
참 (ch'am)	*very*
창구 (ch'anggu)	*window, cashier window*
치- (ch'i-)	*to play* (tennis, table tennis etc.)
침대 (ch'imdae)	*bed*
침대방 (ch'imdaebang)	*room with bed*
청바지 (ch'ǒngbaji)	*blue jeans*
청소하- (ch'ǒngso ha-)	*clean, clean up*
촌사람 (ch'onsaram)	*country bumpkin, yokel*
-처럼 (-ch'ǒrǒm)	*like*
처음 (ch'ǒǔm)	*at first*
출발 (ch'ulbal)	*departure*
출발하- (ch'ulbal ha-)	*depart*
자- (cha-)	*sleep*
자동차 (chadongch'a)	*car*
재작년 (chaejangnyǒn)	*the year before last year*
재미있- (chaemi iss-)	*is interesting, is fun*
재료 (chaeryo)	*stuff, (raw) material*
재수 (chaesu)	*luck*
재수없- (chaesu ǒps-)	*have no luck, have bad luck*
자주 (chaju)	*often, frequently*
잘 (chal)	*good, well* (adverb)

잘못 (chalmot)	*wrongly, mis-*
잠 (cham)	*sleep* (noun)
잠바 (chamba)	*jumper*
잠깐 (chamkkan)	*a little (while)*
잠깐 기다리세요 (chamkkan kidariseyo)	*please wait a moment*
잔 (chan)	*cup*
작년 (changnyŏn)	*last year*
잡지 (chapchi)	*magazine*
잡쉬보- (chapswo-bo-)	*try eating* (honorific form)
잡수시- (chapsushi-)	*eat* (honorific equivalent of *mŏk-*)
자리 (chari)	*seat*
제 (che)	*my* (humble form)
제 생각에는 (che saenggag-enŭn)	*in my opinion*
제과점 (chegwajŏm)	*bakery*
제일 (cheil)	*the most*
지배인 (chibaein)	*manager (of hotel or facility)*
지금 (chigŭm)	*now*
직원 (chigwon)	*employee*
지하 (chiha)	*basement*
지하 식당 (chiha shiktang)	*basement restaurant*
지점 (chijŏm)	*branch*
직접 (chikchŏp)	*direct(ly)*
직행 (chikhaeng)	*fast train, express train* (also called *saemaŭl(ho)*)
질 (chil)	*quality*
질색이- (chilsaeg-i-)	*(really) hate*
진짜 (chinccha)	*really*
집 (chip)	*house*
집사람 (chipsaram)	*wife*

저 (chǒ)	me
저- (chǒ-)	that one (a long way away, old English 'yon')
저⋯ (chǒ ...)	er ..., hmm ...
좋지 않- (cho-ch'i anh-)	is not good (from choh-)
좋은 생각이네요 (cho-ǔn saenggag-ineyo)	that's a good idea
좋아하- (choa ha-)	like (stem)
좋아요 (choayo)	good, fine, okay (polite style)
죄송하지만 (choesong ha-jiman)	I'm sorry, but; excuse me, but ...
죄송합니다 (choesong hamnida)	I'm sorry; I apologize; excuse me
저기 (chǒgi)	(over) there
적어도 (chǒgǒ-do)	at least
조금 (chogǔm)	a little, a bit
조금 전 (chogǔm chǒn)	a little while ago
좋- (choh-)	good (stem)
저희 (chǒhǔy)	humble form of uri 'our, my'
좀 (chom)	a little; please
점심 (chǒmshim)	lunch
전 (chǒn)	before
전하- (chǒn ha-)	communicate
전할 말 (chǒn ha-l mal)	something to say/pass on/communicate
전에 (chǒn-e)	previously
전기 면도기 (chǒngi myǒndogi)	electric shaver
정말 (chǒngmal)	really
정하- (chǒngdo)	extent, about (approximately)
정도 (chǒng ha-)	decide

종로 (chongno)	*Chongno* (one of the main streets in Seoul, north of the Han river)
종류 (chongnyu)	*type, sort, kind*
정류장 (chŏngnyujang)	*bus stop*
종업원 (chongŏbwon)	*waiter, assistant*
전광판 (chŏngwangp'an)	*electronic noticeboard*
전화 (chŏnhwa)	*telephone*
전화하- (chŏnhwa ha-)	*telephone* (verb stem)
전신 (chŏnshin)	*the whole body*
저녁 (chŏnyŏk)	*evening*
저런 (chŏrŏn)	*oh dear!, o my!*
졸업하- (chorŏp ha-)	*to graduate*
졸음 (chorŭm)	*sleepiness, drowsiness*
조심하- (choshim ha-)	*be careful, be cautious*
주- (chu-)	*give* (stem)
주차하- (chuch'a ha-)	*to park*
주차한 (chuch'a han)	*parked*
즉시 (chŭkshi)	*immediately*
주문하- (chumun ha-)	*order* (stem)
주무시- (chumushi-)	*sleep* (honorific equivalent of cha-)
중국 (chungguk)	*China*
중요하- (chungyo ha-)	*be important*
중요한 (chungyo han)	*important* (modifier form, like an adjective)
주세요 (chuseyo)	*please give* (polite request form)
좌회전 (chwahoejŏn)	*left turn*
좌회전한 다음에 (chwahoejŏn han taŭm-e)	*after doing a left turn*
좌석 (chwasŏk)	*seating, places*
취소하- (chwiso ha-)	*cancel*

데이트하− (deit'ŭ ha-)	*to date*
디자인 (dijain)	*design*
−도 (-do)	*too, also* (particle, attaches to nouns)
동안 (dongan)	*during*
두 (tu)	*two* (pure Korean number)
−에 (-e)	*at (a certain time)*
−에 (-e)	*each, per*
−에 (-e)	*to* (preposition, attaches to nouns)
−에 (-e)	*about, concerning*
−에 대해서 (-e taehaesŏ)	*about, concerning*
−에게 (-ege)	*to*
에이 (ei)	*hey, come off it!*
−에서 (-esŏ)	location particle (place in which something happens); *from*
하− (ha-)	*do* (verb stem)
할말 (ha-l mal)	*something to say*
하러 (ha-rŏ)	*in order to do*
했어요 (haessŏyo)	*did* (past tense form of *ha-* do)
해요 (haeyo)	*do* (stem plus polite ending *-yo*, irregular form)
−하고 (-hago)	*and*
학과 (hakkwa)	*department (of college/ university)*
학교 (hakkyo)	*school*
할머니 (halmŏni)	*grandma*
함께 (hamkke)	*together*
한 (han)	*one* (pure Korean, when used with a counter or measure word)

한 (숫자/시간) 쯤 (han [number/time] cchŭm)	about, around, approximately
하나 (hana)	one
항상 (hangsang)	always
한국말 (hangungmal)	Korean language
한국 (hanguk)	Korea(n) (pronounced hanguk)
한자 (hanja)	Chinese characters
한식당 (hanshiktang)	Korean restaurant (serving Korean food)
-한테 (-hant'e)	to, for (a person)
한영 (han-yŏng)	Korean–English
할아버지 (harabŏji)	grandfather
할인 (harin)	discount
할인하- (harin ha-)	give a discount
하루 (haru)	one day (duration)
하루에 (haru-e)	per day
힘 (him)	strength, energy
회 (hoe)	raw meat
회사 (hoesa)	company
혹시 (hokshi)	maybe, perhaps, possibly
홈 (hom)	platform
혼자 (honja)	alone, on one's own
호텔 (hot'el)	hotel
흡연석 (hŭbyŏnsŏk)	smoker (compartment)
확인하- (hwagin ha-)	check, confirm
활동적인 (hwaldongjŏg-in)	modifier form of the below (like an adjective)
활동적 (hwaldongjŏk)	casual, active
환불하- (hwanbul ha-)	reimburse
훨씬 (hwolsshin)	by far, far and away
후 (hu)	after

훌륭하- (hullyung ha-)	*is excellent, great*
현대 자동차 (hyŏndae chadongch'a)	*Hyundai car (company)*
이 (i)	*two*
이- (i-)	*this one* (+ noun), *this noun*
이번 (i-bŏn)	*this time*
일 (il)	*matter, business, work*
일하- (il ha-)	*work* (verb stem)
일 끝내고 (il kkŭnnago)	*after finishing work*
일방통행 (ilbang t'onghaeng)	*one way*
일방통행로 (ilbang t'onghaengno)	*one-way street*
일본 (ilbon)	*Japan*
일본말 (ilbonmal)	*Japanese language*
일찍 (ilcchik)	*early*
읽- (ilk-)	*read*
일요일 (iryoil)	*Sunday*
일요일날 (iryoillal)	*Sunday* (longer form)
-인분 (-inbun)	*portion*
인천 (inch'ŏn)	*Korean port near Seoul*
입구 (ipku)	*entrance*
-이랑 (-irang)	*with* (-rang after vowel)
잃어버리- (irŏbŏri-)	*lose*
이렇게 (irŏk'e)	*like this*
이름 (irŭm)	*name*
이상 (isang)	*more than*
이상하- (isang ha-)	*is strange, bizarre*
이상하네(요) (isang ha-ne[yo])	*(it is) strange!*
있- (iss-)	*1 exist, there is/are* (stem) *2 have* (stem)

있어요 (issŏyo)	as above, polite style
있으시- (issŭshi-)	*have* (honorific of *iss-* in its meaning of possession)
이따가 (ittaga)	*in a little while*
-이요 (-iyo)	(used to check information, 'you mean?')
-지 마세요 (-ji maseyo)	*please don't*
카드 (k'adŭ)	*a card*
큰 (k'ŭn)	*big*
가- (ka-)	*go* (verb stem)
가방 (kabang)	*a briefcase, a bag*
가보- (ka-bo-)	*go and see, visit (a place)*
같이 (kach'i)	*together*
가게 (kage)	*shop*
가격 (kagyŏk)	*price*
가지 (kaji)	*kind, example* (counter for the noun *chongnyu*)
가족 (kajok)	*family*
가죽 (kajuk)	*leather*
가져가- (kajyŏga-)	*take*
갈- (kal-)	*change (a towel, a platform, clothes etc.)*
갈비 (kalbi)	*marinated and fried meat, usually beef or pork*
가는 (kanŭn)	*going to, bound for*
갈아입- (kara-ip-)	*change clothes*
갈아타- (kara-t'a-)	*change (platform, trains etc.)*
가르치- (karŭch'i-)	*teach*
같- (kat'-)	*be the same, be similar; seem like*
갖고 계시- (katko kyeshi-)	*have, possess* (for honorific person; polite style = *katko kyeseyo*)

같은 (kat'ŭn)   *same*

같은 것 (kat'ŭn kŏt)   *(a) similar thing, something similar*

가요 (kayo)   *go (stem plus polite ending -yo)*

게다가 (kedaga)   *on top of that*

기다리- (kidari-)   *wait*

길 (kil)   *road, route*

-기만 하세요 (-ki-man haseyo)   *just do (verb)*

김치 (kimch'i)   *classic Korean side dish, marinated cabbage*

기억 (kiŏk)   *memory*

-기로 했어요 (-kiro haessŏyo)   *decided to*

-까지 (-kkaji)   *until*

깎아주- (kkakka-ju-)   *cut the price (for someone's benefit)*

꾀병을 부리지요 (kkoebyŏng -ŭl purijiyo)   *you're making it up! (feigning an illness)*

꼭 (kkok)   *exactly, certainly, precisely*

꼭 (kkok)   *without fail, definitely*

끝나- (kkŭnna-)   *finish*

끝내- (kkŭnnae-)   *finish (verb stem, to finish something)*

꾀병 (kkwoebyŏng)   *a feigned illness*

거 (kŏ)   *thing, object, fact (abbreviation of kŭt, spelt kŭs)*

-고 (-ko)   *and (to join clauses)*

-거든요 (-kŏdŭnyo)   *(see Unit 8, Grammar 13, note 6)*

거기 (kŏgi)   *over there (nearer than chŏgi)*

고장 나- (kojang na-)   *break down*

고장 났어요 (kojang nassŏyo)   *be broken down*

걱정하지 마세요 (kŏkchŏng ha-ji maseyo)   *don't worry! (colloquial form: kŏkchŏng maseyo)*

걱정 (kŏkchŏng)	*worry, concern*
걱정하- (kŏkchŏng ha-)	*be worried*
걸리- (kŏlli-)	*takes* (time duration)
걸려요 (kŏllyŏyo)	*it takes* (polite style)
골목 (kolmok)	*alley, small road*
고맙습니다 (komapsŭmnida)	*thank you*
검정 (kŏmjŏng)	*black*
건 (kŏn)	*thing, object* (abbrev of *kŏt* + topic particle)
-고 나서 (-ko nasŏ)	*after* (added to verb stems)
건강 (kŏngang)	*health*
건너편 (kŏnnŏp'yŏn)	*opposite side*
걸어서 (kŏrŏsŏ)	*on foot*
걸었어요 (kŏrŏssŏyo)	*dialled* (past tense of *kŏl-*, irreg. verb)
곳 (kos)	*place*
거의 (kŏuy)	*nearly, almost*
그- (kŭ-)	*that one* (nearer than *cho*)
그 다음에 (kŭ-daŭm-e)	*after that*
그건 (kŭ-gŏn)	*that thing* (topic)
그것 보라고! (kŭ-gŏt porago!)	*you see!*
그저 그래요 (kŭjŏ kŭraeyo)	*so-so*
국 (kuk)	*soup*
글쎄요 (kŭlsseyo)	*I dunno, I'm not sure, who knows?*
금연석 (kŭmyŏnsŏk)	*non-smoking compartment*
근처 (kŭnch'ŏ)	*district, area, vicinity*
근사하- (kŭnsa ha-)	*look super, look good*
그냥 (kŭnyang)	*simply, just*
그래도 (kŭraedo)	*however, nevertheless, but still*
그러세요? (kŭrŏseyo?)	*so what?*
그래요(?) (kŭraeyo [?])	*really (?), is it/it is so (?)*

그리고 (kǔrigo)	*and (also)* (used to begin a sentence)
그리고 나서 (kǔrigo nasǒ)	*after that*
그렇지 않아요 (kǔrǒch'i anayo)	*of course not*
그렇게 (kǔrǒk'e)	*like that*
그럼 (kǔrǒm)	*then, in that case*
그런 (kǔrǒn)	*such a, that (particular)*
그러니까 (kǔrǒnikka)	*therefore, because of that*
그런 편이에요(kǔrǒn p'yǒn-ieyo)	*(we) tend to be so/do so (it's usually like that, etc.)*
그릇 (kǔrǔt)	*dish*
구식 (kushik)	*old style, old fashioned*
과일 (kwail)	*fruit*
관련(kwallyǒn)	*relation, link*
과로 (kwaro)	*overwork*
권 (kwon)	*volume (measure word)*
계획 (kyehoek)	*plan(s)*
계시- (kyeshi-)	*exist* (honorific of *iss-* in its existential *there is/are* meaning)
교회 (kyohoe)	*church*
결정하- (kyǒljǒng ha-)	*decide*
경찰 (kyǒngch'al)	*policeman*
경찰서 (kyǒngch'alsǒ)	*police station*
경우 (kyǒngu)	*circumstance, situation*
겨우 (kyǒu)	*only*
마찬가지에요 (mach'angaji -eyo)	*be the same, be identical*
-마다 (-mada)	*each, every*
매일 (maeil)	*every day*
맥주 (maekchu)	*beer*

매운 (maeun)	spicy
맞- (maj-)	to fit well (maj + nŭnda = man-nŭnda)
말 (mal)	language
말하- (mal ha-)	speak, say
말한 대로 (mal han taero)	as (I) said, like (I) said
말씀 (malssŭm)	words, speech
말씀하- (malssŭm ha-)	speak, say (of someone honorific, often in phrase malssŭm haseyo!)
말씀하세요 (malssŭm haseyo)	please tell me, please say it (I'm listening!) (honorific)
말씀 많이 들었어요 (malssŭm mani tŭrŏssŏyo)	I've heard a lot about you
만 (man)	10,000
-만 (-man)	only
만병통치약 (manbyŏngt'ongch'iyak)	cure-all medicine, miracle cure
많지 않아서 (man-ch'i anasŏ)	since there aren't many (written manh-ji anhaso)
만들- (mandŭl-)	make (l- irregular verb like p'al, nol- etc.)
만들었어요 (mandŭrŏssŏyo)	be made of (past tense of mandŭl-, l- irregular verb)
-만에 (-man-e)	within, in only (two or three months)
많- (man[h]-)	is many (h is not pronounced, polite style = manayo)
많이 (man[h]i)	much, many, a lot
만나- (manna-)	meet (stem)
만나서 반갑습니다 (mannasŏ pangapsŭmnida)	pleased to meet you
마른 안주 (marŭn anju)	dried snacks

마시- (mashi-)	drink
맛이 없는데도 말이에요 (mashi-ŏmnŭnde-do mar-ieyo)	I'm saying (stress) that even the food tasted bad
맛이없- (mash-i ŏps-)	be tasteless, be unpleasant (to eat)
마음 (maŭm)	mind, heart
마음에 (꼭) 들어요 (maŭm-e (kkok) tŭrŏyo)	I (really) like it
마음에 들지 않아요 (maŭm-e tŭl-ji anayo)	I don't like (her) (maum-e an turoyo)
미국 (miguk)	America
미니바 (miniba)	mini-bar
모두 (modu)	altogether, everything, everyone
몰라요 (mollayo)	I don't know
몸 (mom)	body
머리 (mŏri)	head
멀어요 (mŏrŏyo)	is far (polite style, irregular stem)
모르- (morŭ-)	not know (stem)
모르겠어요 (morŭgessŏyo)	I don't know
멋있- (mŏshiss-)	be stylish, be handsome
못 (mot)	cannot (NB mot + m- = mon m-)
못 알아듣겠다고 하- (mot ara-dŭt-ket-tago ha-)	say that (one) couldn't understand
먹- (mŏk-)	eat
묵- (muk-)	stay, lodge, spend the night
물 (mul)	water
물건 (mulgŏn)	goods
물냉면 (mul naengmyŏn)	thin noodles in cold soup, spicy and refreshing!
문 (mun)	door

문제 (munje)	problem
무엇 (muŏs)	what (full form of mwo)
물어보- (murŏ-bo-)	ask
무슨 (musŭn)	what (kind of), what, which
무뚝뚝하- (muttukttuk ha-)	be stubborn, be blunt
뭐 (mwo)	what?
뭘 (mwol)	what (object form)
면 (myŏn)	cotton
-면 (-myŏn)	if
면도(를) 하- (myŏndo [-rŭl] ha-)	shave
면허증 (myŏnhŏcchŭng)	(driving) licence
-면서 (-myŏnsŏ)	while (see Unit 12, Grammar 22, note 5)
몇 (myŏt [myoch'])	what (number)?
몇 시 (myŏt shi)	what time
나 (na)	I/me
-나 (-na)	approximately, about; or
나아지- (naaji-)	get better
내 (nae)	my
내- (nae-)	pay
내일 (naeil)	tomorrow
냉장고 (naengjanggo)	refrigerator
냉면 (naengmyŏn)	thin noodles with vegetables
나가- (naga-)	go out
날씨 (nalssi)	weather
남- (nam-)	be left (over), remain
남대문 (Namdaemun)	Great South Gate (in Seoul), Namdaemun
남자친구 (namja ch'ingu)	boyfriend
남편 (namp'yŏn)	husband

나오- (nao-)	*come out*
네 (ne)	*yes*
넣- (nŏ[h]-)	*put down, leave*
놀라- (nolla-)	*to be surprised, be shocked*
놀리- (nolli-)	*make fun of*
놀리지 마세요 (nolli-ji maseyo)	*don't joke, don't kid me, don't tease*
너무 (nŏmu)	*too (much)*
농담 (nongdam)	*joke (noun)*
농담하- (nongdam ha-)	*jokes (verb)*
노래 (norae)	*a song*
노래방 (noraebang)	*'karaoke' singing room*
노래하- (norae ha-)	*sing*
노력하- (noryŏk ha-)	*make effort, strive*
누가 (nuga)	*who? (subject form)*
누구 (nugu)	*who?*
느끼- (nŭkki-)	*to feel*
눈 (nun)	*an eye*
늦게 (nŭtke)	*late*
오- (o-)	*come (stem)*
어쨌든 (ŏcchaettŭn)	*anyway*
어디 (ŏdi)	*where?*
어디 가는지 아세요? (ŏdi kannŭnji aseyo?)	*do you know where (she) has gone?*
어딘가 (ŏdinga)	*somewhere or other*
외환 (oehwan)	*exchange*
외환은행 (oehwan ŭnhaeng)	*Korea Exchange Bank*
왼 (oen)	*left*
오히려 (ohiryŏ)	*rather, on the contrary*
어이 (ŏi)	*hey! (used to call close friends and colleagues)*

어제도 마찬가지였고요 (ŏje-do mach'angaji-yŏtgoyo)	it was exactly the same yesterday as well
오징어 (ojingŏ)	squid
얼마 (ŏlma)	how much
얼마 동안 (ŏlmadongan)	how long?
얼마 동안 묵으시겠어요? (ŏlma-dongan mug-ŭshigessŏyo?)	how long will you be staying?
얼마 남지 않았습니다 (ŏlma nam -ji anassŭmnida)	there are only a few spaces left
업무 (ŏmmu)	business, service
없는것 같은데 (ŏmnŭn kŏt kat'ŭnde)	it doesn't look as though there is anything/are any
온돌방 (ondolbang)	room with bed on floor
엉망 (ŏngmang)	rubbish, awful, appalling
언제 (ŏnje)	when
어느 (ŏnŭ)	which one
오늘 (onŭl)	today
오래 (orae)	long
오래간만이에요 (oraeganman-ieyo)	long time no see!
오락실 (orakshil)	amusements (electronic games, etc.)
오른 (orŭn)	right
어서 오세요 (ŏsŏ oseyo)	welcome!
어때요? (ŏttaeyo?)	how is it?
어떻게? (ŏttŏk'e)	how?
어떻게 생겼어요? (ŏttŏk'e saenggyŏssŏyo?)	what does it look like?
어떨까요? (ŏttŏlkkayo?)	how would it be?
어떤 (ŏttŏn)	certain, some (as a question word = which?)
어울리- (ŏulli-)	suit (a person)
파전 (p'ajŏn)	Korean-style pancake
팔지만 (p'aljiman)	they sell, but ...

파는 거 (p'anŭn kŏ)	*item for sale, items sold*
팔아요 (p'arayo)	*sell (polite style form, stem is irregular)*
파티 (p'at'i)	*party*
피로 (p'iro)	*fatigue, weariness*
필요하- (p'iryo ha-)	*is needed (p'iryo ha- also exists but is less common)*
필요있- (p'iryo iss-)	*is necessary, is needed*
필요없- (p'iryo ŏps-)	*is not necessary, is not needed, has no need of*
포함되어 있- (p'oham doeŏiss-)	*be included*
퍼센트 (p'ŏsent'ŭ)	*per cent*
표 (p'yo)	*ticket*
표지 (p'yoji)	*a sign, a signpost*
표지판 (p'yojip'an)	*a signpost*
편도 (p'yŏndo)	*single (ticket, way)*
편하- (p'yŏn ha-)	*is comfortable, is convenient*
편지 (p'yŏnji)	*letter*
배 (pae)	*double, (two) times*
배 (pae)	*stomach*
배달하- (paedal ha-)	*deliver*
백화점 (paekhwajŏm)	*department store*
바꾸- (pakku-)	*change*
밝은 (palgŭn)	*bright*
발생하- (palsaeng ha-)	*occur, happen*
밤 (pam)	*night*
방 (pang)	*room*
반갑습니다 (pangapsŭmnida)	*pleased to meet you*
방금 (panggŭm)	*just now*
방향 (panghyang)	*direction*
밥 (pap)	*rice (cooked rice)*
밥먹- (pap mŏk-)	*have a meal*

바쁘- (pappǔ-)	is busy
바쁜 (pappǔn)	busy
바로 (paro)	directly
받- (pat-)	to receive
비빔 (pibim)	mixed
비가 오- (pi-ga o-)	rains, is raining
빌리- (pilli-)	borrow
빌려주- (pillyǒ-ju-)	lend
빈 (pin)	empty, vacant, free (of seats and rooms)
비싸- (pissa-)	is expensive
비싼 (pissan)	expensive (adjective)
비슷하- (pisǔt ha-)	look similar
보- (po-)	see, look (sometimes = meet)
-보다 (-poda)	more than
보관하- (pogwan ha-)	keep
벌 (pǒl)	(counter for clothes)
벌금 (pǒlgǔm)	a fine, a penalty
번 (pǒn)	number
번 (pǒn)	time (as in first time, second time, many times)
보내- (ponae-)	send
버리- (pǒri-)	throw away
버스 (pǒsǔ)	bus
보여주- (poyǒ-ju-)	to show
빨간 (ppalgan)	red
빨리 (ppalli)	quickly
빵 (ppang)	bread
-뿐 (-ppun)	only
부작용 (pujagyong)	a side-effect
불친절하- (pulch'injǒl ha-)	be unhelpful, be unkind, be impolite

불고기 (**pulgogi**)	*Korean spiced marinated beef*
불국사 (**pulguksa**)	*Pulguksa (Korean Buddhist temple, near Kyongju)*
불평하- (**pulp'yŏng ha-**)	*complain*
분 (**pun**)	*minute*
부르- (**purŭ-**)	*call*
부탁하- (**put'ak ha-**)	*make a request*
-부터 (**-put'ŏ**)	*from*
봐주세요 (**pwa-juseyo**)	*please look at*
봐요 (**pwayo**)	*see, look (polite style, irregular)*
별일 (**pyŏlil**)	*a special matter, something particular*
별일 없으면… (**pyŏlil ŏpsŭmyŏn ...**)	*if you don't have anything special on ...*
별로 (**pyŏllo**)	*not particularly, not really (+ negative)*
별로 없-(**pyŏllo ŏps-**)	*have almost none, scarcely have any*
병원 (**pyŏngwon**)	*hospital*
-러 (**-rŏ**)	*in order to*
사- (**sa-**)	*buy (verb stem)*
색 (**saek**)	*colour*
생각 (**saenggak**)	*thought*
생각 (**saenggak**)	*idea*
생각나- (**saenggang na-**)	*remember, it comes to mind*
생기- (**saenggi-**)	*to occur, happen, take place; look like*
생일 (**saengil**)	*birthday (normal form)*
생신 (**saengshin**)	*birthday (honorific form)*
생선 (**saengson**)	*fish*
사거리 (**sagŏri**)	*crossroads*
사과 (**sagwa**)	*apple*

사이 (sai-e)	*between*
사장(님) (sajang(nim))	*manager* (honorific form)
사전 (sajŏn)	*dictionary*
사무실 (samushil)	*office*
산 (san)	*mountain*
상자 (sangja)	*box*
상업 (sangŏp)	*trade*
상업은행 (sangŏp ŭnhaeng)	*Commercial Bank* (*lit*: trade bank)
사업 (saŏp)	*business*
사람 (saram)	*person*
사랑하- (sarang ha-)	*love*
사실 (sashil)	*fact (the fact is ...)*
사우나 (sauna)	*sauna*
사요 (sayo)	*buy* (stem plus polite ending -*yo*)
세 (se)	*three* (pure Korean)
시 (shi)	*o'clock*
시간 (shigan)	*time, hour*
식어 있- (shigŏiss-)	*be cool, get cold*
시작하- (shijak ha-)	*begin, start*
시장 (shijang)	*market*
식- (shik-)	*get cold*
식후 (shikhu)	*after meal*
시끄러워요! (shikkŭrŏwoyo!)	*shut up!, be quiet!*
식사하- (shiksa ha-)	*have meal*
식당 (shiktang)	*restaurant*
실례합니다 (shillye hamnida)	*excuse me, please*
실례지만… (shillye-jiman ...)	*excuse me, but ...*
실수 (shilsu)	*mistake*
실수하- (shilsu ha-)	*make a mistake*
심하- (shim ha-)	*be serious*

시내 (shinae)	town centre
신문 (shinmun)	newspaper
싫어하- (shirŏ ha-)	to dislike
시설 (shisŏl)	facility
쉽게 (shwipke)	easily
셔츠 (shyŏch'ŭ)	shirt
쇼핑(하-) (shyop'ing (ha-))	shopping (do/go shopping)
서- (sŏ-)	stop (stem)
서비스 (sŏbisŭ)	service
소개하- (sogaeha-)	to introduce
소주 (soju)	soju, Korean wine/vodka
솔직히 (solchikhi)	frankly, honestly
솔직히 말해보세요 (solchikhi mal hae-boseyo)	tell me the truth!
솔직히 말해서 (solchikhi mal hae-sŏ)	honestly speaking; to tell the truth; in fact ...
손님 (sonnim)	customer
서류 (sŏryu)	document
서울 (sŏul)	Seoul
싸- (ssa-)	is cheap
싼 (ssan)	cheap (adjective)
-씩 (-sshik)	each, per (see notes)
썩었어요 (ssŏgŏssŏyo)	has gone bad, has gone off (polite style, past tense)
쓰- (ssŭ-)	write
쓰게 (ssŭ-ge)	usable
수고하세요 (sugo haseyo)	work hard! (said to someone doing their job)
수건 (sugŏn)	towel
수건을 갈아달라고 했어요 (sugŏn-ŭl kara-tallago haessŏyo)	I asked (her) to change the towel
술집 (sulchip)	pub
스타일 (sŭt'ail)	style

스탠드바 (sǔt'endǔba)	bar (standing bar)
스트레스 (sǔt'uresǔ)	stress
수영하- (suyǒng ha-)	swim
수영장 (suyǒngjang)	swimming pool
타- (t'a-)	take (transport), travel on (transport)
탁구 (t'akku)	table tennis
다 (ta)	all, everything
대구 (Taegu)	Korean city
대해서 (taehaesǒ)	about, concerning (noun e taehaeso)
대학 (taehak)	university
대학교 (taehakkyo)	university
대사관 (taesagwan)	embassy
대신 (taeshin)	instead, on behalf of
달 (tal)	month
당장 (tangjang)	immediately
당신 (tangshin)	you (often between husband and wife)
다리 (tari)	leg
다르- (tarǔ-)	be different (polite style = tallayo)
다른 (tarǔn)	another, different
다시 (tashi)	again
다음 (taǔm [daǔm])	after, next
데 (te)	place
더 (tǒ)	more
도봉산 (tobongsan)	Tobongsan (Korean mountain in Seoul)
되- (toe-)	become
더 이상 (tǒ isang)	any more

독서 (toksŏ)	reading
돈 (ton)	money
동창 (tongch'ang)	colleague (fellow student in this case)
동대문 (tongdaemun)	Great East Gate (in Seoul), Tongdaemun
돌아오- (torao-)	come back, return
더럽- (tŏrŏp-)	be dirty (polite = tŏrŏwoyo, p- verb like kakkap- etc.)
도와주- (towa-ju-)	to help
더워서 (tŏwosŏ)	because it is hot, because you're hot
때 (ttae)	time (when)
딱 질색이에요 (ttak chilsaeg-ieyo)	hate, is awful (to me)
따라 (ttara)	follow
또 (tto)	again; moreover, also
똑 (ttok)	exactly, precisely (often used with kat'-)
두 (tu)	two (pure Korean number)
둘 (tul)	two (when you mean 'the two of them', 'both')
등산 (tŭngsan)	mountain climbing
드릴까요 (tŭrilkkayo)	would you like? (lit: shall I give you?)
들어 있- (tŭrŏ iss-)	be contained, be included
들어오- (tŭrŏo-)	to enter
두통 (tut'ong)	headache
우체국 (uch'eguk)	post office
우회전 (uhoejŏn)	right turn
우회전한 다음에 (uhoejŏn han taŭm-e)	after doing a right turn

음료수 (ŭmryosu)	*drink*
음료수 하시겠어요? (ŭmryosu hashigessŏyo?)	*would you like some thing to drink?*
음식 (ŭmshik)	*food*
응 (ŭng)	*yes (casual form)*
은행 (ŭnhaeng)	*bank*
은행원 (ŭnhaengwon)	*bank clerk*
운전수 (unjŏnsu)	*a driver*
우리 (uri)	*we/our*
우리 둘만 가요? (uri tul-man kayo?)	*is it just the two of us going?*
-으로 (-ŭro)	*towards, in the direction of (-ro, after vowels)*
우산 (usan)	*umbrella*
우선 (usŏn)	*first*
-의 (-ŭy)	*belonging to*
의견 (ŭygyŏn)	*suggestion, opinion*
의논 (ŭynon)	*discussion*
의논하- (ŭynon ha-)	*discuss*
우연히 (ŭyŏnhi)	*by chance, coincidentally*
와! (wa!)	*wow!*
왜요? (waeyo)	*why?*
와인 (wain)	*wine*
왕복 (wangbok)	*return*
완행 (wanhaeng)	*slow train*
왔어요 (wassŏyo)	*came (past tense form)*
와요 (wayo)	*come (polite style form)*
웨이터 (weit'ŏ)	*waiter*
위험하- (wihŏm ha-)	*be dangerous*
원 (won)	*won (unit of Korean currency)*

원하- (won ha-)	*want, require*
원인 (wonin)	*reason, cause*
원숭이 (wonsungi)	*monkey*
애기하- (yaegi ha-)	*talk, tell*
약을 먹어야겠어요 (yag-ŭl mŏgŏyagessŏyo)	*I'll have to take some medicine*
약 (yak)	*medicine*
약국 (yakkuk)	*chemist, drugstore*
약사 (yaksa)	*pharmacist, chemist*
약속 (yaksok)	*appointment*
양주 (yangju)	*spirits, western liquor*
양말 (yangmal)	*socks*
양식당 (yangshiktang)	*Western restaurant*
예 (ye)	*yes* (politer form of *ne*)
예약하- (yeyak ha-)	*reserve, book*
여보세요 (yŏboseyo)	*hello* (on the telephone)
여기 (yŏgi)	*here*
여기서 (yŏgi-sŏ)	*from here* (abbrev. of *yogi-esŏ*)
요금 (yogŭm)	*fee, fare*
여자친구 (yŏja ch'ingu)	*girlfriend*
요즘 (yojŭm)	*nowadays*
요즘 재미가 어떠세요? (yojŭm chaemi-ga ŏttŏseyo?)	*how are you doing?, how are things these days?*
요즘 사업은 어때요? (yojŭm saŏb-ŭn ŏttaeyo?)	*how is business these days?*
열 (yŏl)	*ten* (pure Korean number)
열두 (yŏldu)	*twelve* (pure Korean number)
열리지 않- (yŏlli-ji an[h]-)	*does not open*
영국 (yŏngguk)	*England/ish, Britain/ish*

영한 (yŏng-han)	*English–Korean*
영화 (yŏnghwa)	*film, movie*
영업 (yŏngŏp)	*business*
영수증 (yŏngsujŭng)	*receipt*
옆 (yŏp')	*next door*
유행하- (yuhaeng ha-)	*be popular, be in vogue*

English–Korean vocabulary

about, concerning	에(-e); -에 대해서(-e taehaeso)
about/around, approximately	한(han) (*number/time*) 쯤(cchŭm)
after (after, next)	후(hu) 다음(taŭm/daŭm)
again (moreover, also, furthermore)	다시(tashi), 또(tto)
all, everything	다(ta)
almost, nearly	거의(kŏŭy)
alone	혼자(honja)
altogether, everything, everyone	모두(modu)
always	항상(hangsang)
and	-하고(-hago)
and (to join clauses)	-고(-ko)
and (also) (used to begin a sentence)	그리고(kŭrigo)
apple	사과(sagwa)
appointment, promise	약속(yaksok)
area, district, vicinity	근처(kŭnch'ŏ)
at (a certain time)	-에(-e)
bag, briefcase	가방(kabang)
bank (bank clerk)	은행(ŭnhaeng) (은행원 [ŭnhaengwon])
basement	지하(chiha)
bed; (room with a bed) (– on the floor, Korean style)	침대(ch'imdae); 침대방(ch'imdae bang), 온돌방(ondolbang)
beer	맥주(maekchu)
before	전(chŏn)
begin, start	시작하-(shijak ha-)

big	큰(**k'ŭn**)
birthday (honorific form)	생일(**saengil**) (생신(**saengshin**))
black	검정(**kŏmjŏng**)
blue jeans	청바지(**ch'ŏngbaji**)
body	몸(**mom**)
borrow	빌리-(**pilli-**)
boy/girlfriend	남자/여자 친구(**namja/yŏja ch'ingu**)
bread	빵(**ppang**)
break down	고장 나-(**kojang na-**)
breakfast	아침식사(**ach'imshiksa**)
breakfast (abbreviated form); (to have breakfast)	아침(**ach'im**); 아침 먹-(**ach'im mŏk-**)
bus	버스(**bŏsŭ**)
bus stop	정류장(**chŏngnyujang**)
business	사업(**saŏp**)
busy	바쁘-(**pappŭ-**)
buy (verb stem)	사-(**sa-**)
by far, far and away	훨씬(**hwolssin**)
call	부르-(**purŭ-**)
cancel	취소하-(**ch'wiso ha-**)
car	자동차(**chadongch'a**)
car (short form)	차(**ch'a**)
careful/cautious	조심하-(**chŏshim ha-**)
change (clothes/trains etc.)	바꾸-(**pakku-**) (갈아입-/타- [**kara-ip-/t'a-**])
cheap	싸-(**ssa-**)
check, confirm	확인하-(**hwagin ha-**)
China	중국(**chungguk**)
Chinese character	한자(**hanja**)
church	교회(**kyohoe**)
clean, clean up	청소하-(**ch'ŏngso ha-**)

colour	색(saek)
come (out)	오-(o-) (나오-[nao-])
comfortable/convenient	편하-(p'yŏn ha-)
company	회사(hoesa)
complain	불평하-(pulp'yong ha-)
cotton	면(myŏn)
country bumpkin, yokel	촌사람(ch'onsaram)
cup	잔(chan)
customer	손님(sonnim)
dangerous	위험하-(wihom ha-)
decide	정하-(chŏng ha-)
deliver	배달하-(paedal ha-)
depart	출발하-(ch'ulbal ha-)
department (store)	학과(hakkwa) (백화점 [paekhwajŏm])
departure	출발(ch'ulbal)
design	디자인(dijain)
dictionary	사전(sajŏn)
different	다르-(tarŭ-)
directly	직접/바로(chikchŏp/paro)
discount	할인(harin)
dish	그릇(kŭrŭt)
dislike	싫어하-(shirŏ ha-)
district, area, vicinity	근처(kŭnch'ŏ)
do (verb stem)	하-(ha-)
document	서류(sŏryu)
door	문(mun)
double, times	배(pae)
drink	마시-(mashi-)
driver	운전수(unjŏnsu)
during	동안(dongan)

each, every (each, per)	-마다(-mada), (-씩[-sshik])
early	일찍(ilcchik)
easy, easily	쉽-(shwip-), 쉽게(shwipke)
eat	먹-(mŏk-)
eat (honorific, equivalent of *mok-*); (*try eating*) (honorific form)	잡수시-(chapsushi-); 잡숴보- (chapswo-bo-)
effort, strive	노력하-(noryŏk ha-)
embassy	대사관(taesagwan)
employee	직원(chigwon)
empty	빈(pin)
energy, strength	힘(him)
England, Britain	영국(yŏngguk)
English–Korean	영한(yŏng-han)
entrance	입구(ipku)
every day	매일(maeil)
everything, everyone, altogether	모두(modu)
eye, snow	눈(nun)
exactly, certainly, precisely	꼭(kkok), 똑(ttok)
exchange (Korea Exchange Bank)	외환(oehwan) (은행[unheng])
excuse me, sorry, but ...	죄송하지만(choesong ha-jiman)
excuse me, please	실례합니다(shilye hamnida)
exist, there is/are (honorific) (stem)	있-(iss-) (계시-[kyeshi-])
expensive	비싸-(pissa-)
express train	직행(chikhaeng)
evening (time as well as meal)	저녁(chŏnyŏk)
everything, all	다(ta)
family	가족(kajok)
feel	느끼-(nŭkki-)
film, movie	영화(yŏnghwa)

(at) first	처음(**ch'ŏŭm**)
fish	생선(**saengsŏn**)
food	음식(**ŭmshik**)
(on) foot	걸어서(**kŏrŏsŏ**)
frequently, often	자주(**chaju**)
(in) front of	앞에서(**ap'esŏ**)
from (location particle, place in which something happens)	-부터(**-put'ŏ**), (-에서[**esŏ**])
fruit	과일(**kwail**)
give	주-(**chu-**)
go (out)	가-(**ka-**) (나가-[**naga-**])
good (stem)	좋-(**choh-**)
good, fine, ok (polite style)	좋아요(**choayo**)
good, well (adverb)	잘(**chal**)
goodbye (to someone who is leaving)	안녕히 가세요(**annyŏnghi kaseyo**)
goodbye (to someone who is staying)	안녕히 계세요(**annyŏnghi kyeseyo**)
graduate	졸업하-(**cholŏp ha-**)
grandfather, old men in general	할아버지(**harabŏji**)
grandma, old women in general	할머니(**halmŏni**)
handsome	멋있-(**mŏshiss-**)
have (stem)	있-(**iss-**)
have (honorific form)	있으시-(**issŭshi-**)
head	머리(**mŏri**)
health	건강(**kŏngang**)
hello (on the telephone)	여보세요(**yŏboseyo**)
help	도와주-(**towa-ju-**)
here (from here)	여기(**yŏgi**) (여기서 **yogi-sŏ**)
hospital	병원(**pyŏngwon**)
house	집(**chip**)

how?	어떻게(ŏttŏlkk'e)
how is it?	어때요(ŏttaeyo?)
however, nevertheless, but still	그래도(kŭraedo)
how much, long?	얼마(ŏlma), (동안dongan)
hurts (polite style)	아파요-(ap'ayo)
hurts (stem)	아프-(ap'ŭ-)
hurting, painful (adjective)	아픈(ap'ŭn)
husband	남편(namp'yŏn)
if	-면(-myŏn)
important	중요하-(chungyo ha-)
in order to do	하러(ha-rŏ)
interesting, fun	재미있-(chaemi iss-)
introduce	소개하-(sogae ha-)
Japan (Japanese language)	일본(ilbon) (말[mal])
joke	농담(nongdam)(하-[ha-])
jumper	잠바(chamba)
just, simply	그냥(kŭnyang)
just now	방금(panggŭm)
kind, type, example	가지(kaji)
Korea	한국(hanguk)
Korean–English	한영(han-yŏng)
Korean language	한국말(hangungmal)
language, word (to speak/say)	말(mal) (말하-[mal ha-])
last year	작년(changnyon)
lately, nowadays	요즘(yojŭm)
least	적어도(chŏgŏ-do)
left	왼(oen)
leg	다리(tari)

lend	빌려주-(pillyŏ-ju)
letter	편지(p'yŏnji)
like (adjective)	-처럼(-ch'ŏrŏm)
like (stem), *I like* (polite form)	좋아하-(choa ha-), 마음에 들어요(maŭm-e tŭrŏyo)
like that	그렇게(kŭrŏk'e)
like this	이렇게(irŏk'e)
little (while, time); *in a little while*	잠깐(chamkkan); 이따가(ittaga)
little, a bit (quantity)	조금(chogŭm)
little, please	좀(chom)
look, see (sometimes = *to meet*)	보-(po-)
look for	찾-(ch'aj-)
look, to look for	찾아보-(ch'aja-bo-)
lose	잃어버리-(irŏbŏri-)
love	사랑하-(sarang ha-)
lunch	점심(chŏmshim)
magazine	잡지(chapchi)
make	만들-(mandŭl-)(l- irregular verb like *p'al, nol* etc.)
manager (honorific form)	사장(sajang) (님(nim))
many (*h* is not pronouced)	많-(man(h)-)
market	시장(shijang)
maybe, perhaps	혹시(hokshi)
me (humble form)	나(na) (저(chŏ))
medicine (pharmacist), (drugstore)	약(yak) (약사[yaksa]) (약국 (yakkuk))
meet (stem) (pleased to meet you)	만나-(manna-) (만나서 반갑습니다(mannasŏ pangapsŭmnida)
mind, heart	마음(maŭm)

minute	분(**pun**)
mis-, wrongly	잘못(**chalmot**)
mixed	비빔(**pibim**)
money	돈(**ton**)
month	달(**tal**)
more (any more)	도(**to**)
more than	이상(**isang**),-보다(**-poda**)
morning	아침(**ach'im**)
most	제일(**cheil**)
mountain (climbing)	산(**san**) (등산[**tǔngsan**])
my (humble form)	제(**che**)
name	이름(**irǔm**)
needed (not needed)	필요하-/있-(없-)(**p'iryo ha-/iss- [ops-]**)
nevertheless, however, but still	그래도(**kǔraedo**)
newspaper	신문(**shinmun**)
next	옆(**yǒp'**)
night	밤(**pam**)
no	아니요(**aniyo**)
noodles in cold soup	물냉면(**mul naengmyǒn**)
not (opposite of -[i]eyo)	아니에요(**anieyo**)
not available, something which is not sold	안 파는 거(**an p'anǔn kǒ**)
not know (stem)	모르-(**morǔ-**)
now	지금(**chigǔm**)
nowadays, lately	요즘(**yojǔm**)
number (times)	-째(**-cchae**)
number (time as in 'first time', etc.)	번(**pǒn**)
o'clock	-시(**-shi**)
office	사무실(**samushil**)

often, frequently	자주(chaju)
okay, right, fine (formal)	알겠습니다(algessŭmnida)
one	하나(hana)
one day	하루(haru)
only	–만(-man), –뿐(-ppun)
opinion (in my) (humble form)	제 생각에는 (che saenggag-enŭn)
opposite side	건너편(kŏnnŏp'yŏn)
order; would you like to order?	주문하–(chumun ha-);
	주문하시겠어요?(chumum
	hashigessŏyo?)
our, we	우리(uri)
our, we (humble form of *wuri*)	저희(chŏhŭy)
over there	고기(kogi)
park	주차하–(chuch'a ha-)
particularly (not), (not) really (negative)	별로(pyŏllo)
per, each	–에(-e)
perhaps, probably	아마(ama)
person	사람(saram)
place	곳(kos)
plan	계획(kyehoek)
play (tennis, piano etc.)	치–(ch'i-)
please don't ...	–지 마세요(-ji maseyo)
please give (polite request form)	주세요(chuseyo)
police (man/station)	경찰/–서(kyŏngch'al/-sŏ)
portion	–인분(-inbun)
post office	우체국(uch'eguk)
previously	전에(chŏn-e)
price	가격(kagyŏk)
problem	문제(munje)
promise, appointment	약속(yaksok)
pub	술집(sulchip)

quality	질(**chil**)
quickly	빨리(**ppalli**)
rains, is raining	비가 오-(**pi-ga o-**)
really (colloquial)	진짜(**chinccha**)
really	정말(**chŏngmal**)
really(?), is it(?), is that so(?)	그래요(?)(**kŭraeyo(?)**)
read	읽-(**ilk-**)
reason, cause	원인(**wonin**)
receipt	영수증(**yŏngsujŭng**)
receive	받-(**pat-**)
red	빨간(**ppalgan**)
refrigerator	냉장고(**naenjanggo**)
request	부탁하-(**put'ak ha-**)
reserve, book	예약하-(**yeyak ha-**)
restaurant	식당(**shiktang**)
return (tickets)	왕복(**wangbok**)
rice, cooked (uncooked)	밥(**pap**) (쌀(**ssal**))
right (direction)	오른(**orŭn**)
road	길(**kil**)
room	방(**pang**)
same/identical	마찬가지(**mach'angaji**)
school	학교(**hakkyo**)
seat	자리-(**chari**)
see, look (sometimes = to meet)	보-(**po-**)
shave	면도(**myŏndo**) (-를[-rŭl] 하-([ha-])
shop	가게(**kage**)
sit (stem)	앉-(**anj-**)
side	쪽(**cchok**)
side dish for drinks or snack	(마른[**marŭn**]) 안주(**anju**)

simply, just	그냥(kǔnyang)
single (ticket, way)	편도(p'yǒndo)
sleep	자–(cha-)
sleep (honorific)	주무시–(chumushi-)
smoker (compartment); *non-smoking compartment*	흡연석(hǔbyǒnsǒk); 금연석 (kǔmyǒnsǒk)
snow	눈(nun)
socks	양말(yangmal)
soft drinks	음료수(ǔmryosu)
something to say	할 말(ha-l mal)
son	아들(adǔl)
song, 'karaoke' singing room	노래(norae)(하–[ha-]), 노래방 (noraebang)
(I'm) sorry, I apologize, excuse me	죄송합니다(choesong hamnida)
so-so	그저 그래요(kǔjǒ kǔraeyo)
soup	국(kuk)
spicy	매운(maeun)
spirits, western liquor	양주(yangju)
squid	오징어(ojingǒ)
start, begin	시작하–(shijak ha-)
stay, lodge, spend the night	묵–(muk-)
stomach	배(pae)
stop (verb stem)	서–(sǒ-)
strange, bizarre	이상하–(isang ha-)
strength, energy	힘(him)
stylish/handsome	멋 있–(mǒshiss-)
suit (a person)	어울리-(ǒulli-)
Sunday	일요일(iryoil)
swim (swimming pool)	수영하–(suyǒng ha- (수영장 [suyǒngjang])

take (time duration)	걸리-(kŏlli-)
take, travel on (transport)	타-(t'a-)
talk, tell	얘기하-(yaegi ha-)
tasty/tasteless	맛이 있-/없-(mash-i iss-/ŏps-)
teach	가르치-(karŭch'i-)
telephone	전화(chŏnhwa)
telephone (verb stem)	전화하-(chŏnhwa ha-)
thank you	감사합니다/고맙습니다 (kamsahamnida/komapsŭmnida)
that one (long way away)	저(chŏ-)
that one (nearer than *cho-*)	그(kŭ-)
(over) there	저기(chŏgi)
therefore, because of that	그러니까(kŭrŏnikka)
thing, object, fact (abbreviation of *kŏt* spelt *kos*)	거(kŏ)
this one (+ noun), *this noun*	이-(i-)
thought, idea (remember, it comes to mind)	생각(saenggak) (나[na-])
three (pure Korean)	세(se)
ticket	표(p'yo)
time, hour	시간(shigan)
times/double	배(pae)
to (preposition, attaches to nouns)	-에(-e)
to	-에게(-ege)
to/for (a person)	-한테(-hant'e)
today	오늘(onŭl)
together	함께(hamkke)
together	같이(kach'i)
tomorrow	내일(naeil)
too, also (particle, attaches to nouns)	-도(-to)

too (much)	너무(**nŏmu**)
towards, in the direction of	으로(**ŭro**)
towel	수건(**sugŏn**)
town centre	시내(**shinae**)
turned out well, it's all for the best	잘 됐네요(**chal twaenneyo**)
two	두(**du**), 이(**i**)
umbrella	우산(**usan**)
understand	알아들-(**ara-dŭl-**)(1/t verb like *tŭl-* listen; *ara-dŭrŏyo*)
unfortunately	안 되겠네요(**an toegenneyo**)
university	대학(**taehak**), 대학교 (**taehakkyo**)
until	-까지(**-kkaji**)
USA	미국(**miguk**)
very	아주(**aju**), 참(**ch'am**)
vicinity, area, district	근처(**kŭnch'o**)
wait	기다리-(**kidari-**)
wait a moment (please)	잠깐 기다리세요(**chamkkan kidariseyo**)
waiter!	아저씨(**ajŏssi**)
waitress! (lit: = girl, unmarried woman)	아가씨(**agassi**)
want, require	원하-(**won ha-**)
water	물(**mul**)
we, our	우리(**uri**)
weather	날씨(**nalssi**)
welcome!	어서 오세요(**ŏsŏ oseyo**)
well, good (adverb)	잘(**chal**)
what (object form) (full form)	뭐(**mwo**) (뭘[**mwol**]) (무엇 [**muos**])

what (kind of, which) (number)	무슨(musŭn), 몇 (myŏt/myŏch')
when	언제(ŏnje)
where	어디(ŏdi)
which one?	어느(ŏnŭ)
while, a little	잠깐(chamkkan)
who? (subject form)	누구(nugu)(누가[nuga])
wife (not a polite form)	집사람(chipsaram)
window	창구(ch'anggu)
with (*irang* after consonants)	-랑(-rang)
word, language (to speak/say) (polite form)	말(mal) (말하-[mal ha-]); 말씀 (malssŭm)
work, matter, business	일(il)
worry (to)	걱정(kŏkchŏng) (하-([ha-])
write	쓰-(ssŭ-)
wrongly, mis-	잘못(chalmot)
yes	네(ne)
yet, still	아직(ajik)
year before last	재작년(chaejangnyŏn)
you (often between married couples)	당신(tangshin)

Taking it further

Websites that can be used for learning Korean:

- Korean@Monash: http://www.arts.monash.edu.au/korean/
- Korean studies at Sogang University: http://korean.sogang.ac.kr/
- Mr Oh's learnkorean.com: http://www.learnkorean.com/
- Learning hangul with Soyongdori: http://library.thinkquest.org/20746/
- Audio files of Korean conversations and narrations at Indiana University: http://languagelab.bh.indiana.edu/korean101.html
- Korean folk tales for kids at the Korean LG company website. This is not designed for language learning, but it has an English version as well as a Korean one. Go to http://www.lg.co.kr/english/ and click on 'LG Korean Folk Tales'.
- Say Hello to the World: www.ipl.org/div/hello
- *An Introduction to Korean* by J. David Eisenberg: http://catcode.com/kintro
- Korean Language Study on Internet: www.interedu.go.kr

Index of grammatical terms

References are to units 'GR' stands for 'Grammar'.